Simon Dickel, Evangelia Kindinger (eds.)
After the Storm

American Studies | Volume 10

Simon Dickel, Evangelia Kindinger (eds.)
After the Storm
The Cultural Politics of Hurricane Katrina

[transcript]

Bibliographic information published by the Deutsche Nationalbibliothek
The Deutsche Nationalbibliothek lists this publication in the Deutsche Nationalbibliografie; detailed bibliographic data are available in the Internet at http://dnb.d-nb.de

© 2015 transcript Verlag, Bielefeld

All rights reserved. No part of this book may be reprinted or reproduced or utilized in any form or by any electronic, mechanical, or other means, now known or hereafter invented, including photocopying and recording, or in any information storage or retrieval system, without permission in writing from the publisher.

Cover layout: Kordula Röckenhaus, Bielefeld
Cover illustration: Lewis Watts, *St. Claude Ave.*,
   Ninth Ward, New Orleans, 2005
Printed and bound in Great Britain by Marston Book Services Ltd, Oxfordshire
Print-ISBN 978-3-8376-2893-7
PDF-ISBN 978-3-8394-2893-1

Contents

Introduction: The Fire Next Time
Simon Dickel and Evangelia Kindinger | 7

New Orleans Suite: A Photographic Essay
Lewis Watts | 21

**Documenting Stories of Reconstruction in New Orleans:
Spike Lee and Jonathan Demme**
Delphine Letort | 25

**Recycling and Surviving in *Beasts of the Southern Wild*:
Screening Katrina as a Magic Realist Tale**
Miriam Strube | 43

**Down in the *Treme:*
Televising Man-made Natural Disaster in the New Millennium**
Kornelia Freitag | 61

Where They At? Bounce and Class in *Treme*
Michael Bucher | 79

**Dance Back From the Grave: Marc Cohn's and Jackson Browne's
Musical Responses to Hurricane Katrina**
Cyprian Piskurek | 97

**Revisiting Place, the Memorial, and the Historical in Tom Piazza's
Why New Orleans Matters and Natasha Trethewey's *Beyond Katrina***
Courtney George | 113

**Natural Hazards, Human Vulnerability:
Teaching Hurricane Katrina Through Literary Nonfiction**
Philipp Siepmann | 131

**Where Y'at Since the Storm?:
Linguistic Effects of Hurricane Katrina**
Katie Carmichael | 149

Life and Luck after Katrina: African American Men, Oral History, and Mentoring in New Orleans, 2010 to 2014
Nikki Brown | 167

The Landscapes of *Man*:
Ecological and Cultural Change Before Hurricane Katrina
Demetrius L. Eudell | 187

Authors | 217

Introduction: The Fire Next Time

SIMON DICKEL AND EVANGELIA KINDINGER

The cover of our book *After the Storm: The Cultural Politics of Hurricane Katrina* shows a photo Lewis Watts took of the veranda of a devastated house in New Orleans after Hurricane Katrina had hit the city in August of 2005. Trash bags are visible in the foreground, and on the veranda, there are a few pieces of defunct furniture. The entrance of the house is spray-painted with the phrase "The Fire Next Time" and the initials "JB." In the media coverage of the storm, the sight of spray-painted verandas was a familiar one. Images of the so-called x-charts, spray-painted by the search-and-rescue teams, illustrated many media reports about the hurricane. This graffito, however, is different. The initials J.B. point to the writer James Baldwin and his 1963 collection of essays *The Fire Next Time* in which he discusses race and religion in the US. It is an abbreviated line from a spiritual, which refers to the Bible. The full line reads "God gave Noah the rainbow sign, no more water, the fire next time."

As a sentence for the graffito, it could not have been more appropriate for the situation of post-Katrina New Orleans, because, after the levees broke, 80% of the city were flooded, which does not let the comparison between the flooded city and the biblical Flood appear far-fetched. By explicitly adding the initials J.B. to the quotation, the spray-painter refers to Baldwin and thus opens a specific perspective on Hurricane Katrina and its aftermath that goes beyond a treatment of the hurricane merely as a natural disaster. The written phrase refers to at least two pre-texts, it signifies on the Bible and the Flood on the one hand, and on James Baldwin, the Civil Rights struggle and the history of race and racism in the US on the other. It opens a perspective that connects African American history and the civil rights struggle to the current political situation in the United States. The x-chart is still visible underneath the word "time." Thus, the act of spray-painting the wall might also be read as an act of emancipation. Like in a palimpsest, the official sign still shines through the new phrase, but it becomes less important through the more urgent quotation. Using spray-paint, the writer takes up and appropriates the same technique the officials used to mark the houses with the x-charts.

Lewis Watts's symmetric black and white documentary photo of the house and the veranda enable the viewer to take in these different dimensions of meaning. Watts chooses the frame of the veranda as a frame for the image itself. The veranda appears as a stage with stairs on the left and the right that lead to and from it. Fittingly, the abandoned pieces of furniture, among them a lamp and a tailor's dummy, are reminiscent of stage props. Cultural negotiations of Hurricane Katrina and its aftermath, the photo seems to suggest, do not take place in a neutral setting. All cultural texts enter a stage that is predetermined by cultural meanings, political struggles, and conflicting discourses. Watts's photo addresses the immediacy of the situation while already pointing at different levels of cultural meanings, for example the official record and the unofficial interpretation of the reason for the disaster. The photo shows a stage with an entrance, an exit, and enough space for new negotiations, and it is for this reason that we consider it the ideal image for this book of essays on the cultural politics of Hurricane Katrina.

Over the nearly ten years since the storm, numerous artists and writers have negotiated the meaning of Hurricane Katrina in a growing number of texts of all genres. Early responses, such as Spike Lee's documentary film *When the Levees Broke* (2006), aimed at presenting personal counter-narratives to the dominant media images that often reinforced stereotypes of race and class. More recent texts, such as Benh Zeitlin's feature film *Beasts of the Southern Wild* (2012), tend to approach the storm and its aftermath implicitly. While Zeitlin's film does not even mention Hurricane Katrina, it can still be read as a text that meditates on the central topics of earlier Katrina narratives, such as race, poverty, and ecology. The Academy Award nominations for this film, the 2011 National Book Award for Jesmyn Ward's *Salvage the Bones* (2011), and the international success of David Simon and Eric Overmyer's TV-series *Treme* (2009-2013) have emphasized the relevance of Katrina for political, cultural, and academic discourses. In addition to documentaries, feature films, TV-series, and novels, authors have turned to genres, such as graphic novel, creative non-fiction, performance art, or music and added other Katrina narratives.

The wide range of cultural texts allows for a manifold access to Hurricane Katrina and its aftermaths. In *Treme* for instance, the creators of the series introduce its audience to a diverse group of characters. Their fate is specified in personal storylines, yet they also share it with all New Orleanians in the city and abroad. This intricate dynamic of individual and communal becomes relevant in the storyline of Creighton Bernette, a university professor who voices his personal frustration and anger about local, state and national post-Katrina crisis management as publicly, loudly and visibly as he can, speaking for himself and the citizens of New Orleans. In one of his YouTube-'rants,' he very pointedly states: "Living now, here, is like a dream, the way that everything in a dream is the same yet not the same. Familiar, yet strange. Not quite right, but you just can't put your finger on it." ("All On A Mardi Gras Day," 50:23-50:39) This collection of essays from different disciplines puts a finger on the effects Hurricane Katrina had on the people of New Orleans and the Gulf Coast, and on the effects it had on writers, filmmakers, and photographers who decided to respond with their art and tell stories of survival, destruction, and perseverance for the local communities, but also for those not directly affected by the storm.

Creighton Bernette's declaration addresses a state of being left in limbo, of the simultaneous experience of familiarity and alienation in one's city, one's home, and even one's nation. One of the predominant public responses to the images of human and environmental devastation after Hurricane Katrina had swept through New Orleans and the coasts of Alabama and Mississippi was incredulity that this was possible in an industrialized, Western nation-state like the United States. The ways in which Hurricane Katrina made economic and social discrepancies visible by natural force can be understood as an awakening from a dream many Americans strongly believed in: the equal access to opportunity and privilege for all American citizens. This rough awakening came unexpectedly to those who believed in this American cultural narrative, yet not to those who have historically been excluded by it: poor and black Americans.

The majority of publications responding to and explaining the economic, social and cultural circumstances that resulted in the post-Katrina crisis concentrate on the poor African American population of the Gulf Coast and of New Orleans specifically. What they all agree on is that those who had to stay behind in the city and seek shelter in the Superdome and the Convention Center were the most vulnerable residents of New Orleans: They were disproportionately poor, black, old, or of poor health (cf. Hartman/Squires 2006). Another aspect agreed upon is that the disaster, which unfolded, might have been natural in its shape – the winds, the rain, the flooding – but at its core, it was human-made.

Both the cultural texts that offer creative responses to Katrina and the academic work that analyzes these texts are produced within a discourse that is firmly rooted in other academic disciplines, such as political sciences, sociology, and geography. The following brief overview of some important studies that have been published since the storm illustrates the intertwining of different approaches and arguments, which have certainly informed the essays featured in this book and which complement these in return. Michael Eric Dyson's *Come Hell or High*

Water: Hurricane Katrina and the Color of Disaster (2006), Chester Hartman and Gregory D. Squires's edited collection *There Is No Such Thing As a Natural Disaster: Race, Class, and Hurricane Katrina* (2006), as well as Jeremy I. Levitt and Matthew C. Whitaker's collection *Hurricane Katrina: America's Unnatural Disaster* (2009), all attest to the unnaturalness of Hurricane Katrina, a storm which uncovered "weaknesses, prejudices, and inequalities throughout the Gulf Coast and within the whole of American society" (Levitt/Whitaker 2009: 2). As Dyson persuasively argues, speaking of Katrina as a mere natural disaster masks the disparities and realities it laid bare for everyone to see, not only in the United States, but also around the world. Natural disasters are ironically liberating of responsibility and of prevention. A natural disaster – supposedly – cannot be prevented, and while it invites anger and empathy, while it might even result in public outrage and relief work, it nevertheless implies that its effects can never be wholly predicted and prevented. Yet as the aforementioned publications show to the point, the aftermaths of the storm could have been prevented if the United States was not still structured by institutional inequalities and segregational politics. Responsibility, thus, cannot be so easily repelled.

The question of state and federal responsibility is vital for the future of the affected regions and respectively the nation as a whole. By taking responsibility for the deeply engrained but long avoided or downplayed questions of race and class in the United States, the social and economic landscape could be shaped anew. The redevelopment of New Orleans is therefore of particular interest to both the public and academic sphere. The interim conclusion is ambiguous so far. Cedric Johnson's edited book *The Neoliberal Deluge: Hurricane Katrina, Late Capitalism, and the Remaking of New Orleans* (2011) reviews private and governmental rebuilding efforts, while Johnson formulates a rather sobering verdict, namely that "the social, economic, and environmental crises that were rendered visible through disaster have been used to further advance neoliberalization" (2006: xvii). Disaster relief, which was overwhelming after the storm hit, is commonly represented as a sign of public care and interest in the so called victims. Yet as Johnson argues, disaster relief was and is mostly privatized, and the same is true for urban re-development. This privatization highlights and reinforces the neoliberal belief that social responsibility is not in the hands of state and federal government, but in the hands of private institutions and individuals. Without discrediting all the privatized disaster relief work, *The Neoliberal Deluge* aims at exposing the inequalities rendered by neoliberalization and calls for government responsibility in times of crises.

Crisis Cities: Disaster and Redevelopment in New York and New Orleans (2014) by Kevin Fox Gotham and Miriam Greenberg, by comparing post-disaster relief and redevelopment in New Orleans and New York City, implies that social disparities are uncovered by different 'kinds' of crises. They ask whether "post-disaster redevelopment [was and is] linked to broader processes of social and spatial restructuring" (viii) and, similar to Johnson and the essays featured in his *The Neoliberal Deluge*, they conclude that New York City and New Orleans, instead of restructuring urban space in sensible, equal and inclusive ways, "have [rather] emerged as 'crisis cities,' representing a 'neoliberal,' or free-market-oriented approach to post-disaster redevelopment that is increasingly dominant for crisis-stricken urban regions around the country and the world" (ix). While Fox Gotham and Greenberg acknowledge and refer to moments of important and potent community activism and organizing, they stress that these efforts – unfortunately – have remained in the margins and were unable to be sustained within the cities' "market-oriented and inequitable redevelopment agenda" (xii).

Hurricane Katrina did not only expose capitalist ideologies, racial segregation, poverty, and governmental mismanagement, it also exposed the fragility of belonging, citizenship, and home. The early media coverage that labeled the residents of New Orleans and the Gulf Coast who had to leave their homes and their hometowns "refugees" has been widely criticized as deceptive and re-assertive of the segregation and disenfranchisement many African American residents were exposed to before, during and after the storm: "The framing of Katrina victims as refugees helped construct a view of the victims as undeserving of government and resources." (Fox Gotham/Greenberg 2014: 71) It helped construct them as non-citizens of the United States, a foreign body in their own homes.

A term sought to be more suitable to the state of forced displacement is "diaspora." The Katrina Diaspora, the waves of people leaving the impacted regions and settling provisionally in other places, spread to every state of the United States (Ericson, Matthew/Tse, Archie/Wilgoren, Jodi 2005: n.p.), and according to journalist Jonathan Tilove, in 2010, 100.000 New Orleanians were still scattered across the United States. Yet "mostly apparent for its absence" (n.p.), the Katrina Diaspora is difficult to grasp, because it is an intra-national and regional diaspora that has become invisible. Supported by organizations devoted to return, such as the federal program Road Home, many diasporans have indeed returned to their homes, but many still live displaced in areas away from home, the road back still difficult for them to take.

In 2012, Lori Peek and Lynn Weber published a collection of ethnographic essays, *Displaced: Life in the Katrina Diaspora*, in which they, among other authors, attempted to give the Katrina Diaspora the visibility it deserves. Interestingly enough, they do not specify how they understand and make use of the term "diaspora," subtly making a claim for the self-evidence of a Katrina diaspora, which does not need further conceptualization. The claim does not have to be so subtle though, the Katrina Diaspora is diasporic in the term's most classic sense: traumatized and displaced by a catastrophic event, a collective, which is (treated like) a minority group is forced to leave the so-called homeland and settle in other, mostly foreign places (cf. Tölölyan 2007; Cohen 1997). The "rhetoric of restoration and return" (Tölölyan 2007: 649), which determines life in the diaspora, is crucial for the community's preservation and for possible return movements "back home." The essays we have assembled here take part in this rhetoric; they create visibility and assess the restoration efforts displayed in various cultural texts and practices.

Although featured prominently in Peek and Weber's book title, the authors do not make further use of the term "diaspora," but rather refer to the people who had to leave their homes as "internally displaced persons" (2012: 2), preferring this terminology to other labels such as "refugees, victims, survivors, evacuees, exiles, and environmental migrants" (ibid.). To be "internally displaced" suggests displacement within the larger structure of the nation-state, it suggests an intra-national diaspora, which imagines the homeland in more regionalized and localized terms, in this case New Orleans and the Gulf region. Internal displacement might also refer to the consciousness and lived experiences of having been displaced, excluded, segregated and kept in the margins of one's homeland: "Experiences of loss, marginality, and exile (differentially cushioned by class) are often reinforced by systematic exploitation and blocked advancement. This constitutive suffering coexists with the skills of survival [...]. Diaspora consciousness lives loss and hope as a defining tension." (Clifford 1994: 312) We dare to suggest that this tension created by internal displacement, coupled with the realization of living apart from, and having no access to the privileges of hegemonic society as experienced by many poor, elderly and African American New Orleanians during and after the storm is actually a displacement they experienced long before Hurricane Katrina.

Lynnell L. Thomas's *Desire & Disaster in New Orleans: Tourism, Race, and Historical Memory* (2014) names tourism a distinct sphere of continuous displacement and exclusion, primarily of African American New Orleanians and their history. The city's tourism narrative has always prioritized the French Quarter and the city's European heritages, stigmatizing the "black areas of the city as dangerous" (1), and thus reinforcing urban and racial segregation. Thomas formulates two contrasting frames that have been utilized to represent local black culture for visiting tourists: the desire to experience "authentic" and "safe" black culture, and the disaster narratives of poverty, crime, immorality and inadequacy that have connoted black culture in the American imagination (cf. ibid: 7). This duality, so runs Thomas's argument, shaped the media coverage and public perception of Hurricane Katrina: "Those who were most responsible for representing the city and its citizens in the aftermath of Katrina did so from a limited perspective that conformed to a narrative perpetuated in tourist representations of the city." (ibid: 2) The focus on a nostalgic, highly fabricated white adaptation of antebellum culture has fostered desire, while displacing and obscuring black history, black agency and inclusive tourist narratives of and in the city. Hurricane Katrina, again, operated as a destructive force laying bare these narratives, as seen in the instant efforts to rebuild New Orleans' damaged tourist attractions like the French Quarter and neglect the poor and black residential neighborhoods such as the Lower 9th Ward.

The question of agency, narrative power, and representation is one we acknowledge in this collection of essays. With regard to diasporas, Khachig Tölölyan emphasizes the importance of "talking back" and becoming "simultaneously objects of knowledge and cosubjects" (2007: 654). Before talking back though, individual and collective voices need to be found, raised and mediated. In the light of all the failures and negligence of federal and state government, and of mainstream (news) media, cultural productions offer space for obscured knowledge and voices, open a dialogue and facilitate "talking back." The conversation this book contributes to is that of the politics voiced by cultural texts. It is also a transnational and interdisciplinary conversation, in which scholars of different academic and biographical origins pay attention to how Hurricane Katrina and its aftermaths are memorized, narrated, structured, visualized and politicized in fictional or personal responses, in the classroom, in the language people use, and in art projects.

This book has evolved from the international conference "After the Storm: The Cultural Politics of Hurricane Katrina" that we organized in Bochum/Germany in December 2013. At the time, many conference speakers from New Orleans and other parts of the United States voiced their surprise that a conference with this particular focus took place in Europe. In turn, we had been surprised and glad about so many participants from the United States and particularly New Orleans who travelled to Bochum to discuss the topic with us. The international and interdisciplinary exchange was so productive that the decision for this collection of essays to document it was an easy one. Our conference and this book are evidence of the growing academic attention to the cultural negotiations of Hurricane Katrina.

Our discussions in this book are inspired by Lloyd Pratt's essay "New Orleans and Its Storm: Exception, Example, or Event?" (2006), in which he warns against the impulse to treat Hurricane Katrina and its aftermath either as an exception from the ordinary course of history or as an example of the way that race and class inequalities have always manifested themselves historically. Both are tendencies to historicize the storm in opposing ways, which, he argues, pose the danger of being inattentive to what is new about the storm. This volume's interdisciplinary approach considers Hurricane Katrina and the way it has been culturally negotiated from a variety of angles. In line with Pratt's deliberations, our aim with both the conference and this publication is a multifaceted take on the meanings of the storm and its cultural negotiations. A considerable number of the essays in this book address fictional texts of different genres. However, the book's scope is not limited to literary studies or film studies. It is broadened by essays, which belong to one or more other academic disciplines, namely linguistics, pedagogy, music, sociology, and philosophy. What is more, two contributors share their creative photographic work and put it in theoretical perspective.

Throughout the book, placed before each individual essay, you find one photo by photographer Lewis Watts, accompanied by a caption to contextualize it. Together with his statement and self-portrait at the beginning of the book, these photos form his contribution "New Orleans Suite: A Photographic Essay." He took some of these black and white photos in New Orleans over the course of ten days, six weeks after Katrina. Some of the photos are of a more recent date, and others depict the city before the hurricane. At the time Katrina made landfall, Watts was supposed to start his work as an artist in residence at the Ogden Museum of Southern Art. As an artist Watts is most interested in documenting the people and their cultural practices. Consequently, his photographic essay does not only show an abandoned and destroyed city but includes portraits of the people of New Orleans.

In "Documenting Stories of Reconstruction in New Orleans: Spike Lee and Jonathan Demme" Delphine Letort compares the documentary style and cultural politics of two documentaries, Spike Lee's *If God is Willing and da Creek Don't Rise* (2010) and Jonathan Demme's *I'm Carolyn Parker, the Good, the Mad and the Beautiful* (2012). Letort states that even though both films build on the participatory and performative modes of documentary filmmaking as defined by film theorist Bill Nichols, Demme and Lee do not convey the same image of New Orleans and its inhabitants. Both films portray everyday life in post-Katrina New Orleans through the focus on individual characters. Letort analyzes how Lee explores the narrative dynamics of serialization to investigate the individual and collective impact of Hurricane Katrina, whereas Demme personalizes his approach through the focus on Carolyn Parker, whom, as she contends, he celebrates as an American model of resilience. Demme's commitment to Carolyn

Parker, Letort argues, stands in stark contrast to Lee's engagement with collective concerns as expressed by the multimodal narrative structure that allows him to interweave different storylines.

Creative responses to Hurricane Katrina, such a complex and overwhelming disaster (whether natural and/or human-made), avail themselves of different styles and methods of narration. Miriam Strube and Kornelia Freitag discuss two different cultural representations that are narrated in a similar tradition, namely in a realist fashion. Yet, as Strube and Freitag show, realist tales can vary; realism as a narrative aesthetic is versatile. In "Recycling and Surviving in *Beasts of the Southern Wild*: Screening Katrina as a Magic Realist Tale," Strube analyzes Zeitlin's film from 2012. She offers a reading of the film by comparing it to classic features of magic realism, a genre that blends what is considered to be real, in this case the ecological vulnerability of places in the Gulf Coast, with magical elements, the sudden and unexpected appearance of prehistoric animals, which are 'tamed' and sent away by the film's adolescent protagonist Hushpuppy. Next to identifying the magic realist features though, Strube goes one step further and discusses the role of the dump and the relevance of trash in the movie, concluding that Zeitlin creates images of community life, commodities and consumerism that counter mainstream American society without romanticizing or abjecting these as unworthy.

Freitag, in her contribution "Down in the *Treme:* Televising Man-made Natural Disaster in the New Millennium," also attends to the realist method of narrating Hurricane Katrina. She reads *Treme* as a series that uses local color strategies, which captivate the viewers by representing the regional specificities or the Otherness of New Orleans' culture. Yet Freitag goes one step further and considers the role, more precisely the absence, of the hurricane in *Treme* – an absence she explains as an effect of the realist aesthetics deployed by the series, aesthetics that place the human being at the center of interest and representation. The materiality of Hurricane Katrina – the storm, the wind, and the flooding – while being mostly obscured nevertheless resurfaces in eerie narrative moments that rupture the realist mode.

Michael Bucher offers a different approach to *Treme*. In "Where They At? Bounce and Class in *Treme*," he discusses the role of music in the TV-series. But rather than focusing on jazz, Cajun music, or the musical heritage of Mardi Gras, all of which feature prominently in the series, he attends to hip-hop and bounce. Both are current African American musical styles, which New Orleans is well-known for, but which are largely neglected in the series. Bucher analyzes the appearances of artists Katey Red and Lil Calliope and states that both are dependent on and sidekicks to the DJ Davis storyline. Based on this analysis,

Bucher makes the argument that the marginalization of bounce and hip-hop is ultimately an exclusion of queer, female and poor subjects from the TV-series.

In his essay "Dance Back From the Grave: Marc Cohn's and Jackson Browne's Musical Responses to Hurricane Katrina" Cyprian Piskurek analyzes two albums about Hurricane Katrina. He argues that among the various representations of Hurricane Katrina and its aftermath, music occupies a special place because it testifies to the centrality of New Orleans within the national and global music scene. His essay starts out with a discussion of contemporary 'telethon culture' which was responsible for many of the most immediate responses to the storm. Whereas songs responding to Katrina are often discussed in isolation as individual tracks, this article calls for closer attention to complete albums influenced by the event, as these texts give more thorough insights into the emergent structures of feeling after the disaster. Piskurek discusses two such responses in detail: Marc Cohn's *Join the Parade* (2007) and Jackson Browne's *Time the Conqueror* (2008). He demonstrates how Cohn interprets Katrina as a natural disaster while Browne takes a more political stance and sees the horrendous consequences as man-made. Although the discussion focuses on only two examples, he argues that evolving patterns of representing the storm can be read off these albums and contribute to our understanding of Hurricane Katrina's cultural politics.

Courtney George's "Revisiting Place, the Memorial, and the Historical in Tom Piazza's *Why New Orleans Matters* and Natasha Trethewey's *Beyond Katrina*" argues for a reconsideration of the binaries history/memory, space/place, and local/global in Southern Studies, which cannot be easily upheld in the aftermaths of Hurricane Katrina. Analyzing two personal approaches to post-Katrina New Orleans (Piazza) and coastal Mississippi (Trethewey), George argues for the physicality of place that has been overshadowed by the understanding that place is merely created in our imagination. There is a crucial interconnectedness of the physical space and imagined place, which Piazza and Trethewey assert in their narratives. Without intending to negate the creation of place through history and memory, George, in a bioregional approach, aims at the reconciliation of imagined, remembered place and the physical space that facilitates imagination and memory. Representations of place, like Piazza's and Trethewey's, allow access to the physical space, especially for those who were dislocated by Hurricane Katrina and for those who lived outside the places affected by the storm.

Philipp Siepmann approaches Hurricane Katrina with a didactic approach, asking how the lessons learned and not-learned from the course of events unleashed by the hurricane can be utilized to introduce high school students to global ecological and socio-political challenges and inequalities while fostering their (inter)cultural and analytic competences. "Natural Hazards, Human Vulnerability – Teaching Hurricane Katrina Through Literary Nonfiction" proposes a didactic model based on the main inquiry of defining Hurricane Katrina as a natural and/or man-made disaster, which students are meant to explore by means of three different texts: the oral history project *Voices from the Storm* (2008), Dave Eggers's *Zeitoun* (2009), and Josh Neufeld's *A.D.: New Orleans after the Deluge* (2009). These texts, according to Siepmann, stand at the crossroads of fiction and nonfiction and thus exemplify the fictionalization and appropriation of personal stories, which are relevant for sensitizing students to the meaning of representation and agency with regard to Hurricane Katrina, and more generally, to cultural texts of all kinds.

Katie Carmichael's essay "Where Y'at Since the Storm?: Linguistic Effects of Hurricane Katrina" offers a linguistic perspective on the effects of Katrina. She has conducted original research on the unique dialects of English in Greater New Orleans, which have long attracted the notice of both linguists and locals alike, but on which only very little research has been conducted so far. In particular, Carmichael asks how the upheaval and large-scale relocation following Hurricane Katrina has affected local speech patterns. In her study, she examines the speech of 57 individuals from St. Bernard Parish, located just east of New Orleans, to determine whether distinctive local linguistic features have remained robust after the storm. In comparing the speech of those individuals who have relocated following Hurricane Katrina and those who have returned to their original homes, she determines that relocation has had little effect on speakers' language use, providing some hope for the future of New Orleans' distinctive linguistic heritage. In her analysis, she suggests that part of the reason for this linguistic retention may be a result of the post-Katrina nostalgia movement creating a revaluing of all things local.

As already mentioned, the disenfranchisement and grave stigmatization of African American New Orleanians was widely discussed after the storm, and Nikki Brown adds another perspective to this discussion, considering photography and oral history. In "Life and Luck after Katrina: African American Men, Oral History, and Mentoring in New Orleans, 2010 to 2014" she focuses on African American men in the city, those men who were nationally denounced as "looters" and "thugs" by the media and the images circulated in the aftermath of the hurricane. Brown displays photographs from her own project "Ordinary Lives, Extraordinary Times: African American Men in New Orleans after Hurricane Katrina, 2010-2014," and valorizes African American men's lives in New Orleans. She stresses their agency by visualizing and arguing for a different kind of crisis management and disaster activism: the mentoring of African American youth by African American men, for example in community-relevant institutions such as the barbershop or in life skills classes offered by Chef Joe at Café Reconcile. Brown's photographs are complemented by interviews she conducted with men who describe their status in the city and counter the mainstream narratives of urban black masculinity.

In his essay "The Landscapes of *Man*: Ecological and Cultural Change before Hurricane Katrina" Demetrius L. Eudell uses Hurricane Katrina as an endpoint to analyze the history of ecological and socio-cultural change in New Orleans. After displacing and transforming Indigenous societies, European settlers had to decide how to establish a different kind of community in such a precarious landscape. Eudell argues that a particular understanding not only of the environment but also a conception of Being Human, that of secular *Man* (if initially only partially so) remained equally relevant. Within the logic of this self/social understanding, a system of levees to address hurricane and storm surge would be implemented, initially with convict and slave labor, and after the Civil War, with poorly-compensated (i.e. 'cheap'), predominantly Black labor. Eudell's analysis asks for a fundamental change: The cultural and environmental questions that emerged in the way of Katrina should compel a rethinking of the viability of contemporary approaches to organizing complex technological societies, especially as it relates to questions of ecological change.

All the essays in this book offer crucial insights to what we have termed the "cultural politics of Hurricane Katrina." We want to thank Hans Niehues, Anne Potjans, and Heike Steinhoff for their help in the various stages of editing this volume. We are grateful to everyone included in this book for their contributions and smooth cooperation on this project. We are happy about the unique opportunity to show Lewis Watts's photographic work on the cover and throughout this book. The graffito shown in the cover photograph offers a meaningful intertextual reference that sets the stage for this collection.[1] In "The Rainbow Sign," Hanif Kureishi talks about an important photo he remembers from his formative years: "On the cover of the Penguin edition of *The Fire Next Time* was James Baldwin holding a child, his nephew. Baldwin, having suffered, having

---

1   Baldwin's use of the phrase "The Fire Next Time" has not only inspired the spray-painter who wrote it on the veranda in Watts's photo, but also other writers and artists, who have quoted it once again to question constructions of race and negotiate the intersections of race, class, gender, and sexuality. Among them are Hanif Kureishi's long autobiographical essay on Pakistani-British identity, and Randall Kenan's collection of essays *The Fire This Time* (2007), both of which pay explicit homage to Baldwin.

been there, was all anger and understanding. He was intelligence and love combined." (1996: 77) By referencing Baldwin's book-title with Lewis Watts's photo on the cover, we suggest that Baldwin's intellectual and emotional range of response to racism in the US – anger and understanding, intelligence and love – motivates the creative and academic work in this book.

BIBLIOGRAPHY

Clifford, James (1994): "Diasporas." In: *Cultural Anthropology* 3/3, pp. 302-38.

Cohen, Robin (1997): *Global Diasporas: An Introduction*, Seattle: University of Washington Press.

Dyson, Michael Eric (2006): *Come Hell or High Water: Hurricane Katrina and the Color of Disaster*, New York: Basic Books.

Ericson, Matthew/Tse, Archie/Wilgoren, Jodi (2005): "Katrina's Diaspora." In: *The New York Times*, February 24, 2015 (http://nytimes.com/imagepages/2005/10/02/national/nationalspecial/20051002diaspora_graphic.html).

Fox Gotham, Kevin/Greenberg, Miriam (2014): *Crisis Cities: Disaster and Redevelopment in New York and New Orleans*, Oxford: Oxford University Press.

Hartman, Chester/Squires, Gregory D. (2006): *There Is No Such Thing As a Natural Disaster: Race, Class, and Hurricane Katrina*, New York: Routledge.

Johnson, Cedric (2011): *The Neoliberal Deluge: Hurricane Katrina, Late Capitalism, and the Remaking of New Orleans*, Minneapolis: University of Minnesota Press.

Kenan, Randall (2007): *The Fire this Time*. New York: Melville House.

Kureishi, Hanif ([1986] 1996): "The Rainbow Sign." In: *My Beautiful Laundrette and Other Writings*. London: Faber and Faber, pp. 72-102.

Levitt, Jeremy I./Whitaker, Matthew C. (2009): *Hurricane Katrina: America's Unnatural Disaster*, Lincoln: University of Nebraska Press.

Peek, Lori/Weber, Lynn (2012): *Displaced: Life in the Katrina Diaspora*. Austin: University of Texas Press.

Pratt, Lloyd (2007): "New Orleans and Its Storm: Exception, Example, or Event?" In: *American Literary History* 19/1, pp. 251-165.

Thomas, Lynnell L. (2014): *Desire & Disaster in New Orleans: Tourism, Race, Historical Memory*, Durham: Duke University Press.

Tilove, Jonathan (2010): "Five years after Hurricane Katrina, 100,000 New Orleanians have yet to return." In: *nola.com: Everything New Orleans*, February 24, 2015 (http://www.nola.com/katrina/index.ssf/2010/08/five_years_after_hurricane_kat. html).

Treme, The Complete First Season, (2011). Created by Eric Overmyer and David Simon. New York: HBO. DVD.

New Orleans Suite: A Photographic Essay

LEWIS WATTS

I have been photographing in New Orleans since 1994 as part of my examination of the African American cultural landscape. An inspiration for this is my own background as the child of parents born in the southern U.S. who migrated west as a result of World War II. I have been interested in the idea of migration – what people bring with them and what they leave behind. Many residents of Louisiana came west in the mid-twentieth century for economic opportunities, and to get away from the segregation of the South. My investigation of New Orleans, other parts of Louisiana and the South is an attempt to compare and contrast what was transferred and transformed and also what remained. In the book, *New Orleans Suite, Music and Culture in Transition* (2013) my co-author Eric Porter and I present a dialog with photographs and written commentary about New Orleans as it was, the effects of Hurricane Katrina on the unique established cultural practices, and the efforts by the cultural workers to ensure that the traditions survive in the face of mass human displacement from the storm as well as efforts by some to commodify these practices.[1]

I was supposed to do an Artist in Residency in New Orleans that was derailed by Hurricane Katrina in 2005. I was able to get into the city six weeks after the storm. I found the destruction much worse than what I had seen in news accounts. I had to be imbedded in the National Guard to gain access to the Lower Ninth Ward, an African American community that sustained major flooding and that was closed to all including former residents right after the storm. I photographed

---

[1] Besides my participation in the "After the Storm" conference, images from *New Orleans Suite* have been exhibited and published internationally, including in the exhibit "Great Black Music" at the Cité de la Musique in Paris in the spring and summer of 2014.

intently what remained for about ten days until I had to stop because of the fact that there were very few people in the city at that time.

It was the people and their cultural practice that I was most interested in and I have tried to continue documenting that reality ever since. Not much was done to repair the damage for the first few years after the storm. Photographing the Mardi Gras Indian Tribes, the Social Aid and Pleasure Clubs, the Brass Bands, and the funeral societies, I have also tried to show the ways that these cultural workers have worked to ensure that many of the century-old traditions endured, especially after so many of New Orleans' residents were displaced by the storm.

Lewis Watts: *Lewis Watts Imbedded with the National Guard*, Lower 9th Ward 2005

BIBLIOGRAPHY

Porter, Eric/Watts, Lewis (2013): *New Orleans Suite: Music and Culture in Transition*. Berkeley: University of California Press.

Lewis Watts: *Glen David Andrews,* Tremé 2008

David is a well-known New Orleans musician who was participating in a second line parade that had originally been banned by the New Orleans police. It took a court order to get the ban lifted. This is an example of the efforts that the cultural workers in New Orleans had to go through to insure that traditions survived.

Documenting Stories of Reconstruction in New Orleans: Spike Lee and Jonathan Demme

DELPHINE LETORT

Spike Lee's *If God is Willing and da Creek Don't Rise* (2010) and Jonathan Demme's *I'm Carolyn Parker, the Good, the Mad and the Beautiful* (2011) articulate the directors' commitment to recovering the stories of New Orleanians behind the headlines that spotlighted Hurricane Katrina's destructive sweep across the Gulf Coast. After the levees surrounding the city broke in the wake of Katrina's landfall on August 29, 2005, causing the lowest quarters to flood and houses to be displaced from their concrete basements, many people found themselves stranded without external help for several days. Rather than delve into the dark hours of Katrina, which have left an imprint on collective memory through intense media coverage, the two films foreground stories of reconstruction. The filmed participants are offered a public platform, which they self-consciously explore to bear witness to Katrina's hidden stories and to voice their opinions on the challenges posed by reconstruction. Although both documentaries explore the participatory mode of filmmaking to convey the directors' engagements with the issues broached by their filmed subjects, the directors' portrayals of the city differ as they call attention to diverging aspects of the local social geography. Whereas Spike Lee's engagement with racial politics informs his characterization of all interviewed New Orleanians, Jonathan Demme characterizes Carolyn Parker as an American model of resilience whose determination he glorifies beyond the color line.[1]

Through a comparative approach that underlines the directors' idiosyncratic filmmaking styles, this article discusses how the two fiction film directors appropriate the documentary genre to shape an intimate narrative of surviving

---

1   The comments on Spike Lee's documentaries draw on the chapters developed in Letort (2015).

after Katrina. Both followed their filmed participants over a five-year time span, thereby investigating the impact of reconstruction on the citizens' everyday life. Whether they film their interaction with the filmed participants, or invite them to speak freely in front of the camera, the directors nonetheless leave their authorial imprint on the documentaries. Not only do they select the testimonies to be incorporated into the narrative, but they also use specific framings to visually express their engagements. While Lee's film is a polyphonic piece that allows him to portray the city from various standpoints, Demme's focus on Carolyn Parker enhances the woman's active role in the community of Holy Cross in the Lower Ninth Ward. As an outspoken character committed to fighting injustice, Parker draws attention to her "house" as a symbol for an enduring collective struggle that resonates with the 1960's civil rights movement. The two films allow powerful role models to emerge among the ordinary characters of New Orleans' social fabric, thereby countering the negative stereotypes associated with Katrina's stranded victims who had been presented as the "underclass" by most mainstream media (Jennings/Jushnick 1999: 6).

EXPLORING THE IMPACT OF KATRINA THROUGH THE "PARTICIPATORY MODE"

Spike Lee and Jonathan Demme investigate the impact of Katrina on New Orleans through interviews with witnesses who are keen to testify in front of the camera. Documentary theorist Bill Nichols argues that this type of filmmaking, which he defines as the "participatory mode," is based on direct interaction between filmmakers and filmed subjects:

Filmmakers who seek to represent their own direct encounter with their surrounding world and those who seek to represent broad social issues and historical perspectives through interviews and compilation footage constitute two large components of the participatory mode. As viewers we have the sense that we are witness to a form of dialogue between filmmaker and subject that stresses situated engagement, negotiated interaction, and emotion-laden encounter. (2010: 187)

The camera explicitly embodies Demme's point of view in *I'm Carolyn Parker, the Good, the Mad and the Beautiful*, enhancing the proximity of the relationship created between himself and Carolyn Parker. The five-year time span covered by the film allows mutual trust and confidence to grow: although he almost never appears on screen, Demme's presence permeates the film. Not only does he employ the voice-over to fashion the film's narrative, giving information to fill in the time gaps between two encounters, he also dramatizes the documentary through subjective comments that arouse the viewers' expectations. The film is a reflective endeavor insofar as Demme's hand-held camera movements are associated with the filmmaker's, which highlights the whole process of filmmaking.

When making the acquaintance of Raymond, the director is keen to indicate that he is shooting a film by drawing attention to the intrusive function of the camera – "Hi Raymond I'm coming in here with a camera rolling" (Demme 2011: 04:23). The camera acts as a tool of mediation that prompts communication between Demme and Parker, for the documentary turns into a playful filmic experience as the woman self-consciously plays her character. "I'm Carolyn Parker" (04:20), she proudly asserts on her first meeting with Demme. Her character overwhelms the film as she actively takes part in her self-representation: she stands in the doorway of her damaged wooden frame home with rollers in her hair and a head scarf on when she invites Demme to take a tour round her house. Parker's easy humor and warmth dismiss the shock expressed by Demme as he asks whether the family really live in the dark broken house. Questions spontaneously crop up in the conversation as he discovers the derelict state of the house Carolyn Parker and her family occupy, betraying the sense of unease created by the unhealthy living conditions he witnesses. "Are you living here now? Like sleeping here now" (05:04) he asks, overtly wondering whether this is a reasonable choice. The woman downplays the shock and dismay of her visitor by responding with humor as she flicks an imaginary switch on, helping Demme and his crew to feel at ease despite the sight of debris. She explains that vandals rampaged through the house after it was flooded, robbing her of all valuable objects, underlining the double injustice of fate.

The film captures the growing complicity between Demme and Parker; the filmmaker shares his angst with the viewer when learning about her double knee replacement surgery and expresses his relief when he sees her walk again: "When we next visited Carolyn seven months later in December '07, we were so happy to see her up on her feet again." (54:20) His comments serve the narrative by providing information filling in the gaps between two visits while also articulating an emotional engagement that keeps rising as time passes. Demme dramatizes the biographical narrative he is shaping by responding personally to Carolyn Parker's story, pointing out her difficulties to express his commitment as a filmmaker concerned with the inequalities that he bears witness to. His repeated visits to the woman and her family make visible his physical engagement to effectively support them. Hand-held camera movements testify to his presence on the ground and to the time spent with Carolyn Parker and her daughter Kyrah. At the end of the documentary, Demme and his film crew sit in the Parkers' living room watching a football match on television as though they were part of the family. The five-year time lapse allows an emotional relationship to blossom, endowing the portrait of Carolyn Parker with a poetic tenderness, which magnifies her qualities of friendship.

Empowerment through the "Performative Mode"

Lee and Demme get involved in a long-term investigation through their respective documentaries, which allow them to develop the characterization of their subjects. The filmed participants are not content with bearing witness in front of the camera; they progressively reveal themselves as subjects countering the reifying gaze of the camera by staging their own testimonies for the camera. The participants' stories and faces become familiar by the end of Lee's four-hour-long documentary entitled *When the Levees Broke: A Requiem in Four Acts* (2006), for their interviews are disseminated throughout the film which thereby broaches the consequences of Katrina from different angles. Lee revisits New Orleans in *If God is Willing and da Creek Don't Rise* (2010); the credit sequence of the latter film evokes the time lapse between the two documentaries by inserting medium-close ups of the same participants, thus arousing curiosity as to what their life has become since Katrina's immediate aftermath. Some faces have grown older and bear the marks of time passing whereas others evoke the lack of progress since Katrina.

Phyllis Montana-Leblanc introduces *If God is Willing and da Creek Don't Rise* in a prologue that spotlights her physical transformation since her last appearance in *When the Levees Broke*: she was sitting inside her trailer then, bending over a poem she had written and read out in a low voice, self-consciously using Lee's camera to make herself heard. Her body language now conveys a stark contrast: she stands and looks straight at the camera, energetically delivering her text like a rap song, drawing a list of demands that characterize her as an activist. The documentary series permits the viewer to measure the distance between the present and the past, hinting at all the events that occurred between 2006 and 2010. Calling for change, Montana-Leblanc's presentation foreshadows the documentary's thematic concerns: poverty, death statistics, education, levee maintenance, politicians' lies, health care, corporate greed, and environmental issues will be tackled, widening the scope of the documentary beyond the racial issues Lee brought to the fore when dealing with Katrina in *When the Levees Broke: A Requiem in Four Acts*.

Her opening lines point to the derogatory prejudices against low-income residents, who bear the brunt of the cold-blooded contempt expressed by the men "in tailored suits" whom she accuses of being responsible for the deaths she metaphorically evokes as "hooded white sheets" (cf. Lee 2010). The recurring line "If God is Willing and da Creek Don't Rise" evokes a natural cycle that cannot be broken, suggesting that New Orleans' fate belongs to forces that are beyond man's power to control. This introduction dramatizes the time gap between the two parts of the documentary series, hinting at a situation that has worsened since 2006.

While Demme uses interviews to relate to his filmed subjects, thereby enhancing Parker's knack for storytelling, Lee exploits them as prompts to probe political issues. There are many moments when the documentarians lend their art of filmmaking to highlighting the words of the filmed participants. Framing thus enhances the "performative mode" of the documentary, in which, according to Jane Roscoe and Craig Hight, "a key focus becomes the prioritisation of the subjective aspects of documentary accounts of reality" (2011: 46-47). Demme builds up a proximity relationship with Carolyn Parker by using an abundance of close-ups throughout the film, capturing the playful look in her eyes and generating a sense of closeness and confidence that counters a voyeuristic look. The filmmaker immerses the viewer in the woman's world, following her movements very closely and using her as a landmark when venturing outside in the Lower Ninth Ward. Lee, on his part, displays the signature shots that identify his presence behind the camera – including high angle shots that dramatize the words of Shelton Shakespear Alexander's rap song (Lee 2006, Part 2: 01:04) and the "racial slur montage" that was made famous in *Do the Right Thing* (1989) in a sequence accusing British Petroleum of misdemeanor in the handling of the Deepwater Horizon oil spill (Lee 2010, Part 2: 01:18:20). Lee explores cinematographic techniques that endow the filmed participants' words with more power, conveying his viewpoint through the *mise-en-scene* and the editing of their speech.

THE POLITICS OF THE DOCUMENTARIES

Although Lee and Demme visit the same neighborhood for their films, they seem to embrace starkly contrasting visual and political landscapes. The original musical score composed for both films creates a different atmosphere: a slow jazz piece generates a sense of doom in *If God is Willing and da Creek Don't Rise*,[2] whereas the light music of *I'm Carolyn Parker, the Good, the Mad and the Beautiful* produces a sentimental, tear-jerking mood. The music connotes the directors' contrasting vision of post-Katrina New Orleans, which is further encapsulated in the interviews selected to shape the narrative arcs of each film.

Lee and Demme frame the issues of reconstruction from different perspectives: while Lee underlines the power struggle that opposed many citizens to the local and federal authorities – including their plans to have housing projects demolished and replaced with mixed-income developments, Demme highlights the determination of Carolyn Parker to fight social injustice by settling back in her ruined house, thereby asserting her right to return in the Lower Ninth Ward.[3] Accompanying her on board the bus that takes her to St. David Church, Demme tells about the gains won through collective struggle:

From our very first trip with Carolyn to St. David at St. Maurice, it had been upsetting to see the membership of these two Ninth Ward cornerstones pitted against each other for the very survival of their churches. It was the marbled, storied elegance of high-society St. Maurice versus the historic, rock-solid vibrancy of St. David. But after 18 months of suspenseful deliberation, through sheer strength of numbers, the power of collective will and the unavoidable fact that they were just so plain determined to get back into their home house of worship, St. David once again opened its doors for Mass two years after the floodwaters of Katrina had filled her walls to the rafters. (54:55)

These voice-over statements affect the image of Carolyn Parker, whom the camera follows walking through the Lower Ninth Ward after her double-knee surgery,

---

2 The music used for the film creates a rich intertextual subtext, referring to *When the Levees Broke* and to *Inside Man* (Lee 2006), since the three films use the same musical score composed by Terence Blanchard.

3 Demme speaks about his encounter with Carolyn in the PBS interview added to the commentary of the DVD: "We first went down to New Orleans about six months after the floods that followed Katrina. I had heard about a small but mighty group of scattered people who were defying the warnings to not go back – that these neighborhoods will be razed, they will be leveled and they will become green space. They will maybe one day become condominiums but they're not going to be the neighborhoods anymore. Yet, there were people who went rushing back in to say 'No, we're here, and even if we're going to live in our gutted house or in a formaldehyde stinking FEMA trailer we're here, we refuse to leave, we have a right to return and we're exercising it.'" (03:12)

turning her individual courage into an icon of the collective fight waged for the reopening of the church. The focus on the woman yet undermines the community efforts that Spike Lee endeavors to make visible. The documentaries therefore appear as a space of negotiation between the filmmakers and the characters, whose statements are incorporated in an overall narrative fashioned by the filmmakers themselves. The overall discourse of the films conveys the documentarians' understanding of the situation: Demme tells a story of collective reconstruction through portraying Carolyn Parker's individual and personal path whereas Lee collects a web of interviews among people whose overtly militant stances he underlines through specific camera movements. Both films address civil rights issues from a different standpoint, underscoring continuous efforts to make justice prevail.

SPIKE LEE'S ACTIVIST STANCE

Lee calls attention to the political underpinning of reconstruction policies by having local activists comment on their analysis of the situation in front of the camera. The film turns into a militant piece when shedding light on the critiques fostered by reconstruction. *If God is Willing and da Creek Don't Rise* broaches an array of specific issues which have emerged in the years that followed Katrina – including the rise in black on black crime, the development of charter schools, the legacy of racial segregation, the damages caused by the 2010 oil spill, among others. Lee builds an overview of these challenging problems which New Orleans has to face as a community by allowing activist citizens to hammer home their views in front of the camera: local fishermen (Albert Andry III, Dustin King, Vietnamese American fishermen), scholars (Douglas Brinkley), journalists (David Shammer, Anderson Cooper), musicians (Dr. John), environmental activists (Lisa Margonelli, Fred Krupp), local attorneys (Scott Bickford, Joseph Bruno), local associations (William Nungesser, Fred Johnson), and official representatives (Ahn "Joseph" Cao) express diverging opinions and bring illuminating insight into the local consequences of a national state of affairs. The documentary calls attention to the actions of concerned citizens who are committed to recovering their place in a city undergoing a rejuvenating process.

Lee exploits the polyphony of voices heard in the documentary to demonstrate that the individuals' return to New Orleans was all too often dependent on their socioeconomic status. The director tracks through the New Orleans landscape, which unveils the economic and political choices undergirding reconstruction: the first episode opens with shots panning the brand new Superdome, which highlight the contrasts to the empty blocks of the Saint Bernard projects, filmed in long tracking shots that enhance the absence of residents. The reconstruction projects of New Orleans prioritized the tourism business to the reopening of social housing – most of which were doomed to demolition even when they underwent minor damage. Lee offers a bleak view of New Orleans, underscoring the sense of loss caused by demolition and reconstruction when filming a child clutching at the wire netting erected around a demolition site. Through the collected interviews, which offer crisscrossing perspectives on reconstruction, Lee underlines the transformation of the social fabric it produces. In *If God is Willing and da Creek Don't Rise* (Part 1), city planner Shawn Escoffery explains from a studio that New Orleans will never be the same, especially the Lower Ninth Ward:

There is not a lot of means to rebuild in parts of the Ninth Ward considering the majority of the population there was extremely poor. Some people sold their home to the Road Home, got a fraction of what it would cost to actually build a new home and they can't come back. Then you have new houses being built up all the time. You have the Make it Right Brad Pitt houses, the Lower Nine NENA and other groups that are working to rebuild the Ninth Ward but the task at hand is daunting. (47:00)

Not only does Lee interview people whose life was improved thanks to the green projects of Brad Pitt's foundation, but he also points to the difficult readjustment of the people who were compelled to stay away. The focus on Parker in Demme's film obstructs a broader perspective, individualizing her plight while simultaneously glorifying her resilience. It seems to suggest that returning to New Orleans is a matter of individual choice whereas many were not able return to their home city because it did not provide the necessary facilities.

CAROLYN PARKER: AN ICON OF NEW ORLEANS

I'm Carolyn Parker, the Good, the Mad, and the Beautiful follows Carolyn Parker's fight to have her house rebuilt, a process that took over five years to be completed. The various stages of her house renovation form the narrative and chronological backbone of the film, which emphasizes the woman's will of strength as she faces one ordeal after another: it took six months for her to obtain a FEMA trailer, two years to have contractors start work on the structure of her house, six months to recover from a double knee replacement surgery. Five years had elapsed since her first encounter with Demme when she could move back in a renovated house. Carolyn Parker's house anchors the film in the Lower Ninth

Ward, which Demme tracks through in search of her address, offering a glimpse at the dreary spectacle of ruined houses in the opening sequence. Demme underlines the metonymical relationship between Carolyn Parker and her house, which exhibits her vibrant character through flashy colors – including the light green of her outside walls and the "Barbie" pink which used to cover the walls of her daughter Kyrah's bedroom.

The woman expresses her attachment to her house, recalling the years she devoted to transform it into a home. She retrieved a few unspoiled artifacts from the ruined house, which she put up on a "wall of remembrance" that visually testifies to the emotional dimension of the family home. The water-spared photographs open a window into the past, conveying the happy life that used to be lived there. Carolyn Parker's testimony provides a glimpse into life in the Lower Ninth Ward, which she embodies on screen as the leading character of the film and as a prominent figure of the quarter, whom her neighbors introduce as a local celebrity before she even appears in person. Geographer J. Nicholas Entrikin argues that place creates a center of meaning, which contributes to shaping identity:

We live our lives in place and have a sense of being part of place, but we also view place as acting separate, something external. Our neighbourhood is both an area centered on ourselves, as well as an area containing houses, streets and people that we may view from a decentered or an outsider's perspective. Thus place is both a center of meaning and the extreme context of our action. (1991: 7)

By developing a trusting relationship and a bond of friendship with Parker, which her home signifies as the place where she invites the film crew, Demme manages to capture this intimate sense of belonging. He thereby becomes complicit with her, trying to counter the sense of estrangement that emerges from the derelict interior of her flood-ravaged living room or the standard setting of her trailer.

While the focus on Parker's individual efforts to have her house refurbished underlines her resilient character, it tends to downplay the structural barriers that prevented many others from returning. The reconstruction of her house parallels Parker's personal struggle to recover her footing after the floods washed away all her belongings, thereby allowing Demme to draw a positive, inspiring portrayal of the woman.[4] The film describes the various stages in the reconstruction of

---

4   In Demme's words: "Now here's this extraordinary portrait of a great person that we're hearing, and a person who personifies a whole segment of American history with a special focus on segregation and a movement away from segregation. One of the things

Parker's house, which emphasize her determination to overcome the barriers erected by structural and institutional factors – including the marginalization of the Lower Ninth Ward in the speeches of the authorities devising reconstruction priorities. Demme's focus on Carolyn Parker reflects his Hollywood approach to filmmaking, turning her empowering story of individual fortitude into an example to be emulated. His questions drive the interviews and point out the difficulties that the woman and her daughter overcame while living in the Lower Ninth, striving to overturn the prejudiced view that might marginalize them. Both embody models of achievement; the two women espouse the work ethics that allow Demme to counter prejudiced views about those New Orleanians who would not abandon their house despite their derelict state.

I'm Carolyn Parker, the Good, the Mad, and the Beautiful portrays New Orleans through the eyes of Carolyn Parker, whose personal and family life is interwoven with the history of the city. She recounts her childhood memories of segregated New Orleans as stories to be passed on through the camera recording her words. She thus plays the traditional role of the African griot, relating stories that cement the community even beyond the screen. Demme invites the viewer to share in the listening experience by standing close to Parker, zooming in on her face to focus attention on her storytelling when she speaks about her first encounter with racism as a little girl whose fair skin caused her to be mistaken for white, and recalls growing up in the bayou as part of the African-American minority. Parker is identified as an activist who pursued her commitment by addressing Mayor Ray Nagin in a public meeting held at the Sheraton Hotel on January 11, 2006. She overtly questioned the plans for reconstruction in the Lower Ninth Ward: "I'm here for those persons who could not get back and I don't think it's right if you try to take our property." (08:28)[5] The authorities decided that

---

I found very poignant about Carolyn and also very inspiring was that she's a woman who, as a child born into segregation, participates in the civil rights movement with the NAACP, helps achieve massive social change, goes to work in an industry and as a black woman achieves notoriety. She's on the job for 30 years; she's a highly respected person in that community. With the arc of this woman's life, to now at this age in her 60s, to have to do battle with the State of Louisiana, the City of New Orleans, the United States of America in order to get back into her house, this is just not right. But she did it. That's the thing that's so amazing. She actually went back to the barricades and won."
(PBS interview added in the commentary of the DVD, 09:00)

5   After he was re-elected in 2006, Mayor Ray Nagin declared that the city would not invest money in the Lower Ninth Ward and New Orleans East: "I've been saying this publicly, and people are starting to hear it: low-lying areas of New Orleans east, stay

houses would be bulldozed when damage was estimated at beyond 51% of their fair market value.[6] Demme underlines Parker's stance of bravery by cutting to archive footage showing her addressing the panel of bureaucrats gathered at the Sheraton. He draws attention to her isolated position as she stands up overtly accusing the local authorities of discriminating against the black residents of the Lower Ninth Ward.

Parker rarely appears outside her familiar setting which seems to be geographically limited to her immediate surrounding. Her speaking in favor of the reopening of St. David Church, which was still a matter of debate when Demme started filming, however, pinpoints the enduring legacy of race and class: Carolyn was compelled to attend mass service at St. Maurice Church, which did not suffer the same damage as St. David because it was located in a more affluent neighborhood. Restricting his approach to New Orleans through Parker's experience in the Lower Ninth Ward permits Demme to enhance the individual commitment of the woman whose determination to stay in her neighborhood and to have her house refurbished is also a strategy that aims to demonstrate and to counter the segregationist policies of the city. Her fight for her house testifies to an engagement that intertwines the personal and the political, highlighting the fact that segregation translates into the private realm.

As an African-American widow who does not have a lot of money to live with, Parker stands for a minority – which the geographical focus on her house emphasizes. Never does Parker confess any economic motives for her decision to remain in the Lower Ninth Ward, although Demme explains in a voice-over that "almost two years after the floods now, Carolyn has finally received the federally provided financial assistance promised to the underinsured homeowners like herself under the increasingly controversial Road Home program" (50:35). The film depicts the Lower Ninth Ward as a black community where few white people venture – apart from contractors hoping to wrench money from the poor.

---

away from... Move closer to the river" (qtd. in Villemoare/Stillman, "Civic Culture and the Politics of Planning for Neighborhoods and Housing in Post-Katrina" 2010: 28). The authors interpret the mayor's declaration: "In effect, therefore, the mayor as authority figure was saying both that people could come back (and even had a right to do so) and that it would be better if they did not (and that the city would not be investing in them, providing services for them, or reintegrating their neighborhoods into the city as a whole)." (ibid)

6 These demolitions happened without prior notice to the owners, which left many homeowners anxiously wondering whether their home might be next (cf. Verchick 2010: 195).

Away from New Orleans

Lee, on his part, examines the city's spatial layout through a collection of interviews and points out the impact of segregation on the landscape of the city, which according to sociologist Mary Pattillo-McCoy underscores the relationship between place and segregation: "Racial segregation means that racial inequalities in employment, education, income, and wealth are inscribed in space. Predominantly white neighborhoods benefit from the historically determined and contemporarily sustained edges that whites enjoy." (1999: 159) Lee's documentary series captures race and class differences through filming the visual landscape of New Orleans, for example using editing to convey the striking contrast between the clean undamaged mansion erected behind Mitch Landrieu with the derelict landscape of the Lower Ninth Ward. Lee travels outside New Orleans to interview evacuees who were compelled to settle in other parts of the country because the lack of social services, including education and health care, made it impossible for them to come back to New Orleans.

In *If God is Willing and da Creek Don't Rise* (Part 1), Clovina "Rita" McCoy and Catherine Montana Gordon explain that their decision to stay in Humble, Texas, was dictated by the special needs of an autistic child that would not be taken care of in New Orleans. The pink wall used as a background to the interview shows no personal item as though the two women had been cut off from their past by moving away from their home city. These testimonies point to the disruption of the affective relationship between individuals and places: the women stand in front of the house they bought in Humble, which however displays their indifference to the place. There are neither trees nor any flowers adorning the garden around the house, which does not seem to have been invested with affection. Humble is the site of no cultural or family memory for New Orleanians who look back at the Big Easy as their home city.

David Harvey explains that places are constructed through socio-spatial practices; home is not just identified as the place where one lives, it is endowed with cultural and social values as individuals weave their individual life stories into the local narrative:

Places are constructed and experienced as material ecological artefacts and intricate networks of social relations. They are the focus of the imaginary, of beliefs, longing and desires (most particularly with respect to the psychological pull and push of the idea of "home"). They are an intense focus of discursive activity, filled with symbolic and representational meanings, and they are a distinctive product of institutionalized social and economic power. (1996: 316)

Clovina "Rita" McCoy keeps repeating that she hates Texas; the outside shots point to the isolation of the house in a humdrum suburb, where all the houses look identical to each other, with clean paths defining the ideal distance between neighbors. The women have not really integrated the local routine and there is no sign of their blending into a state that represents their uprootedness. Their house therefore symbolizes the alienation produced by displacement after Hurricane Katrina, which Carolyn Parker strives to resist by insisting on her right to return.

Lee's documentary conveys a bleak picture of New Orleans, giving voice to those characters who were not able to recover their place in the city, whereas Demme's film relates an enlightening tale of how Carolyn Parker managed to surmount the obstacles to have the house renovated. She embodies the self-reliant ethic that draws admiration and respect. Her life story fits a preconceived narrative of individual empowerment that allows Demme to turn her into the heroine of his biographical film. Although the documentary is no biopic, it derives from the genre and emphasizes the personal over the political. Carolyn Parker is therefore portrayed as an exemplary individual rather than as a committed political figure. Through using a wide range of interviews, Lee challenges the biographical mode of narration and makes for a more complex and contradictory experience.

CONCLUSION

The documentaries made for television by Lee and Demme enrich the portrayal of African-Americans on screen, challenging the stereotypes that came to the forefront in the wake of Katrina. Many survivors were framed in negative terms by the media, which adopted a "blame the victim"-approach, passing moral judgment on those families who could not evacuate before the storm. The focus on Carolyn Parker allows Demme to overturn the "underclass" image that struck many viewers watching the scenes of despair unfolding outside the Convention Center on their small screen. Delving into the Lower Ninth Ward through her guidance, Demme offers an intimate insight into the quarter and challenges its reputation of danger.

While circumstances enhance Parker's victimization, the film overturns this image by spotlighting her determination to overcome the barriers on her path: identified as a victim of social injustice since neither her house nor her quarter were taken into account by the local authorities' initial plans for reconstruction, Parker comes out as a strong character who will fight for her right as an American citizen and as a Christian. In the words of Demme, the film portrays Parker as "a woman who is driven by her vision of social justice, the difference between right and wrong, how people should be dealt with. Her fuel was much drawn from religious beliefs, from her relationship with God." (cf. "Filmmaker Interview") Her church going provides a leitmotif throughout the film with the still camera observing moments of religious fervor, using diegetic music to share her piety.

Lee does not aim to establish this proximity with his interviewees, for he builds a militant piece setting forth political views that Demme does not engage with. While Lee's concern with racial issues taints his approach to New Orleans' reconstruction policies, enhancing the structural legacies of segregation on the present, Demme eschews political debates by prioritizing the emotional dimension of Carolyn's story.

The two documentaries nonetheless offer empowering stories of individual strength by arousing interest in the lives of ordinary characters. Both Carolyn Parker and Phyllis Montana-Leblanc embody inspiring models of strength. Demme's camera expresses his personal fascination for a woman whose life was devoted to fighting injustice whereas Lee's filmmaking turns every individual statement into political comment. Aestheticizing every shot to leave his recognizable imprint on the film, Lee explores the sociological power of documentary filmmaking, recording those testimonies, which provide an intimate look at the events that hit the headlines. Demme does not broach the controversies that Lee tackles, turning Carolyn Parker into an American hero whose racial background matters less than her will of strength. The documentary downplays the notion of race by calling attention to the supposedly all-American ideal or myth of the power of the individual will and perseverance embodied by Parker.

BIBLIOGRAPHY

Entrikin, J. Nicholas (1991): *The Betweenness of Place: Towards a Geography of Modernity*, Baltimore: Johns Hopkins University Press.
Harvey, David (1996): *Justice, Nature and the Geography of Difference*, Oxford: Blackwell.
I'm Carolyn Parker, the Good, the Mad and the Beautiful, (2011). Dir. by Jonathan Demme. Alexandria, Va.: PBS. DVD.
If God is Willing and da Creek Don't Rise, (2010). Dir. by Spike Lee. New York: HBO Documentary Films, 40 Acres and a Mule. DVD.
"I'm Carolyn Parker: Filmmaker Interview with Jonathan Demme," 28 August, 2014 (http://video.pbs.org/video/2260782771/).
Jennings, James/Jushnick, Louis (1999): "Poverty as Race, Power and Wealth." In: Louis Jushnick/James Jennings (eds.), *A New Introduction to Poverty: The*

Role of Race, Power, and Politics, New York: New York University Press, pp. 1-12.

Letort, Delphine (2015): *The Spike Lee Brand: Study of Documentary Filmmaking*, New York: SUNY Press.

Nichols, Bill ([2001] 2010): *Introduction to Documentary*, Bloomington: Indiana University Press.

Pattillo-McCoy, Mary (1999): *Black Picket Fences: Privilege and Peril among the Black Middle Class*, Chicago: University of Chicago Press.

Roscoe, Jane/Hight, Craig (2011): *Faking It: Mock Documentary and the Subversion of Factuality*, Manchester: Manchester University Press.

Verchick, Robert R. M. (2010): *Facing Catastrophe: Environmental Action for a Post-Katrina World*, Cambridge: Harvard University Press.

Villemoare, Adelaide H./Stillman, Peter G. (2010): "Civic Culture and the Politics of Planning for Neighborhoods and Housing in Post-Katrina New Orleans." In: M. B. Hacker (ed.), *Culture after Hurricanes, Rhetoric and Reinvention on the Gulf Coast*, Jackson: University Press of Mississippi, pp. 17-43.

When the Levees Broke: A Requiem in Four Acts, (2006). Dir. by Spike Lee. New York: HBO Documentary Films, 40 Acres and a Mule. DVD.

Lewis Watts: *To the Ancestors*, Guardians of the Flame Arts Society, Harrison family home, Upper 9th Ward on Mardi Gras morning 2007

On the 2nd celebration of Mardi Gras after Hurricane Katrina, this was a ceremony using the Yoruba practice of pouring libations to honor those who came before. Also the children in Mardi Gras Indian suits show the promise that the traditions will endure. I gained access to this and other customs, after I exhibited my early work from New Orleans along with other artists from there. They felt that my work warranted access that was not easily given. I have been very grateful for their generosity.

Recycling and Surviving in *Beasts of the Southern Wild*: Screening Katrina as a Magic Realist Tale

Miriam Strube

Prologue: The Man on the Dump

The movie *Beasts of the Southern Wild* (2012) is placed in an incongruous setting: on a dump amidst nature. This placement connects it to the modernist project of showing decay, disillusionment, a wasteland. Even more, as I want to show, it can be connected to a very complex – and somewhat ambivalent – approach to trash, junk, the dump. The poem "The Man on the Dump" (1942) by modernist writer Wallace Stevens provides a helpful reference to open and motivate my argument, allowing me to introduce the intricate structure of the film as well as to incorporate a layer of criticism.

In "The Man on the Dump" Stevens presents imagery showing that being on a dump might not be such a bad place. Moreover, it is his version of an elegy, a poetic form highly fashionable in his time. Like other modernists, Stevens judges the classical elegy, which is of the deceased of high origin, to be outdated. Departing from Thomas Gray's Romantic poetry in the early 1740s, especially Gray's epochal "Elegy," modernism shifted the focus to the deceased of common origin and "to the events occurring in the mind of the poetic persona contemplating that death. […] This facilitates the shift in emphasis from the deceased to the mourner." (Dolan 1997: 209)

Similarly, Stevens turns his elegiac reflection to the obscure, the low, the common, the quotidian, as the poem says: "the janitor's poems / Of every day, the wrapper on the can of pears, / The cat in the paper-bag, the corset, the box" ([1942] 1997: 184). In this modernist version of the elegy, the high is no longer valued, but is supplanted by the common, therefore, the humble: "Did the nightingale torture the ear, / Pack the heart and scratch the mind?" The answer in "The Man on the Dump" is that indeed the once conventional and traditional image of the nightingale is no longer valued but becomes supplanted by the "crow's voice" (ibid: 185), in which the speaker finds solace. Similarly, *Beasts of the Southern Wild* goes beyond the conventional imagery of what is generally valued, turning to the common, and literally to animals' voices.

However, in "The Man on the Dump," Stevens goes further and refuses to simply reproduce the modernist elegy, which John Dolan convincingly terms a self-centered elegy. Indeed, the poem displays a self-conscious gesture refusing to mourn the dead for poetic gain; a gesture that ironically picks up the popular style of Edgar Lee Masters's modernist elegy, but it places the speaker not in a country graveyard but in a city dump.

In what follows, I will turn to a filmic dump,[1] namely the city dump in the movie *Beasts of the Southern Wild*. Structurally being led by the challenges posed by Stevens's poem "The Man on the Dump," my essay will first turn to the discursive function of this specific dump. In the main part, I thus analyze the film's social comment on post-Katrina America. While there have been no publications on this film from academia, it has been widely reviewed by online critics and viewers, usually in a (sometimes too) celebratory manner. Many claim – and rightly so – that, as Steven Rea puts it in *Inquirer*, the "specter of Hurricane Katrina and its aftermath hovers over the story – if not literally, then metaphorically" (2012: n.p.). As Stephen Whitty points out the film "never actually mentions Katrina, or the Ninth Ward, [nevertheless] it's clearly invoking that disaster, and identifying with the poorest of its victims. The native Louisianans we meet here are resourceful, stubborn, suspicious survivors." (2012: n.p.) This connection has also created some criticism. In his online article published in *Time Out*, Joshua Rothkopf, for example, asks: "How can a movie so steeped in post-Katrina imagery eschew even the smallest comment about social responsibility? Maybe that was deemed too earnest, a decision that makes zero sense when a twinkling score [...] is ladled on like instant pathos. Real people aren't beasts, nor do they require starry-eyed glorification." (2012: n.p.)

In contrast to this criticism, which does not seem to understand the literary reference of the film's title, my reading analyzes the movie's more or less subtle social comment. In order to do so, it is helpful to read it as a magic realist film that places the protagonist and her community on a dump. In showing this marginalized community on a dump, the film renders visible how not only discarded objects but people as well can be judged or turned into trash by mainstream

---

1 Throughout the text, I will not differentiate between the dump and the junkyard, reading them both as places that pile up discarded objects as junk.

society; but the movie also displays how this community refuses this very position, similarly as the speaker in "The Man on the Dump" refuses to see the dump as merely bad.

In the epilogue, I will return to Stevens's poem, of which I have claimed that it also goes beyond the modernist project in commenting on the writer's ambivalent role when displaying the dead, even if the ordinary dead, for poetic gain. This final part thus reflects on the role of the artist or scholar incorporating the dump. In this contemplation I also turn to the film philosopher Stanley Cavell, "the only major American philosopher who has made the subject of film a central part of his work" (Rothman 2009: 344). In this meta-reflection, Cavell's insights are particularly important to my question of what it means to *screen* 'ordinary' people on a dump. I thus contemplate the double meaning of screening that Cavell has focused on. In this context it should be pointed out that his "writings on film are capable of helping academic film study free itself to explore regions that have remained closed to it – capable of inspiring the field to think in exciting new ways about film and its history" (ibid.).[2] More specifically, he helps in posing film *ontological* questions rather than simply giving a set of instruments for analyzing film.[3] But I am not only interested in what Cavell has to say about film ontology, especially his notion of screening as I will explore in the final part of this essay, but also in what Cavell continuously does in his writing, namely pointing to the self-reflective dimension of *writing* about film.

THE GIRL ON THE DUMP

The film *Beasts of the Southern Wild* was made in 2012 by Benh Zeitlin and the New Orleans-based collective called Court 13.[4] Following the devastating effects of Hurricane Katrina, Zeitlin and his Court 13 cohort went to New Orleans and

---

2   Thus, for instance, when analyzing the comedies of remarriage in *Pursuit of Happiness*, he differs from readings that assume these films as escapist fairy tales for the Depression era. Rather, he argues that this genre is a way of thinking that not only affirms the possibility, but even claims a necessity of social change for gender roles.

3   For example, in *Pursuit of Happiness* he sees "the specific difficulty of philosophy and calls upon its particular strength, to receive inspiration for taking thought from the very conditions that oppose thought." (41-42)

4   Among the awards *Beasts of the Southern Wild* received are the top award for dramatic (fiction) film and for cinematography at the Sundance Film Festival, and the Caméra d'Or prize for best first feature at Cannes.

first shot a short movie, *Glory at Sea* (2008), a fantasy about a group of mourners who build a raft out of debris and rescue their loved ones trapped beneath the waves.[5] In *Beasts of the Southern Wild*, his first feature film, Zeitlin continued this idea yet connected it to the play *Juicy and Delicious* (2012) by Lucy Alibar, who (in cooperation with Zeitlin) also freely adapted this play to the screen, keeping the original play's mix of childhood wonder with the harsh realities of the adult world at the margins of the United States.

Beasts of the Southern Wild has been called a small miracle of deliberate outsider art that entranced and exhilarated audiences during its limited theatrical run after its opening night. Unruly, unbound by studios or the usual Hollywood conventions, this paean to childhood perception and human resilience exists in its own hermetically sealed world, physically and metaphorically. Zeitlin made the movie on a $1.8 million shoestring in southern Louisiana with hand-held cameras, jury-rigged sets, untrained actors and a grass-roots collective of artists (cf. Lidz 2012). The movie ignores some of the usual rules for feature films by including outdated techniques such as 16-millimeter camera and casting non-professionals for all the roles.[6]

The plot of *Beasts of the Southern Wild* follows the young girl Hushpuppy (Quvenzhané Wallis) and shows what happens when a Katrina-like storm hits the narrow and ruggedly beautiful Isle de Jean Charles, a fictional place known affectionately by the locals in the film as The Bathtub, located beyond the levees that keep the delta dry. Hushpuppy's mother is long gone; now she and her sick and drinking father Wink (Dwight Henry) are living together, if in separate sheds. As her father succumbs to illness and alcohol – and with a hurricane on the way – Hushpuppy has to figure out how to survive, if necessary even on her own. The confluence of Hushpuppy's father being sick with Bathtub's flooding creates the arc of the storyline.

---

5   As Murray Bookchin's politically oriented approach to environmentalist philosophy argues, ecological crises "offer a powerful incentive to pursue the transformation of social and political institutions and processes in a non-hierarchical, anarchistic direction" (qtd. in Meyer 2001: 30).

6   Not in its style but in terms of the protagonist, Richard Corliss sees the movie's antecedents in the "intensity of Terrence Malick's early films, the conflicts and tenderness of the multiracial kids in David Gordon Green's *George Washington*, the family antagonisms in Kasi Lemmons' *Eve's Bayou* and, further back, Robert Flaherty's 1948 *Louisiana Story*, the proto-indie tale of a Cajun boy whose life is upended by the construction of a nearby oil rig" (2012: n.p.).

The film's opening sequence introduces the setting and gives a sense of the protagonists, Hushpuppy and her father. The soundtrack first concentrates on natural sounds, introducing the protagonists' life in close proximity to nature. Then a glockenspiel is added, musically pointing to the girl protagonist (in a rather clichéd fashion, as it is often used to introduce a young character). Indeed, it is Hushpuppy who is then displayed not only as the main protagonist but also as the narrator who gives voice-over comments. While using Hushpuppy's voice-over to comment on animals and her relationship to them, the visuals focus not only on Hushpuppy herself but also on old spare tires, broken car pieces and other objects on the dump that have been used to build both Hushpuppy's and her father's shed or which lay around nearby. Interestingly, living on a dump, having recycled thrown-away material, being surrounded by objects others have found obsolete is not reflected upon – those objects seem as 'natural' to Hushpuppy as nature itself.

The film is set on a muddy, tiny island in the Mississippi Delta that is shown to be just one levee away from being under water. In the distance, Hushpuppy and her father see an industrial city, presumably New Orleans, with smokestacks and electrical towers. In contrast, in The Bathtub, they are surrounded by wilderness and animals and earth, making good use of obsolete objects from the other side of the levee. It is a place of magic and junk, joy and mourning, excess and awareness. Not only does it show The Bathtub's survival on the other side of a levee that protects the things of mainstream culture, but it also presents it as an alternative: a world, as Hushpuppy's voice-over emphasizes, with "fish stuck in plastic wrappers" (05:33), "babies stuck in carriages" (05:39), and without regular work or means of production.

The Bathtub's community, with its different take on materialism and living, is further characterized by its multi-ethnic make-up. Having introduced Hushpuppy and her father, the opening sequence picks up speed and noise. Here the interracial community is not only displayed visually but also aurally by zydeco music, a southwestern Louisiana genre that merges Cajun music, blues and rhythm and blues. Yet, even this celebratory opening sequence ends with an ambivalence that runs through the whole movie. The Bathtub community can be seen as an alternative to mainstream culture, living and surviving on thrown-away objects, in close connection to nature (including animals that are both food and friends), and on self-made liquor. While the connection between poverty and closeness to nature might be seen as stereotyped as the sequence's music, there is a subtle irritation that is not stereotypical. The community is not shown as altogether happy; most of the community's members – including Hushpuppy – are shown drinking alcohol or getting drunk. The film does not celebrate or expose that fact, yet it does not condemn it either. Rather, it shows The Bathtub as a place of complex people; they are diverse, different from the mainstream, but despite their problems they are worthy of celebration, as the opening sequence's ending shows in the community's festivity with fireworks and triumphant music that moves from being diegetic to non-diegetic, and is reminiscent of the celebration of winners.

However, following the climax of the film's opening, a much darker side is soon introduced when Hushpuppy's teacher Miss Bathsheba (Gina Montana) warns of global warming, of floods, and of the arrival of wild creatures. Indeed, after the South Pole's ice caps have melted, Hushpuppy eventually faces these creatures called aurochs, fearsome prehistoric behemoths that will reclaim the earth as the ice caps melt.

I would argue that in combining these two levels – real-world problems like poverty and global warming as well as fantastic creatures – Zeitlin uses the mode of magic realism, an aesthetic style originally known from literature and from a Latin American or postcolonial background. Here, magical elements are blended into a realistic atmosphere, which is enhanced by the hand-held camera and rigged sets. In this blending, fantastic elements are displayed as ordinary occurrences and are thus shown in a straightforward manner, allowing an "amalgamation" of the "real" and the "magical" (Hegerfeldt 2005: 37), which thereby is accepted in the same stream of thought. Magical realism, moreover, attempts to access a deeper understanding of reality, or as Anne Hegerfeldt points out in the title of her study on magical realism, "lies that tell the truth."

Although the film depicts fantastic prehistoric animals and a protagonist who communicates with her absent mother, the film tells some truths in Hegerfeldt's sense. First of all, it obviously points to environmental problems like global warming when discussing the melting of the South Pole's ice caps. Global warming, as Ross Gelbspan emphasizes, partly created by the use of carbon fuels, such as coal and petroleum, "has contributed to rising sea levels and stronger tropical storms. Hurricane Katrina is a harbinger of what global warming might bring in the future." (2006: 50)

Secondly, another truth the film implicitly explores is the fact that during Katrina and earlier storms the people in the poor neighborhoods were treated as being unimportant. Spike Lee's documentary *When the Levees Broke: A Requiem in Four Acts* (2006) discusses the 1965 Hurricane Betsy. Lee interviews various people from politicians to John Barry, author of *Rising Tide* (1997), and suggests through the montage of the interviews that during Hurricane Betsy a levee near a poor neighborhood in New Orleans had consciously been dynamited – resulting in peoples' deaths – in order to save richer neighborhoods. Although The Bathtub's community is interracial, placing a black girl and her father at the center points to environmental racism, which is defined by an "unhealthy environment in which a disproportionately large share of poor people and people of color live" (Bullard/Johnson/Torres 2011: 9).[7] Similarly, as David Boaz claims, "Government at all levels – federal, state, and local – failed in responding to Hurricane Katrina. Government officials failed to adequately plan for the hurricane, failed to spend enough money on levees and flood control, and failed to deliver disaster relief in a timely manner or to maintain order following the hurricane." (2006: 30) Walter Ellis likewise points to the race and class divide revealed by Hurricane Katrina: "New Orleans, the city hardest hit by the storm, is one of the poorest cities in the United States; flood victims there were predominantly poor and black. [...] Half the households have an income of less than $22.000; nearly 30 per cent of the population lives officially in poverty." (2006: 15, 16)[8]

Thirdly, the film focuses on the existence of communities living and surviving literally on the margins and on the recycled objects thrown away by mainstream society. Communities as in *Beasts of the Southern Wild* exist and have existed for a long time, for example they did so in large numbers during the Great Depression. These shantytowns for the homeless were so common that they were given a name, namely Hooverville (as they sprang up during the years of President Hoover).

However, it is important to stress that *Beasts of the Southern Wild* is explicitly not a documentary, and makes no claims on *social* realism. The theme of the aurochs runs through the whole movie. I therefore would like to list a number of magical realist features that are at play in *Beasts of the Southern Wild*: 1) It is told in a matter-of-fact tone often from the perspective of an unusual focalizer, such as a child. 2) It is set in a realist setting (it could be near New Orleans), yet combines realist and magical happenings. The screen is filled with magic, from the motes glowing in the air to visions of aurochs. Hushpuppy is also convinced that animals and her absent mother, who "swam away" (12:54) years earlier, talk to her, sometimes in code. 3) It presents an alternative conception of reality, thereby re-evaluating modes of knowledge production (thus The Bathtub that from a mainstream perspective is little more than a dump with broken pieces and people is seen and declared as the most beautiful place on earth by its inhabitants). 4) It rethinks the dominant Western worldviews (namely that you need work, holidays, plastic wrappers and strollers). 5) It regards reality as empirically not perceivable (in

---

7 On environmental racism see also Luke W. Cole and Sheila R. Foster, *From the Ground Up* (2000) as well as Laura Westra, Bill E. Lawson, and Peter S. Wenz, *Faces of Environmental Racism* (2001).

8 In a similar vein, Wickham DeWayne argues that both "race and class played a role in the fate of poor blacks victimized by Hurricane Katrina and the government's poor response. [...] Poverty is the new Jim Crow." (2006: 40, 41)

Hushpuppy's reality her absent mother and the extinct aurochs are present although they do not belong to our empirical world and her mother cannot even be seen by others within the diegetic framework of the film). 6) It expresses a world fissured, distorted, made incredible by cultural displacement (here, the community separated by the walls of the levee). 7) By combining the magical with local legend and imagery to represent cultures that have been unsettled by invasion, occupation or political corruption, Zeitlin uses the magic effect to indict the violence of both empire and its aftermath. In *Beasts of the Southern Wild,* despite mandatory evacuations, The Bathtub's people resist leaving their drowning home – in part out of skepticism, but also out of a fear of tearing the community apart by turning their backs on their home. Instead, the community sings songs, drinks heavily, and celebrates the richness of their lives until officials invade and forcefully relocate the Bathtub people to an emergency shelter on the dry land, which they will escape from as soon as they can to return to The Bathtub.

It also becomes clear that it is not a dream or Hushpuppy's imagination but – being magical realism – the magical is a real part of the story. Thus, when the aurochs run towards a group of girls they all run away until Hushpuppy decides to confront them and to make peace with the aurochs who consequently move away on her order. This is part of the film's rethinking of the dominant Western worldview. Hushpuppy and her community see The Bathtub as decidedly beautiful, not as a place of poverty dependent on junk, not themselves as poor or displaced. The objects placed on their dump become both a means of transportation (such as the fishing boat fashioned out of an old Chevy pickup) and thus of survival as well as objects of resignification.

For Hushpuppy and her community, junk means freedom, self-definition, self-reliance, a positive alternative to the capitalist principles of production (including planned obsolescence) and consumption (in the form of buying), which characterize mainstream society's everyday dynamics and values. Thus, The Bathtub is a complex place, vulnerable but also resistant to cataclysm. Therefore, in a moment of reversal and civil disobedience, one sequence shows the Bathtub people, including Hushpuppy's father and his friends, destroying the levee that keeps the nearby city dry and The Bathtub immersed. But in contrast to the wealthy destroying a levee, as after Hurricane Betsy (and as conspiracy theory has it, also after Hurricane Katrina), they resort to this means not for money but for survival: after the storm, water floods the Bathtub area, and dead animals float in this water bringing diseases and possible death. Rather than buying into the capitalist logic, the Bathtub people simply use junk for their self-reliance and pleasure. This different logic and aesthetic is further underlined by the film's visual mode: consciously shot with hand-held cameras on 16-millimeter film rather than in a digital format, and aided by its ingenious cinematographer, Ben Richardson, the film finds and transports a rugged beauty that is not stylized but is portrayed as untouched and natural.

This alternative of perspectives and values also includes the father-daughter-relationship, which is full of love and care, yet also different from the mainstream's social branding of parenting when he disappears for days or gives her alcohol to drink. That the film reflects parental love can already be seen in the film's title *Beasts of the Southern Wild*, a line from William Blake's poem "The Little Black Boy" (1789). The poem is a strong expression of motherly love vis-à-vis the dualisms of life, played out in the poem as the oppositions between black and white, southern wild and English, earth and heaven, child and adult:

And we are put on earth a little space,
That we may learn to bear the beams of love,
And these black bodies and this sun-burnt face
Is but a cloud, and like a shady grove.

For when our souls have learn'd the heat to bear
The cloud will vanish we shall hear his voice
Saying come out from the grove my love & care,
And round my golden tent like lambs rejoice. ([1789] 2006: 9-10)

As the mother acknowledges that the black child cannot live in acceptance, she is at pains to stress that life on earth is short, "a little space." Like "a cloud" that passes by "black bodies," i.e. the material – racialized – body, will be left behind. In Blake's poem, this only happens in the afterlife when "his voice" can be heard and life continues, rejoicing and in innocence (the lamb being an important symbol representing innocence and purity, if not even Christ Himself). The dualisms built up in the poem, most importantly here between black and white, will be overcome, but only after the child's death.

In contrast, the film's magical realism consciously subverts simple dualisms. The Bathtub's community is not black, but a colorful mixture of different races, an idealized or utopian mixed-race community that is displayed as uncorrupted by politics, religion or consumerism. In this community, there is no typical parental love, no love characterized by bourgeois rules. Hushpuppy's father does love her, however, he is shown as rough, trying to teach her lessons, lessons to make her survive after his death, to be as independent and self-reliant as a grown-up man. Furthermore, in contrast to Blake's poem, the hardship of life is not to be accepted as if heaven were waiting after death. Despite all the junk on the dump, The

Bathtub includes so many animals, so much of the natural world and is depicted as sensual, to be lived with in close relationship with nature. In the opening sequence Hushpuppy's father makes sure that she also gives some food to the dog, but he later also teaches her how to fish by hand and eat crawfish. The structure within this interspecies community is dictated by the food chain – the strong eat the weak. But survival also depends on another basic principle articulated by the teacher Miss Bathsheba, who tells the children: "The most important thing I can teach you – you gotta learn to take care of people smaller and sweeter than you are." (44:05)

More than taking care of only people, Hushpuppy has learned to take care of animals as well. Although she and her father do not have much food (or clothes, or anything else, for that matter) in the opening sequence of the film, her father asks her to share her food with the dog. This collective is not only diverse, it is an interspecies collective, in which human beings and animals live side by side. Indeed, Hushpuppy is convinced that she sometimes can understand what the animals are saying. Despite all its complexity and ambivalence, The Bathtub is perceived as somewhat magical: despite the thrown-away lumber, scrap metal and junk, The Bathtub is almost shown as a kind of Eden where man and beast, nature and junk are side by side. Chickens and pigs roam freely around Hushpuppy's home, sometimes companions and sometimes dinner. Thus, in contrast to Blake's poem, for Hushpuppy, the magical annihilation of dualisms takes place not in heaven but on earth.

Nevertheless, it should be stressed that The Bathtub is not displayed as Eden as the story continues. Death looms large, both for Hushpuppy's father and the community. What might look like a romanticization of The Bathtub in some scenes is counterbalanced by Hushpuppy's fear, her sense of loneliness when talking to her absent mother and her drinking alcohol, as well as the others' heavy drinking. Again, a magical level and a realist level merge in the characterization of The Bathtub and its inhabitants, creating an ambivalent picture more than a simple romanticization.

The film's magic further emphasizes that reality is not empirically perceivable – there always are myths and mythmaking. Indeed, Hushpuppy takes on a form of mythmaking when she draws her own kind of cave art on a thrown away cardboard box. Imagining the archeological discovery of her cave art, she says "I'm recording my story for the scientists. In a million years when kids go to school they're gonna know once there was a Hushpuppy and she lived with her Daddy in the Bathtub." (17:11) Using the third person although talking about herself not only shows her imaginative storytelling, but even in partaking in a crucial element of culture production – in the art at the center of early mankind, namely mythmaking. Moreover, referring to herself as "a Hushpuppy," places her in the midst of this interspecies community; after all, as a hushpuppy originally was a piece of food to be thrown to dogs to hush them during a hunt, Hushpuppy's name – and her objectification when using it in this scene – significantly points to her as part of the food chain, part of a larger scheme of things.

Towards the end the film assumes a more spiritual tone (reminiscent of Terrence Malick's recent films as *The New World* or *Tree of Life*), letting Hushpuppy realize the universe's interconnectedness: "The entire universe depends on everything fitting together just right. If you can fix the broken piece, everything can go right back." (50:14) When the aurochs finally reach The Bathtub, the other children run away. Hushpuppy, however, turns to face them, resolute in her knowledge that she's "a little piece of a big, big universe." (1:30:11) "You are my friends, kind of, but I gotta take care of mine" (1:24:23), she tells them, the beasts retreating as Hushpuppy tends to her moribund father. At the end, after their return from the dry side to The Bathtub and after her father's death, she acknowledges her place in the larger scheme of things. Recognizing the material and metaphysical truth about the interconnectedness of all things, Hushpuppy believes her highest calling is to care for others, in particular the Bathtub people. Thus, while the realist part of this magic realist movie directs attention (without offering political solutions) to the social and environmental habits and effects of a throw-away culture, the magic elements point to the facts that a different (interspecies) community with a different way of life is possible. Moreover, it underlines that even when consumer culture and climate change happened to make (some or all) humans obsolete in the sense of supplanting them with new forms of life, the "big universe" Hushpuppy reflects upon will continue in any case.

EPILOGUE: THE SCHOLAR ON THE DUMP

Screening and contemplating the poverty, junk, and subversive communities on view in *Beasts of the Southern Wild* is an important endeavor, making visible the relationship between the values and lifestyles of mainstream culture and their social and ecological effects. However, when taking Cavell's film philosophy into account, screening such communities is no easy or simple task.[9] As Cavell argues

---

9   As Espen Hammer points out, "on first reading, Cavell's work may seem to have little to offer by way of political reflection" (2006: 164). Nevertheless, Hammer rightly argues that the more one reads Cavell, "the clearer it becomes that most of his thinking, even when its distance from the political seems to be considerable, actually is

in *The World Viewed*, screening has a double meaning: on one level screening means to show something on the screen, yet on another level it functions in a very different way because a "screen is a barrier. What does the silver screen screen? It screens me from the world it holds – that is, makes me invisible. And it screens that world from me – that is, screens its existence from me." (1979b: 24) Any film including different or poor communities for telling a story that also displays environmental awareness has to deal with this paradoxical double structure of screening. In *Beasts of the Southern Wild* we see The Bathtub and its glory as well as its problems, yet we are also screened from the very problems it displays: the audience is watching, it is not and does not become a part of it.

Thus, in a Cavellian mode of self-reflexivity when writing about film, let me return to Stevens's "The Man on the Dump." While Stevens shares the modernist aversion to celebrating the grand and the so-called high, he is also suspicious of the modernist elegy that stages an epiphany when the derelict landscape is transformed into decorative literary meaning. Rather, Stevens makes fun of it when taking the modern elegy from the rural graveyard to the city dump. As one continues, it becomes clear that the speaker is continuously uncomfortable:

One sits and beats an old tin can, lard pail.
One beats and beats for that which one believes.
That's what one wants to get near. Could it after all
Be merely oneself, as superior as the ear
To a crow's voice?
[...]
Is it a philosopher's honeymoon, one finds
On the dump? (1997: 185)

As the speaker wonders, is the democratic impulse of turning from the high to the low just pretense, is it just self-serving for the philosopher, scholar or artist? The poem plays with images of ripeness and freshness – and the speaker ends up on a self-serving quest for some fresh material, in which junk is screened (in the double sense of Cavell, thus both named but kept at a distance). A democratic merging with the common and humble therefore is a mere façade.

As in the modernist elegy, recent years have shown a heightened interest in the dump, in junk, in trash. Most of these do express an interest in environmental

---

inseparable from some form of socio-political articulation" (ibid.). Cavell himself agrees with this assessment of his work, pointing to the pervasiveness of the political in his work (cf. 2006: 288).

politics or ecological philosophy. This interest might be best symbolized by Slavoj Žižek, who (like Stevens's speaker) places himself literally next to a garbage dump when being filmed for the documentary *Examined Life*, telling the audience in his interview segment to embrace our trash if we want a "real political ecology" (cf. Taylor 2008). So are we just dealing with a new academic topic or is there more to the scholar on the dump?

When contemplating this question I again would like to turn to Cavell, especially his *Philosophy the Day after Tomorrow*. Screening a community living on a dump can also be seen as what he calls a passionate utterance. He defines a passionate utterance as "an invitation to improvisation in the disorders of desire" (2005: 19; cf. also 185). In contrast to J. L. Austin's performative utterance, in which the "I" is central, in a "passionate utterance, the 'you' comes essentially into the picture. [...] In hate speech, the other, the you in question, is a group and the aim is precisely not to elicit a response in kind but to dictate or to stifle response, to make 'we' impossible." (Cavell 2006: 271)[10] *Beasts of the Southern Wild* is decidedly no hate speech, a fact that has some online reviewers as Lisa Kennedy argue that The Bathtub's community is "romanticized and therefore condescended to" (2012: n.p.). In contrast, I would argue that despite or rather because of the decidedly beautiful, intriguing and at times romanticizing images, *Beasts of the Southern Wild* is a passionate utterance trying to create a "we" by envisioning this partly magical and partly critical as well as anarchical Bathtub community.

Thus, in order not to end up as a version of the self-serving philosopher or artist speaking from the comfort of his or her screened-off armchair, artists – as well as the scholars among us who interpret their work – might be well advised to include the kind of self-reflection displayed in Stevens's poem and consider its political and ecological implications more clearly. As a Cavellian defense of sociality would have it, "human beings find themselves (initially) unburdened with responsibilities to one another, and that it is the business of political or moral philosophy to identify, explain, and justify what responsibilities they ought to assume" (Norris 2006: 12). In *Beasts of the Southern Wild*, filmmaker Benh Zeitlin does not include an obvious self-reflection as Stevens does in his poem, but his magic realism considers larger political and moral responsibilities in post-Katrina America. The film therefore does not end up as self-serving or simply using or abusing Katrina as a fresh topic; it rather calls for a changed mode of being, both with each other in a world of diversity and with the natural world. This changed

---

10 Similarly, the emphasis on intersubjectivity in *The Claim of Reason* (especially in part IV) shows that Cavell underlines the role of the other in the journey toward the realization of one's (future) self.

mode, the film seems to suggest, is the only way to avoid further catastrophes such as Hurricane Katrina.

Bibliography

Alibar, Lucy (2012): *Juicy and Delicious*, New York: Diversion Books.

Barry, John M. (1997): *Rising Tide: The Great Mississippi Flood of 1927 and How It Changed America*, New York: Touchstone.

Blake, William: ([1789] 2006): "The Little Black Boy." In: *Songs of Innocence and of Experience*, London: Tate, pp. 9-10.

Beasts of the Southern Wild, (2012). Dir. by Benh Zeitlin. Los Angeles: Fox Searchlight Pictures. DVD.

Boaz, David (2006): "Hurricane Katrina Revealed the Ineffectiveness of Big Government." In: William Dudley (ed.), *Hurricane Katrina*, Detroit: Greenhaven Press, pp. 30-35.

Bullard, Robert D./Johnson, Glenn S./Torres, Angel O. (2011): *Environmental Health and Racial Equity in the United States: Strategies for Building Environmentally Just, Sustainable, and Livable Communities*, Washington: American Public Health Association Press.

Cavell, Stanley (1979a): *The Claim of Reason: Wittgenstein, Skepticism, Morality, and Tragedy*, Oxford: Oxford University Press.

Cavell, Stanley (1979b): *The World Viewed*, Cambridge: Harvard University Press.

Cavell, Stanley (1981): *Pursuits of Happiness: The Hollywood Comedy of Remarriage*, Cambridge: Harvard University Press.

Cavell, Stanley (2005): *Philosophy the Day after Tomorrow*, Cambridge: Harvard University Press.

Cavell, Stanley (2006): "The Incessance and the Absence of the Political." In: Andrew Norris (ed.), *The Claim to Community. Essays on Stanley Cavell and Political Philosophy*, Stanford: Stanford University Press, pp. 263-317.

Cole, Luke W./Foster, Sheila R. (2000): *From the Ground Up: Environmental Racism and the Rise of the Environmental Justice*, New York: New York University Press.

Corliss, Richard (2012): "*Beasts of the Southern Wild*: A Child's Garden of Wonders." In: *Time*, June 26, 2012 (http://entertainment.time.com/2012/06/26/beasts-of-the-southern-wild-a-childs-garden-of-wonders/).

Dolan, John (1997): "A Refusal to Mourn: Stevens and the Self-Centered Elegy." In: *Journal of Modern Literature* 21/2, pp. 209-222.

Ellis, Walter (2006): "Hurricane Katrina Revealed America's Social and Economic Inequalities." In: William Dudley (ed.), *Hurricane Katrina*, Detroit: Greenhaven Press, pp. 15-20.

Examined Life, (2009): Dir. by Astra Taylor. New York: Zeitgeist Films. DVD.

Glory at Sea, (2008): Dir. by Benh Zeitlin. New Orleans: Court 13 Pictures.

Gelbspan, Ross (2006): "Hurricane Katrina Revealed the Seriousness of the Global Warming Problem." In: William Dudley (ed.), *Hurricane Katrina*, Detroit: Greenhaven Press, pp. 50-55.

Hammer, Espen (2006): "Cavell and Political Romanticism." In: Andrew Norris (ed.), *The Claim to Community: Essays on Stanley Cavell and Political Philosophy*, Stanford: Stanford University Press, pp. 165-185.

Hegerfeldt, Anne C. (2005): *Lies That Tell the Truth: Magic Realism Seen Through Contemporary Fiction from Britain*, Amsterdam, New York: Rodopi.

Kennedy, Lisa (2012): "*Beasts of the Southern Wild* Triumphs With Child Hero." In: *Denver Post*, July 13, 2012 (http://denverpost.com/ci_21055216/bracing-beauty-beasts-southern-wild-triumphs-child-hero).

Lidz, Franz (2012): "How Benh Zeitlin Made Beasts of the Southern Wild." In: *Smithsonian Magazine*, February 24, 2015 (http://www.smithsonianmag.com/arts-culture/how-benh-zeitlin-made-beasts-of-the-southern-wild-135132724/?all).

Meyer, John (2001): *Political Nature: Environmentalism and the Interpretation of Western Thought*, Cambridge: MIT Press.

Norris, Andrew (2006): "Introduction: Stanley Cavell and the Claim to Community." In: Andrew Norris (ed.), *The Claim to Community: Essays on Stanley Cavell and Political Philosophy*, Stanford: Stanford University Press, pp. 1-18.

Rea, Steven (2012): "*Beasts of the Southern Wild*: A Magical Trip to Bayou Country." In: *philly.com*, July 13, 2012 (http://philly.com/philly/entertainment/movies/20120713__Beasts_of_the_Southern_Wild___A_magical_trip_to_bayou_country.html?c=r).

Rothkopf, Joshua (2012): "*Beasts of the Southern Wild.*" In: *Time Out*, June 26, 2012 (http://www.timeout.com/us/film/beasts-of-the-southern-wild).

Rothman, William (2009): "Stanley Cavell." In: Paisley Livingston/Carl Plantinga (eds.), *The Routledge Companion to Philosophy and Film*, New York: Routledge, pp. 344-355.

Stevens, Wallace ([1942] 1997): "The Man on the Dump." In: Frank Kermode/Joan Richardson (eds.), *Collected Poetry and Prose*, New York: Library of America, pp. 184-186.

Westra, Laura/Lawson, Bill E./Wenz, Peter S. (2001): *Faces of Environmental Racism: Confronting Issues of Global Justice*, Lanham: Rowman and Littlefield.

When the Levees Broke: A Requiem in Four Acts, (2006): Dir. by Spike Lee. New York: HBO Documentary Films, 40 Acres and a Mule. DVD.

Wickham, DeWayne (2006): "Racism Played a Part in America's Response to Katrina." In: William Dudley (ed.), *Hurricane Katrina*, Detroit: Greenhaven Press, pp. 40-42.

Whitty, Stephen (2012): *"Beasts of the Southern Wild."* In: *NJ*, June 27, 2012 (http://www.nj.com/entertainment/movies/index.ssf/2012/06/beasts_of_the_southern_wild_review_deep-fried_dysfunction.html).

Lewis Watts: *Skeleton Krew*, Mardi Gras Day, Tremé 2008

There is a direct connection between Haiti, Santiago de Cuba and New Orleans, as Haitians brought much of the aesthetics of carnival with them after being exiled from Haiti and then Cuba, ending up in New Orleans.

Down in the *Treme:* Televising Man-made Natural Disaster in the New Millennium

KORNELIA FREITAG

David Simon and Eric Overmyer's HBO drama series *Treme* (2010-2013) tells the story of New Orleans in the aftermath of Hurricane Katrina.[1] As pointed out by the producers, the critics, and New Orleanians alike,[2] the show strove for and achieved great realism by including local residents, writers, and consultants in the production and in the cast, and by referencing real-life New Orleans natives in the fictional fates of some of the protagonists. Yet after the first overwhelmingly positive reactions, criticism started to be raised concerning "formulaic" and problem-belittling plot lines (Miley 2011: 99-101), an imbalance of black and white stories (Rathke 2012: 262-263), or the tendency to cater to the very same touristic gaze the show itself denounces (ibid: 261-267; Thomas 2012: 213-220).

In fact, both the praise as well as the criticism are well founded. As I will argue, the reason for the contradictory assessment seems to reside less in the inability or unwillingness of the producers to 'get things right' (as basically all critics insinuate) but more in the primarily realist narrative strategy of the show. In the first part of my article, "'Buck jumpin' and having fun'[3]: Local Color in *Treme*," I will take a closer look at this strategy and the reason for the mixed messages it seems to be sending. In the second part, "Containing the Storm: Natural and Technological Haunting in *Treme*," I will turn to the marginalization of nature's role in the catastrophe by *Treme*'s focus on the drama in the life stories of the various protagonists, and I will demonstrate that this marginalization of the

---

1 The article refers mainly to the first season that is devoted to the time directly following Katrina, starting three months after the storm.
2 Cf. the running commentary by Dave Walker in *The Times-Picayune* (http://topics.nola.com/tag/treme-explained-season-1/posts.html).
3 "The Treme Song," theme song of the series by John Boutté.

hurricane's role is a direct effect of the show's overall realism. While I will argue that the flood itself does get short thrift due to the series' realist narrative strategy, I will also show that various stark narrative and visual interruptions in the flow of the human (interest) stories *do* nonetheless reference the material impact of the storm on the community of New Orleans, even if they are so smoothly embedded that they have been mostly overlooked or dismissed so far. I will argue that it is exactly the anti-realist or non-realist moments of *Treme* that contradict its general anthropocentric thrust and make the hurricane surface – every now and then – in all its man-made natural horror.

"BUCK JUMPIN' AND HAVING FUN": LOCAL COLOR IN *TREME*

As has been pointed out, for instance in the discussions by Anthony N. Smith, Herman Gray, and Lynnell L. Thomas, *Treme*'s narrative strategy is intricately connected to the possibilities and restrictions of "quality TV" and the general make-up and expectations of its viewers. Smith, for instance, specifies that *Treme*, just like other cable network series, could "develop narratives less intensely paced than those founded in network contexts" (2012: 152) because no breaks for advertisements were necessary. Turning towards more critical effects of the show's venue, Gray argues that "because it makes for compelling quality television" and aims at boosting the city's failing reputation, *Treme* "through no fault of its own, displaces critical engagement with public policy choices and state-centered redress for economic, cultural, and social injustice and inequality" (2012: 268). Thomas, focusing on the effect of the TV series' position "between cultural reproduction and theatrical production" discusses the related "tension between the welcome recognition and celebration of New Orleans black expressive culture and its spectacularization and commodification" (2012: 213).

One might argue that the same problems and limitations of prime time cable TV should have also applied to David Simon and his co-producers' *The Wire*. Yet, the celebrated HBO production on the Baltimore drug scene, which preceded the show about the aftermath of Katrina in New Orleans, has been positively compared to *Treme* by almost all of the latter's detractors. Wade Rathke, for instance, complains: "One would think that anyone, especially an astute observer of urban space like Simon, would be able to see that post-Katrina New Orleans has much more on its mind than a second line and a cold Abita." (2012: 101) This very formulation helps, in fact, to pinpoint one of the underlying problems of *Treme*'s failure to live up to the expectations. Simon may be "an astute observer of urban space" but New Orleans is not primarily staged as urban space in *Treme*. Instead, it is staged as regional, non-urban space. And the fact that it is not staged as a city, I argue, was not purely a deliberate decision made by the producer, but rather predetermined by existing New Orleans discourses.

In his statement for the *Times-Picayune* in April 2010, Simon declared his production team had made an effort "to be honest" and expressed his conviction that "[b]y referencing what is real, or historical a fictional narrative can speak in a powerful, full-throated way to the problems and issues of our time" (2010: n. p.), that is, of New Orleans after the storm. By "what is real, or historical [in] a fictional narrative" he was referencing not just the destroyed houses and the plight of the slowly returning inhabitants of the city but also the New Orleans *discourses* as they existed before, and persisted after the storm. One powerful pre-Katrina discourse on New Orleans was that it was a great and exceptional tourist space, full of special history, food, and music. This is the very opposite of the pervasive discourse on the American inner city – an urban, crime-infested, and problematically 'raced' space – like it was shown in *The Wire*. The completely different discourse on New Orleans as a great tourist space did not disappear with the storm but found its continuation in a post-Katrina version: Before the storm New Orleans was a tourist spot in the far South of the country, and after the storm the city had become a ravaged, troubled spot in the far South of the country that needed its tourists back. This narrative underlies the show from its very beginning.

What is even more, in the national imagination, New Orleans has always been imagined as regional space on the margins of the nation. A comparison of the post-Katrina discourse on New Orleans and the discourse on New York after 9/11, drawn by Rubén Peinado Abarrio, strikingly illuminates the continuation of New Orleans' role as different from the nation's center:

[W]hile 9/11 has been widely (and superficially) regarded as a tragedy that united the whole nation and enhanced patriotism – for better or worse – (Jackson 2011, Ross 2005), the aftermath of Katrina was characterized by different factions playing the blame game (Bibler 2008, Harris 2006). (2012: 117, sources original)

As Abarrio underlines by quoting Michael P. Bibler, the different approach to the two cities leads to

the national media portray[ing] black New Orleanians [as if] these weren't Americans struggling to survive, like we saw in New York on September 11, but rather people who fell victim to their own collective negligence and lawlessness. (qtd. ibid: 117)

Yet, and according to Abbario, one has to give credit to Simon and Overmyer that he and his production team took great pains to avoid the 'blame game' (i.e. accuse New Orleanians, who 'had it coming') and successfully created in *Treme* a "stark narrativ[e] where racial problems related to institutionalized violence, displacement, media representation or denied citizenship occupy a prominent place" (ibid: 125).

The show self-referentially highlights its rejection of New Orleans as a *provincial* city when the viewer first gets to meet (and bond) with Creighton Bernette (John Goodman) down at the New Orleans waterfront, 17 minutes into the pilot episode in season one. The clear-sighted and militant university professor is an expert on New Orleans history and vigorously points out in an interview with an obviously clueless reporter that the disaster was a "man-made catastrophe, a federal fuck-up of epic proportions" (2011: 17:25-17:30). Moreover, he discredits the reporter's arrogant claim that "New Orleans *was* a great city" (18:32-18:36, original emphasis), the music having "seen its day," the food "rather provincial" (18:43-18:51). He asks the rhetorical question why, then, the reporter had even come down to do an interview – the suggestion clearly being that the reporter is a detestable snob and would not have been sent if people elsewhere did not care about New Orleans. Finally, for added emphasis (and spectacle), the enraged Bernette wrests the microphone and the camera from the shocked reporter and his crew, and throws the equipment into the floods of the Mississippi river (19:08-19:25). No better way of highlighting that New Orleans will be respected and even treasured in the show. Three of the storylines are devoted to a chef, a musician, and a Mardi Gras Indian respectively, and performances of New Orleans music are featured in each episode. Prof. Bernette's outbreak underlines that Simon and Overmyer did *not* intend to dissociate their series from its music, its food, and its history, i.e. the regional, non-urban discourse of New Orleans, but that they would build upon them.

Consequently, Simon and Overmyer chose the very genre for their series that has served to stage regions since the nineteenth century: local color, today also called regionalism. Local color, far from being the superficial entertainment it has sometimes been taken for (Foote 2003: 26), was an important contribution to the nineteenth-century literary scene and did especially relevant cultural work after sectional strife had boiled over in the Civil War. Local color writers like Sarah Orne Jewett, Bret Harte, Charles Waddell Chesnutt and others strove "to make each part of the country and each phase of our civilization known to all the other parts," as William Dean Howells, the so called Dean of American Letters put it in 1887 (1983: 98). And in order to reach this aim, nineteenth-century local color required, according to Richard Brodhead's more recent definition, a setting outside the world of modern development, a zone of backwardness where locally variant folkways still prevail. Its characters are ethnologically colorful, personifications of the different humanity produced in such non-modern cultural settings. Above all, this fiction features an extensive written simulation of regional vernacular, a conspicuous effort to catch the nuances of local speech. (1993: 115-116)

In fact, *Treme* employs and updates the nineteenth-century strategies of national mediation described by Howells and the narrative techniques characterized by Brodhead. If the latter's definition is slightly adjusted to fit the TV series, the show is easy to recognize:

It [presents] a setting outside the world of [urban] development, a zone of [difference] where locally variant folkways still prevail. Its characters are ethnologically colorful, personifications of the different humanity produced in such non-[urban] cultural settings. Above all, this fiction features an extensive [...] simulation of regional vernacular, a conspicuous effort to catch the nuances of local speech [as well as of music and food]. (ibid.)

Understanding how regional fiction has been doing its cultural work since its inception in the nineteenth century may explain the controversy about the cultural politics of the series.

A look at the characterization of the narrative and the political mechanisms of nineteenth-century regional writing shows that an authenticating strategy that relies on creating mixed, even contradictory messages about a region and its inhabitants has been the prerequisite of local color from its inception: On the one hand, local color is closely related to, or even a subcategory of literary realism, and it shares the latter's aim of creating reality effects. The readers, just as today's viewers of a series like *Treme*, were meant to think that 'this is how it is.' Authentication strategies, 'to get the details right,' are crucial to achieving this effect. This explains why *Treme's* 'authenticity' (i.e. the comparison of fiction to fact, the 'truth' of the series) was so important for the producers, why it seems so important to the critics, and why it made the authentication by the 'regional dwellers,' i.e. the New Orlenians, centrally important for the series to work. On the other hand, local color – and this is what distinguishes it from other forms of realism – depends on highlighting regional cultural *difference* from the national (supposedly) more encompassing norm. Hence the majority of readers – who did not live in the region (Foote 2003: 30-31) just like most of today's viewers of *Treme* do not live in New Orleans – were meant to think that 'this is how it is *there* and [luckily or unfortunately] *not here*.' In other words, enabling a touristic gaze was an important part of the narrative, and it is an important part of why *Treme* elevates the local Hubrig pie to mythical status (cf. Simon 2011: n. p.), or features an impressive throng of real jazz performers as an expression of New Orleans' overdetermination by Jazz and its history. Musical and culinary differences become prime sites of exhibited cultural difference. Getting the pie and the music 'right' highlights the Southern locality's difference from the economic, political, and cultural center of the USA.

Cultural difference is the major feature of regional narrative. Traditionally, it is a non-threatening, alluring difference that makes it interesting for addressees who do not dwell in 'the region.' The very highlighting of cultural difference – in a place where the 'Indians' are black, a particular kind of deep-fried pastry is called a "Beignet," and Jazz is not a musical style but a form of life – produces a certain nostalgia (ibid.). It signals that the text is *not* about the center but about the margin of the economy, politics, and culture of the nation.

A narrative-cultural economy of centrality and marginalization, of sophistication and homeliness surfaces clearly in the role that New York plays in *Treme*. This becomes especially evident in the unlucky stint of chef Janette Desautel (Kim Dickens) as a cook in Manhattan in the second season of the show but also plays itself out in the difficult relationship between Albert "Big Chief" Lambreaux (Clarke Peters), who lives for Mardi Gras in New Orleans, and his son Delmond (Rob Brown), a young trumpet player who is enchanted by New York's metropolitan flair and promise. The series sets New Orleans' regional economy against New York's urban economy, a juxtaposition that has not been adequately addressed by the critics. The repeated and impressive staging of the urban/non-urban difference is hard to overlook. The affluent but skyscraper-cold, hectic, and distant 'cool' New York is clearly set off against the hard-pressed but vibrant life in and around the historic district, in restaurants and jazz joints, and on the colorful streets during parades and second lines in 'warm' New Orleans. The presentation of this contrast in both plots and images is a crucial signal not only with regard to the regional strategy but also of the national project of the show. The goal of this project is comparable to its literary predecessors after the Civil War: to bring the nation together in understanding and appreciation of the struggle of a regional community, in this case of New Orleans.

This aim is crucially different from the former and much lauded project of Simon's, *The Wire*. The cultural economy of margin and center, which exceeds the cultural market and is part of the greater cultural imaginary of the USA, allows – if it does not even prescribe – very different strategies for cultural centers and cultural margins, especially if one makes a show for HBO. The crime show, set in the urban center Baltimore and thereby functioning as stand-in for political corruption and urban crime throughout the USA, was neither in need of special negotiations of difference nor of extra authentication – a fictive story was enough.

New Orleans with its special status as a Southern and, what is even more, Creole region lent itself to a different staging. Its TV appearance, imbued with regionalism with an extra dose of authenticating docudrama, suited and highlighted the difference from the center. This is not to say that the series stages New Orleans as if it was outside the USA. There are plots and visual elements that insinuate that, for instance, incompetence and corruption work 'like everywhere' else in the States, yet scenes that indicate nationwide negative experiences with the police, state or city officials are mostly set in nondescript offices, administration buildings or outdoor spaces. Not only are they so indistinct that they are not discussed in the criticism of the series, but they function mostly as a neutral background that highlights the overwhelming regional difference displayed there.

Treme is a regional realist narrative, and this also explains the surprisingly contradictory evaluative judgments of the show. If one surveys what has been written so far about *Treme*, it might well be two, not one media event. Appreciation of the "Oppositional Strategies in *Treme*," as in Katie Moylan's title (2012), contrasts with acerbic criticism of the show's "broach[ing] of political issues that subvert the status of the series as entertainment" (Letort 2013: 5; cf. Miley 2011: 95-101). Some herald *Treme* as offering "a wider picture of a neighborhood where racial difference is an inescapable reality," where "characters like Davis McAlary and Albert Lambreaux challeng[e] the audience's expectations regarding racial construction and in doing so anticipat[e] exciting new possibilities" (Abarrio 2012: 125), while others find a lot of fault with the racial politics of the show and especially the two protagonists Albert Lambreaux and Prof. Bernette. Miley, for instance, calls the end of Prof. Bernette a "cliché" (2011: 99) and claims that Lambreaux's decision to opt out of politics "rob[s] the show of all its political momentum" (ibid: 100). One critic even attributes to the show a "race-blind approach to New Orleans society" and bemoans that it did not "suggest any alternative path of action or resistance" (Letort 2013: 7). While a thorough discourse analysis of the interweaving of "Fiction and reality in HBO's *Treme*" results in the observation that it "is both an act of denunciation and an act of testimony [...] *Treme* is a meta-act of political engagement" (Dessinges/Gendrin/Hajjar 2010: 185), one of the show's detractors points out that it gives "no voice [...] to the people who were evacuated and unable to return to New Orleans" (Letort 2013: 9-10). A seventeen-page analysis of the representation of the Mardi Gras Indians in the series which – notwithstanding the "extent to which it reflects a dominant ideology from white producers and production executives" (Gendrin/Desssinges/Hajjar 2012: 304) – "reveals an emancipatory and liberative narrative necessary to their cultural revival" (ibid: 290), stands against the blunt accusation that the show exploits the "nostalgia of jazz funerals and eschew[s] race and class issues" (Letort 2013: 11). Consequently, questions remain: whether the show supports or undercuts progressive politics, whether it captures racial difference or is "race blind," whether it has a middle-class bias or not, and whether it shows culture as an important force of revival or is, in the words of Rathke, just "a sanitized version of the city and its people with an appealing sound track" (2012: 261).

The activist's disappointment results from comparing real-life disaster management with its televised image, but his criticism highlights the same features that turn regional stories into tourist spectacles. Regionalists have always tampered with (i.e. "sanitized") real-life evidence in order to produce empathy by way of nostalgia in the reader. This is part of their strategy to catch the attention of an otherwise uninvolved public; a way of raising sympathetic interest in people on the margins who do not otherwise concern the people at the center of the nation (cf. Foote 2001: 3). Moreover, as Stephanie Foote has argued, "claims for recognition and representation by marginal people" (ibid: 4), and this applies particularly to people marginalized due to race and class, have been addressed in regional writing since the nineteenth century. This regionalism took the activities of people outside the urban centers seriously and "developed strategies to transform rather than to passively resist the meaning of the social and economic developments of late-nineteenth century urban life" (ibid.), but it was neither utopian nor protest literature. Instead, regionalism mostly hid the common economic and political mechanisms that had produced the unequal power relations between the center and the margins.

Treme also follows this double-edged policy. It represents and acknowledges New Orleans' people and their culture, it even registers some of the racial and class differences in great detail – especially in the stories involving Antoine Batiste (Wendell Pierce) and his ex-wife LaDonna (Khandi Alexander), as well as Albert "Big Chief" Lambreaux. The characters' everyday heroism – and occasional failure – is certainly highlighted, but what is presented as regionally different in the first place thus becomes even further specialized: The highly *regionalized* and *personalized* plot is certainly supportive of progressive politics, perceptive to racial and class-related injustice, and appreciative of culture as an important force of revival, but at the same time, the underlying *systemic* economic and political failures that could not be remedied by regional or individual efforts are glossed over and displaced. Hence, time and again the series prefers to show individual instead of common political action, display race and class problems from the perspective of the middle-class ideology of self-help and individual responsibility, and it favors cultural over economic and political solutions. The aim is clearly not to disturb too much – too poor or too radical a protagonist might skew the regional image. Hence, regionalism's great attention to detail and its very nuanced textual strategy, which captures the minutiae of regional class, race and gender differences, is what the supporters of the series focus on. The inherent stress on portraying differences, however, is anathema to taking an interest in the underlying national structural problems regarding racial, class, and gender politics, and this is what is lamented by the critics of the series.

CONTAINING THE STORM: NATURAL AND TECHNOLOGICAL HAUNTING IN *TREME*[4]

If one compares the plot and the characters of the show to the *real* acts of *real* people in New Orleans "just want[ing] [their] city back" after the hurricane, as character Davis McAlary (Steve Zahn) puts it in one memorable scene of the third episode of the show (2011: 6:22), the analysis of the series is reduced to matching the overall realist narrative strategy with a realist reading strategy. It leads to overlooking the fact that there are other, surrealist or even anti-realist elements in the show that undercut nostalgia and the touristic gaze. I am referring to sounds, cuts, images and plot lines that twist the celebrated realism, prompt questions, and direct attention away from human fate and fault to man's natural and technical environment, from man-made to natural catastrophe or rather, to the amalgamation of the two.

It is difficult to find scenes that do not show people in *Treme*, yet in the few shots that are at least briefly devoid of people, the effects of the storm are showcased in a drastic manner. Strong reminders of the raw power of the water that flooded and destroyed human habitations and lives appear in the introductory close ups of moldy and wasted interior and exterior walls (overlaid by the credits) or the views of semi-destroyed buildings in a ghost city to which the camera cuts immediately after Prof. Bernette has thrown the press equipment into the Mississippi river (and through which the daughter of "Big Chief" Lambreaux chauffeurs her father). The uncanny interconnection between natural and man-made – scientifically predicted, technically mediated, yet not controllable – disaster becomes palpable in the constant hum of helicopters which accompanies

---

4   My thanks to Jon R. Hegglund (Washington State University) who opened my eyes to the possibility of reading the haunting in *Treme* in ecological terms by his talk "Stack City: The Shipping Container as Nonhuman Actant" at a symposium at the Kulturwissenschaftliches Institut in Essen in 2013.

the after-storm outdoor scenes, as well as in the first season's final episode's long and confusing flashback to the hours before the storm that includes fast cuts of people glued to the TV weather forecast, people leaving New Orleans, people boarding up their houses in order to stay, people lost, or being taken into police custody in the emptying streets before the hurricane hits, and the beeping phone in an empty house with windows that are storm-whipped by dripping twigs.

Moments like these, as well as the disturbing, only thinly motivated plot twist of Creighton Bernette's suicide, hint at what Felix Guattari has called in an essay entitled "The Three Ecologies," "human relationships with the socius, the psyche, and 'nature'" that "are increasingly deteriorating" (1989: 134). The French theorist calls for understanding each of these relationships (and not only man's relationship to nature) as an "ecology." He names the ecology of the society, the ecology of the individual and the psyche, and the ecology of the environment: "social ecology, mental ecology, and environmental ecology" (1989: ibid.). Most importantly – and contrary to the foregrounding of the first two "ecologies" and the repression of the last one in *Treme* – he cautions that they are not "discrete domains" but are tightly interlaced and that it is necessary to "apprehend the world through the interchangeable lenses of the three ecologies" (ibid.).[5] Katrina and its effect on New Orleans can certainly be seen as one of the many recent cases of "[n]ature kick[ing] back" (ibid.), telling us that – again in the terminology of Guattari – "temporalities of both human and non-human nature will demand […] an existential reorientation" (ibid: 133). As becomes clear from the quotes, the French philosopher sees humanity and nature as intertwined, hence he demands "if we are to understand the interactions between ecosystems, the mechanosphere, and the social and individual universes of reference, we have to learn to think transversally" (ibid: 135). In other words, 'we' – whoever that is – have to decenter man from the prominent place as the one and only mover and shaker of the world, 'we' have to figure nature and even man-made science/technology as equal players into the equation that results in catastrophes.

Realist narratives, no matter whether regional or not, have not traditionally lent themselves to this "transversal" project. In the narrative method of realism, the social, in the form of the subject's perspective, is dominant by definition. Realism, as Catherine Belsey has pointedly noted, "tends to offer as the 'obvious' basis of its intelligibility the assumption that character, unified and coherent, is the source of action. Subjectivity is a major – perhaps the major – theme" (2001: 67). This is why Katrina is translated in *Treme* into the stories of a number of

---

5 The three ecologies are for Guattari both social and individual practices and concepts of the world, i.e. cognitive tools.

characters/subjects who are meant to represent the racial, class, and gender "ecology" of New Orleans society. The human protagonists are also the points of entry which the show offers to its viewers for identification and judgment (and which, in turn, allows them to feel as subjects too).

What is even more, the show consciously takes as its credo the initial proclamation of Creighton Bernette that Katrina was not a natural disaster, not "a hurricane pure and simple. The flooding of New Orleans was a man-made catastrophe, a federal fuck up of epic proportions, it had decades in the making" (2011: 17:20-17:32). Katrina, it is argued in minute 19 of the series, was caused by the negligence of administrators, contractors, and politicians, i.e. by the irresponsibility of the people in charge – and in episode after episode this is reiterated. What is suppressed by this powerful political argument is the fact that the environment (a.k.a. nature in its technologically and scientifically 'enhanced' state) *did* play a part in the destruction. The argument that Katrina might have had something to do with the powers of nature is even ridiculed in the series, because it is put forward by the unsympathetic reporter in the interview. Of course, nature was not the origin "pure and simple," i.e. not the only reason and not at all an apology for human mismanagement of the flood protection system. Yet the outright denial of nature's contribution to Katrina, were it not so powerfully argued by the professor, seems hard to uphold.

With the best of intentions – in order to boost the image of the failing city and reach the widest possible audience – the show consciously puts the blame on the human agents at hand and thereby excludes the role played by what Guattari calls "the environment" and what Jane Bennett has recently called *Vibrant Matter* in her homonymous book. She explains that to "highlight the active role of *nonhuman* materials in public life" (2010: 2, original emphasis) may help "understand [...] agency as a confederation of human and non-human elements" (ibid: 212). Contrary to Prof. Bernette's claim, she stresses that accepting nature's role in natural catastrophes – here she is referring to the massive power outage in the USA and Canada in August 2003 (ibid: 24-38) – does not necessarily mean freeing humans from responsibility: "The notion of a confederate agency [of human and non-human actants] does attenuate the blame game, but it does not thereby abandon the project of identifying (what Arendt called) the sources of harmful effects." (37)

I will show in the rest of the article how in *Treme* the realist foregrounding of human agents and agency is time and again undercut by the uncanny recurrence of symptoms of non-human or environmental agency. Despite the constant domestication of the environment by harnessing it to a human point of view, "vibrant matter" and the effects of the power of "vibrant matter" keep popping up throughout the series. They surface not just in the images and sounds mentioned above, but also in the efforts of every single protagonist to "get [his/her] life back" – which means for some of them, like "Big Chief" Lambreaux, the chef Jeannette, or bar owner LaDonna, literally wresting their houses (homes and businesses) back from the fecund nature in Louisiana.

The realist-anthropocentric strategy of the show represses and belittles nature's power, and it even denies that nature played any role in Katrina in the scene between Bernette and the reporter. Their clash foregrounds man, and it is visually supported by the *mis-en-scene*, with the grand Mississippi river (nature) and the steel bridge (a product of man's ingenuity in subduing nature) across it, forming a calm, inanimate (and local color) backdrop to the human sound and fury. Thus, from the very beginning, the human-centered politics of the show are out in the open, while the repressed – as Freud described it – recurs in the form of gothic hauntings that trouble the clear-cut social message and rupture the calm 'natural' surface of the representation. This becomes apparent in the sequence of cuts and shots following the scene between the professor and the reporter. The camera cuts from furious Professor Bernette on the calm river front to a tracking shot of a deserted, devastated lower part of town – a haunting demonstration of the result of the 'calm' river's fury. Yet, this shot is itself contextualized and bound to the point of view of "Big Chief" Lambreaux and his daughter driving through the destroyed quarter, thereby successfully binding environmental power back to human agency and thus ensuring the unity of the realist strategy of the show.

The gothic haunting in *Treme* has not been totally overlooked in recent discussions, but it is only mentioned in passing, like in the criticism by Letort quoted above, which reads in full:

No voice is given to the people who were evacuated and unable to return to New Orleans even though *the traces of their absence darken the tone of the series and generate suspense by metaphorically representing narrative gaps to be filled*. A case in point is the enigmatic story behind the death of Daymo who has been missing since Katrina. (2007: 9-10, emphasis mine)

This comment is highly perceptive, not only because it mentions a gothic element of the story, but because it pinpoints a way in which the series *does* manage to reference absence (although the critic, again, following the realist prompts of the show, refers here only to absent people). Absence is indeed rendered present in "traces" and a "darken[ing of] the tone" by Daymo's story, which I will discuss in the final pages of the article.

Daymo's story is about an innocent black man who is caught up and lost in a police and penal system that is understaffed and overworked, unreliable and corrupt. The system breaks down under the added pressure of the storm and is unwilling to face up to its failure afterwards. The viewer does not actually see Daymo until episode seven, when he turns out to be one of the bodies in a morgue. This means that for the greater part of the series, Daymo's story may be *about* Daymo, but it is, in fact, the story *of* his stubbornly persistent sister LaDonna, who, with the help of the equally stubbornly persistent lawyer Toni Bernette (Melissa Leo), defies the penal system, finds (the body of) her brother, and makes sure that he at least gets a decent burial in the family tomb. Daymo's story works thus on the one hand to support the overall message of the show: New Orleanians re-inhabit their city, face problems, and sort them out. The success in finding and reclaiming Daymo's body is all due to the shrewdness and persistence of two women, i.e. to "character, unified and coherent" that "is the source of action" (Belsey 2001: 27).

The little rupture in the realist scheme is that Daymo himself is not shown as the subject of his own story. Moreover, as already mentioned, he is not even visible for most of the show, entering the scene towards the end of episode seven as a blistered face and upper part of a corpse in a partly opened body bag (2011: 47:45-50:30), and really acting just in a few scenes of the penultimate flashback in the final episode of the season. There, he is shown as one of the many people leaving their houses, rushing out of the city, then booked for running a red light, and finally captured by the camera dressed in orange prison garb in an iconic close up of suffering – before the scene shifts abruptly to his funeral and the second line at his wake, which disperses him for good and brings the first season to its close.

While the narrative thus illustrates and highlights realism's inevitable movement "towards closure, which is also disclosure, the dissolution of enigma through the re-establishment of order" (Belsey 2001: 65), the movement from body that is irritatingly missing to found but dead body, on to active living and victimized body, to a body that is securely entombed, at second glance, is a disconcerting reversed order of 'things,' or rather the gothic horror story of a resurrected dead man walking, before he is securely put down in his grave. Daymo's story – as is clear by now – is only barely a story with a social and individual ecological perspective, since, as revealed in the last episode of the series, the being that is at its center had already lost its animate quality before the first episode even started, three months after the storm. Daymo is a truly gothic threshold figure – between life and death, human and non-human, man and matter – less a subject than a site where "human and non-human nature" (Guattari 1989: 133) cross and are crossed.

This becomes strikingly clear in the memorable scene where his sister, accompanied by her lawyer, is finally allowed to try to locate Daymo in the makeshift government morgue on the banks of the Mississippi in episode seven. The two women are led to a container by an employee, they enter, a body bag is opened and Daymo's face, only slightly affected by decay, becomes visible; LaDonna acknowledges him as her brother and flees the scene. Struggling to regain her composure, she fumbles for a cigarette and – suddenly – becomes aware that she has exited only *one* of a long row of identical, ghostly white shipping containers, arranged neatly side by side in the painstakingly secured area. Each of the containers, we know from having seen the inside of one, is stacked with unidentified and therefore unclaimed bodies, zipped orderly into black plastic body bags and safeguarded for months from natural decay by buzzing cooling systems. While the viewer's perspective is bound to LaDonna's – following the realist-humanist narrative strategy of *Treme* – what is seen in two point of view shots is neither men nor nature nor technology "pure and simple." It is a ghostly, horrifying symptom of the somehow artificially stopped "assemblage" (Guattari's and Deleuze's term) or "ad hoc groupin[g] of diverse elements, of vibrant matters of all sorts" (Bennett 2010: 23), a sign of the ill-fated interaction of humans, natural forces, and technology in Hurricane Katrina that is here stopped dead in its tracks and forcibly re-assembled in a futile effort to contain the forces of the "three ecologies," which cannot be contained.

I have argued that *Treme* – notwithstanding New Orleans' status as a city in twenty-first-century America – is employing the narrative strategy of regional realism and thereby continuing a tradition of staging non-urban regions that began in the nineteenth century. On the one hand, this strategy's aim of mediating between center and margin by highlighting endearing regional differences enables and actually demands the detailed attention to ethnic, class, and cultural specificities that has been lauded in *Treme*. On the other hand, the need to evoke empathy and understanding for the inhabitants of the region results in a nostalgic tint of this display of differences, one that forbids radical social and cultural critique, a criticism that has been made of the show. Finally, I have argued that the most problematic outcome of the realist method of *Treme* is its anthropocentric message that tends to belittle the ecological problems that gave rise to the devastating effects of Katrina in the first place. Based on Guattari's and Bennett's ideas, I have shown that – notwithstanding the realist confines of the series – there are gothic elements that haunt the human-centered politics of *Treme*. In particular the search for Daymo (a dead body between animate and inanimate state, a dead man who has stopped acting and suffering) drives much of the action in the first season. His story is staged as resulting not only from human failure but also from the disastrous interplay of nature and technology during the storm. It is both the product and the representation of the dangerous amalgamation between man, nature and technology that is beyond human control.

If Daymo's story still remains tied to what *was once* an animate and acting *human* being, and if most of the shots of the raging storm and the failing technology are *bound back* to various horrified *human* onlookers in a shot/countershot technique, the ultimately revealing moment of the indissoluble powers of what Guattari has called "the three ecologies" comes when Daymo's sister LaDonna has left the container that keeps his and many other unclaimed bodies from decomposing after she identified her dead brother. She is shown standing small among the rows and rows of towering similar containers. It is at this moment that the clear-cut division between active man as opposed to reactive technology and nature collapses. While the viewers (with LaDonna) seem to be securely outside the uncanny otherness of the technical battle against natural decay over Daymo's already dead body, by a change of perspective they become bound (and by sharing LaDonna's perspective on her brother's dwelling place literally 'related') to the assemblage in which the human element is only one, and certainly not the most powerful participant. From the first slow camera pan to the second slow camera pan, the rows of angular white boxes crowd out the horizon, take away our (human) perspective, and – stare back at us. The containers' threatening gaze "highlight[s] the active role of *nonhuman* materials in public life" (Bennett 2010: 2, original emphasis) and might make us begin "to learn to think transversally" (Guattari 1989: 135) about Katrina, New Orleans, and televising man-made natural disasters in the new millennium.

BIBLIOGRAPHY

Abarrio, Rubén Peinado (2012): "'Like Refugees in Their Own Country': Racial Formation in Post-Katrina U.S." In: *Odisea: Journal of English Studies* 13, pp. 113-127.
Belsey, Catherine ([1980] 2001): *Critical Practice*, London: Routledge.
Bennett, Jane (2010): *Vibrant Matter: A Political Ecology of Things*, London: Duke University Press.
Brodhead, Richard (1993): *Culture of Letters: Scenes of Reading and Writing in Nineteenth-Century America*, Chicago: University of Chicago Press.
Dessinges, Catherine/Gendrin, Dominique/Hajjar, Wendy (2010): "Fiction and Reality in HBO's *Treme*: A Narrative Alchemy at the Service of Political Truth." In: *TVSeries*, February 24, 2015 (http://www.academia.edu/962345/

Fiction_and_Reality_in_HBOs_Treme_A_Narrative_Alchemy_at_the_Service_of_Political_Truth), pp. 163-186.

Foote, Stephanie (2001): *Regional Fictions: Culture and Identity in Nineteenth-Century American Literature*, Madison: University of Wisconsin Press.

Foote, Stephanie (2003): "The Cultural Work of American Regionalism." In: Charles L. Crow (ed.), *A Companion to the Regional Literatures of America*, Malden, MA: Blackwell, pp. 25-41.

Gray, Herman (2012): "Recovered, Reinvented, Reimagined: *Treme*, Television Studies and Writing New Orleans." In: *Television & New Media* 13/3, pp. 268-278.

Guattari, Felix (1989): "The Three Ecologies." In: *New Formations* 8, pp. 131-147.

Howells, William Dean (1983): *Editors Study*. Ed. James W. Simpson, Troy: Whitston.

Letort, Delphine (2013): "The Tales of New Orleans after Katrina: The Interstices of Fact and Fiction in *Treme*." In: *Alphaville: Journal of Film and Media* 5, (http://www.alphavillejournal.com/Issue5/HTML/ArticleLetort.html), pp. 1-15.

Miley, Mike (2011): "*Treme* & The Battle for a Certified New Orleans." In: *New Orleans Review* 37/1, pp. 94-101.

Moylan, Katie (2012): "'Is Space Political'?: Oppositional Strategies in *Treme*." In: *Mediascape* (Winter), (http://www.tft.ucla.edu/mediascape/winter2012_treme.html).

Rathke, Wade (2012): "*Treme* for Tourists: The Music of the City without the Power." In: *Television & New Media* 13/3, pp. 261-267.

Simon, David (2011): "HBO's 'Treme' Creator David Simon Explains It All for You." In: *The Times-Picayune*, February 24, 2015 (http://www.nola.com/treme-hbo/index.ssf/2010/04/hbos_treme_ creator_david_simon.html).

Smith, Anthony N. (2012): "Putting the Premium into Basic: Slow-Burn Narratives and the Loss-Leader Function of AMC's Original Drama Series." In: *Television & New Media* 13/3, pp. 150-166.

Thomas, Lynnell L. (2012): "'People Want to See What Happened': *Treme*, Televisional Tourism and the Racial Remapping of Post-Katrina New Orleans." In: *Television & New Media* 13/3, pp. 213-224.

Treme, The Complete First Season, (2011). Created by Eric Overmyer and David Simon. New York: HBO. DVD.

Lewis Watts: *Wake*, Iberville Housing Project 1994

On my first visit to New Orleans, I was walking near the French Quarter and I heard some music. I investigated and came about a wake where a group of young musicians was playing to honor the son of the woman with the t-shirt who is facing the camera. The trumpet player is Kermit Ruffins, who has become one of New Orleans's best-known players. These "kids" played better than many of my adult musician friends. This was my first introduction to the musical culture of New Orleans and also the unique way of celebrating life and death.

Where They At? Bounce and Class in *Treme*

MICHAEL BUCHER

Music, alongside food, is presented as the most important site of cultural production in David Simon and Eric Overmyer's high profile HBO series *Treme* (2010-2013), and thus music is of crucial importance for the claims for New Orleans exceptionalism that the series makes throughout in its fictionalization of New Orleans life after hurricane Katrina.[1] The Tremé – the show drops the diacritic – is the neighborhood across Rampart Street from the touristic French Quarter; it is often referred to as the oldest African-American neighborhood in the country and plays an important role in the emergence of the musical genres that are part of the city's heritage. The choice of name therefore also indicates on which side the show imagines its own place in its negotiation of the line it purports to erect between the authentic and the touristic. And indeed the show is enjoyable for many reasons, for example its great cast of actors. *Treme* is commendable for depicting the precarious economic situation of the people struggling to make a living in these sectors as it includes a wide array of both the city's cultural heritage and its contemporary scene. Through its frequent and mostly diegetic use of music, *Treme* has proven thoroughly educational for the non-American viewer – me – since it presents and discusses a wide array of jazz, second line brass band music, Mardi Gras Indian chants, and Cajun music. And while it gives a striking demonstration of the ubiquity of music in New Orleans, it provides extra pleasure as soon as one decides to find out more about the music and the musicians it features – for example the late Coco Robicheaux, who performs a voodoo ritual on the radio show of one of the series' main characters, Davis McAlary ("Meet de

---

1   Barbara Eckstein analyzes claims for New Orleans exceptionalism in affective terms in her book *Sustaining New Orleans* (2006). She calls not for a debunking of such claims, but for their interpretation as "active participants" (29) in the discursive production of the city.

Boys," 01:37-03:26); or Donald Harrison and Dr. John, whose record *Indian Blues* (1991) provides the blueprint for the fusion of Mardi Gras chants and Jazz that is at the center of the Lambreauxs' storyline in season two.

Given *Treme*'s obvious and contagious delight in the music of New Orleans, the show's treatment of hip-hop comes as a surprise, for hip-hop is only relevant in the second out of four seasons: Its first season ignores hip-hop, with maybe the single exception of the aforementioned DJ Davis's indictment of President Bush's handling of the aftermath of hurricane Katrina in the song "Shame, Shame, Shame" (Season 5, Episode 1). The second season attempts to rectify this omission and presents an entire storyline that focuses on hip-hop. This storyline, driven by DJ Davis's interest, reveals a lopsided view of New Orleans hip-hop and thereby, as we will see, dramatizes the full extent of *Treme*'s ambivalence towards African-American culture. In the third season hip-hop has disappeared, its status as a slightly obscure interest with shock value now filled by metal.[2] Hip-hop makes a brief reappearance in the season's finale when DJ Davis finally has a hit called "I Quit." For the fourth and final season HBO only agreed to finance six episodes to wrap up the show, and – at this point it is no longer really a surprise – hip-hop once more is of little significance. It pops up in one scene that is to illustrate the failure of DJ Davis's musical ambitions as his one-hit wonder fame wanes ("Yes, We Can," 19:11-22:11). Throughout its four seasons and despite its repeated depictions of individual musicians' struggles to make ends meet, in its half-hazard portrayal of New Orleans hip-hop *Treme* misses out on an important chance to address music in a social context. This failure manifests itself in the show's approach to bounce, New Orleans' own contribution to hip-hop history.

Treme's scant treatment of hip-hop thus warrants commentary for three reasons. Firstly, at some 30 years of age, hip-hop may be one of the youngest additions to the musical genres that are relevant to the city's history, but it has a vital presence in the city and is as ubiquitous and mainstream as any of the other genres. Since about 1996, it has been New Orleans' biggest selling export with stars like Mystikal, Juvenile, and Lil Wayne. And what is more, locally, New Orleans has produced its own variant of hip-hop, a subgenre called "bounce," and has been a pioneering site for the development of queer hip-hop with "sissy

---

2 New Orleans has a vibrant metal scene that certainly warrants inclusion in the show. The city has been especially important for the development of sludge metal, a Southern variant of metal influenced by doom metal and hardcore punk. Well-known New Orleans metal bands are Eyehategod, Crowbar, Goatwhore and Exhorder. However, given the show's ambivalences concerning African-American cultural production, it feels odd to see hip-hop replaced by a largely white genre.

bounce." New Orleanians often refer to bounce simply as "that beat" (Miller 2012: 1). *Treme* fails to present both the ubiquity and the exceptionalism of New Orleans hip-hop. Secondly, when *Treme* does address hip-hop, it does so as an interest of its white protagonists. Next to Davis, this is Sofia Bernette, the daughter of lawyer Toni Bernette and professor of literature Creighton Bernette, played by the series two biggest stars, Melissa Leo and John Goodman. Sofia has posters announcing bounce concerts on the walls in her room, and when she takes up her late father's tradition of posting video rants on the political situation after Katrina on Youtube, "Drop & Gimme 50," a song by the local bounce artist 10th Ward Buck is playing in the background ("Accentuate the Positive," 10:29-11:30). We soon learn that it is not Sofia playing that song on her stereo, but DJ Davis, who is playing it on his radio show at a job he will soon lose because he is playing too much bounce, and Sofia is listening to his show. Unfortunately, we never learn anything specific about Sofia's bounce fandom, and it is Davis who takes center stage.[3]

The black characters in *Treme* seem surprisingly unimpressed by hip-hop, although most of them are members of the hip-hop generation, a term defined by Bakari Kitwana (2002) as referring to African-Americans born between 1965 and 1984 (that is between the passage of the Civil Rights Act and the assassination of Malcom X, and the global success of hip-hop). These people grew up with hip-hop as a continuous presence in African-American culture. But the only instance in *Treme* where a black main character acknowledges hip-hop as an evident presence in his life is when Randall Batiste, the younger son of LaDonna Batiste-Williams and Antoine Batiste, who would be second-generation if we follow Kitwana's terminology, says he would much rather prefer turntables to the brass instrument his estranged father suggests he start learning. The third reason why *Treme*'s treatment of hip-hop requires commenting concerns the ways in which New Orleans hip-hop highlights class. Bounce, New Orleans' original contribution to the landscape of hip-hop, is an original product of the city's housing projects; so much so, that New Orleans rapper Kilo refers to it as "project music" (Miller 2012: 177). Bounce is working-class culture and has its closest relation to the poorer section of the working class. It has emerged from the block parties and DJ-ing events associated with the projects, and most of its artists come from the projects. Bounce lyrics are often "shout-outs" to the projects and

---

3   Thus it seems that Sofia's interest in bounce is a mere signifier of her fascination with rough, outsider types and serves to prepare the viewer for her tattooed white musician boyfriend in season three. The inclusion of such desire in the show is of course perfectly legitimate, but the presentation of hip-hop masculinities would clearly have benefitted had this theme been fully explored.

associated high schools, neighborhoods, and wards (ibid: 151). Several artists reference the projects and the respective city wards in their names, like the late Magnolia Shorty or the aforementioned 10th Ward Buck. *Treme* adopts this strategy by naming the hip-hopper added to the cast for season two "Lil Calliope," thereby indicating he is or was a resident of the Calliope projects in the 2nd Ward.

The city of New Orleans had already started closing down the housing projects before Katrina hit. The St. Thomas projects, for example, were dismantled prior to Katrina. But the political fallout of Katrina has been especially devastating for public housing in New Orleans since the flood provided a pretext for getting rid of the remaining projects. In 2007, the city council decided to demolish 4500 of 5100 public housing units in New Orleans, which even included the uptown projects that received very little damage from Katrina: Magnolia, Melpomene, and Calliope (cf. NO Projects). 2013 saw the destruction of the last of the fully intact projects, Iberville. The Iberville projects are located in the 4th Ward, adjacent to Kongo Square and Louis Armstrong Park, just across Basin Street and in direct vicinity to the French Quarter, which makes them a prime target for city developers. *Treme* addresses the paradox situation of public housing with Mardi Gras chief Albert Lambreaux's one man protest against the impending demolition of the projects amidst housing shortage in its first season. But the show remains lukewarm as towards bounce as a cultural expression of the actual inhabitants of the projects.[4]

Bounce, more so than the city's other musical genres, throws class relations in New Orleans into sharp relief. But none of the series' main characters is a resident of the housing projects. The music performers the series celebrates are, even though their economic situations are often precarious, reliant on long, venerable traditions and family lines. And while they are often working class – the Mardi Gras Indian tradition, for example, is an African-American working-class tradition – they partake of these family traditions that are linked to dignity of labor, craftsmanship, and respectability. Again, names are important markers: Antoine Batiste carries the name of one of those New Orleans families with a long musical tradition. According to Miller, this access to tradition and filiation is an important element that structures the reception of the musical landscape of New Orleans:

---

4 This is also striking since *The Wire*, Simon's highly acclaimed previous production for HBO, does not shy away from depicting the projects in detail for the entirety of its first season and features a lot of diegetic use of hip-hop. But then *The Wire* is a crime series, and drug trafficking in the Baltimore projects being the topic of its first season, hip-hop is apparently considered to provide the desired sonic authenticity.

[F]ew of the rappers, producers, and entrepreneurs involved with rap music in New Orleans have the family history of musical practice that is so central to studies of Jazz and R&B in the city. [...] While some of the participants in the rap scene can claim family members with musical backgrounds, most of them have accrued their sense of 'New Orleans-ness' from the atmospheric background of the city's musical practices rather than from any direct connection to prior musical forms. (2006: 20)

Treme's musical politics are shaped by a highly problematic reverence for authenticity and respectability and it is only in such a context that Sofia's and Davis's fascination with bounce could be construed as transgressive. Lynnell Thomas has pointed out that in its "focus on heritage music" to the detriment of hip-hop, *Treme* adopts the curatorial practices of the established music festivals (notably Jazz Fest) and venues (2012: 218). Thomas cites Eric Porter's work on "Jazz and Revival" to make the point that by these practices "inequalities [are] obscured through an emphasis of history and an erasure of the present" (Porter 2009: 604; Thomas: ibid.). The ambivalence manifests itself, according to Thomas, on the one hand in the celebration of the uniqueness of New Orleans's black heritage, whereby the implicit case is made that this culture must be restored. But on the other hand, this celebration of black heritage by no means precludes "an aversion to another mode of blackness (and a large, frequently displaced population), deemed transgressive, violent, parasitical, and a threat to the city's return" (Porter 2009: 610; Thomas: ibid.).

As concerns this manifest ambivalence, *Treme*'s second season adds insult to injury by what it lets happen in the Sofia Bernette storyline, that storyline that first introduces hip-hop to the show with 10th Ward Buck's "Drop & Gimme 50" played as an inspiration for Sofia's first Youtube rant, but then immediately abandons it as a topic. To redeem her behavior as a wayward teenager, Sofia, helped by her mother's connections, begins as an intern for city council president Oliver Thomas, who resigned in 2007 and pleaded guilty to bribery charges. In a scathing review of this storyline (and the entire show), political science scholar Adolph Reed writes about the rehabilitation of Oliver Thomas implied by his sympathetic inclusion in the show:

[S]ix months after the storm, in response to protests that displaced poor people were not being helped to return to the city, [Oliver Thomas] complained that government agencies and programs had 'pampered' the black poor and infamously declared that 'We don't need soap opera watchers now.' [One would n]ever know from *Treme* that Thomas had been centrally instrumental in the long-term campaign to cleanse the Lower Garden District of the St. Thomas project. (2011: n.p.)

In failing to adequately address New Orleans hip-hop, discarded together with the rabble of the projects, the series subscribes to what Eric Porter refers to as its "good negro, bad negro" dynamics (610). But before I continue to further develop my argument about *Treme* and the specifics of these exclusionary practices, I want to briefly address developments within New Orleans hip-hop.

Since its early days at the beginning of the eighties, hip-hop has been produced in New Orleans. While the first decade of hip-hop was dedicated to building an infrastructure of clubs, parties, radio shows, labels and recording studios, in the early nineties hip-hop production in New Orleans moved from emulating the styles of the East Coast and West Coast centers of hip-hop, towards developing its own variant. According to Miller, whose 2012 book *Bounce: Rap Music and Local Identity in New Orleans* is the most detailed study of the genre so far, bounce privileges rhythm over melody, and tends to substitute hip-hop's narrative content for "chanted, repeated phrases" (151). As a result, bounce is often dismissed as simple and devoid of political content. The chanting often takes the form of call and response, an element derived from West African culture (cf. Levine 1977: 20) that, like the dance moves associated with bounce, illustrates the importance of audience interaction in bounce and points to its roots in local dance and partying contexts. Bounce lyrics are often exhortations to dance.

MC T. Tucker and DJ Irv's 1991 single "Where They At" is usually considered to be the first bounce release. Soon after its release, bounce artists began to sell bigger than national hip-hop artists in New Orleans. The city's relative geographical isolation and the fact that its tastes are not always representative for the nation, so far has kept major labels from opening offices in the city. This situation allowed for the emergence of strong independent hip-hop labels in New Orleans, the most successful of them being No Limit Records and Cash Money Records. In the second half of the nineties, these independent labels enjoyed national success with artists like Mystikal, Juvenile, and Lil Wayne. None of these national success stories were, strictly speaking, bounce productions, but especially the Cash Money recording artists displayed their bounce influences. Of the two labels mentioned, only Cash Money made it into the new millennium, and its main producer, Mannie Fresh, has a guest appearance in *Treme* when Davis tries to convince him to contribute a track to his hip-hop sampler ("Slip Away," 28:02-30:52).[5]

---

5   Mannie Fresh is not in the office but talks to Davis and Aunt Mimi on the phone. Cash Money's success story has continued with artists like Drake and Nicki Minaj added to its roster.

In a manner not unrelated to its working-class roots, bounce is blatantly sexual. While early bounce is dominated by men and indeed often sexist, there have always been outspoken women assertive of their own sexuality in bounce. These women present their take on male-female sexual relationships and the conflicts involved as a standard element of bounce lyrics. One example is Cheeky Blakk, whom we see at the end of season three when she and Davis record his surprise hit "I Quit" ("Tipitina," 06:21-08:44).[6] Here, Blakk is lending long-sought-for credibility to Davis's hip-hop endeavors. Blakk rose to prominence in New Orleans when she engaged in sexually outspoken rap battles with her partner Pimp Daddy over their relationship.[7]

Angela Davis points out the importance of expanding the notion of what may contribute to feminist discourse. In *Blues Legacies and Black Feminism* (1998), she warns of dismissing peremptorily the female voices in what we envision as hopelessly misogynist discourses, for "what are constituted as black feminist traditions tend to exclude ideas produced by and within poor and working-class communities, where women historically have not had the means or access to publish written texts" (xi-xii). Writing on 1920's blues singers who were frowned upon by many of the Harlem Renaissance artists, Angela Davis maintains: "because women like Bessie Smith and Ida Cox presented and embodied sexualities associated with working-class black life – which, fatally, was seen by some Renaissance strategists as antithetical to the aims of their cultural movement – their music was designated as 'low' culture" (xiii). Bounce is explicitly sexual not only in its lyrics but also in its dancing styles, which corroborates its low status.[8] In New Orleans, however, twerking, p-popping, and other bounce dance moves, which may be traced back to Caribbean and West-African influences, are

---

6   This collaboration is based on the real-life collaboration of Blakk with Davis Rogan, the New Orleans musician on whom DJ Davis's character is modeled.

7   Pimp Daddy started this public family dispute with the 1993 song "Boo-Koo Bitches," to which Cheeky Blakk then responded. For a brief account of their public rap battles see David Dennis (2013).

8   Bounce moves were scandalized on a national level in 2013 when Miley Cyrus was twerking on stage at the MTV Video Music Awards ceremony. While that media scandal was largely about the perceived inappropriateness of a sexualized performance by a former Disney star, Cyrus was also criticized for appropriating African-American culture. In this context, Cash Money recording artist Nicki Minaj's 2014 performance at the Video Music Awards, which also featured extensive twerking, may be read as a response to Cyrus's earlier performance.

central to a queer-feminist appropriation that began as early as 1999 and that recalls the strategies of the early-90s punk-influenced Rrriot Grrrl scene.

Beginning in 1999, when bounce is almost a decade old and national interest in hip-hop from New Orleans begins to fade, bounce is taken over by queer artists in a movement that has been referred to as "sissy bounce." *New York Times* journalist Jonathan Dee inscribes sissy bounce within the narrative of New Orleans' sexual exceptionalism when he writes: "Inside New Orleans, the genius of sissy bounce is how perfectly mainstream it is; in the world beyond, the genius of sissy bounce is how incredibly alternative it is." (2010: n.p.) In the rest of the nation, queer hip-hop, or homo-hop, remains an alternative interest until it first achieves mainstream status with Frank Ocean's coming-out in 2012. The first of the so-called sissy bounce artists is transgender rapper Katey Red who released her first EP "Melpomene Block Party" on Take Fo' Records in 1999. The title song is a typical bounce track in that it combines exhortations to dance with sexually explicit lyrics. For example, Red raps about prostitution: "I'm a punk under pressure, when we finish put my money on the dresser." Another sissy bounce artist is Big Freedia, who was especially prolific in reviving the New Orleans hip-hop community after Katrina. Big Freedia gives workshops on bounce dancing which celebrate it as female sexual expressiveness. At sissy bounce shows, which are predominantly frequented by women, touching is not allowed when the dancers bend over and shake their asses. The MCs strictly uphold this rule, a strategy reminiscent of Riot Grrrl punk rock concerts, where all-female mosh pits were created while the boys were asked to stand in the back (cf. Vukadinović 2013: 110). Punk is gay slang for a person who takes the bottom role in a sexual act, and thus Katey Red's use of the term has a sexual denotation. However, given that Big Freedia likes to reference punk fashion in her clothing styles and hair-dos, the above quote from Katey Red might also be read as a reference to punk as a cultural movement, thus suggesting that the similar strategies at sissy bounce concerts and Riot Grrrl concerts are more than mere coincidences.

Mia X, a star from the early days of bounce, comments on bounce dancing practices as follows: "It's not sexual; dancing to bounce is about freedom." (Miller 2012: 99) Sissy bounce artists like Big Freedia agree with the liberating function, but go further since they embrace the sexual aspects of bounce dancing as part of what is liberating about bounce as collective cultural production. Big Freedia, who considers herself an ambassador for New Orleans as she explains at the beginning of her 2014 video for the song "Explode," and who has set herself the goal of achieving national mainstream success, describes the impact of bounce dancing in the first season of her reality TV show: "Asses certainly are a celebration of life."

Most of this, however, is lost on *Treme* and its rather conventional sexual politics. Still, Katey Red and Big Freedia make a short and pronounced appearance in season two, where hip-hop enters *Treme* in a twofold manner in the Davis McAlary storyline. A main character in all four of *Treme*'s seasons, Davis is a connoisseur of New Orleans music, which he celebrates with tremendous energy. He is from a rich white uptown family, a bit of a family outsider, who lives the bohemian lifestyle down in the Tremé. Davis thus embodies a fascination with letting loose that New Orleans tends to encourage in the imagination of middle-class America. If *Treme*, with its diverse cast, has something like a main character, I would argue it is Davis, who often acts as a guide to the city – literally so when he starts his musical heritage tour. Davis constantly explains the city to strangers and friends alike. He is also, I would say, the most obnoxious character in the series. In season two, Davis is bent on hip-hop fame, which he intends to achieve by two means. With the money of his Aunt Mimi he starts a record label, the first release on which is to be a bounce sampler. Sissy bounce is to be on the sampler, and in episode four we see Katey Red in a recording studio booth, with Big Freedia to her left and Sissy Nobby to her right ("Santa Claus," 35:26-36:47). Aunt Mimi from "past Jackson" is dressed with a baseball hat to match her new entrepreneurial adventure.[9] The producer sitting next to Davis is Don Bartholomew, a real life hip-hop producer in New Orleans and the son of the rhythm and blues musician Dave Bartholomew. At the beginning of the scene, Aunt Mimi is still in the recording booth, drinking and practicing dance moves with Big Freedia, who exhorts her: "Werk it, girl!" Davis, visibly annoyed, asks them: "Ladies, can we – please, please, *please* – put down one track before midnight?" Aunt Mimi leaves the booth and moves over to the side of the producers, but attentiveness is still not where Davis would like to see it, and in a short altercation with Katey Redd he says, near exasperation: "If you'd stop texting, and start writing, and –" Don Bartholomew intervenes and puts on a beat. Katey Red likes it and over this beat repeats what she has just told Davis and adds another sentence: "I'ma tell you when I'm ready, when I'm ready I'ma tell you. I'ma tell you when I'm ready, when I'm ready I'ma tell you. You're bugging me, and you're ug-e-ly, you're ug-e-ly, you're ug-e-ly, and you're bugging me." Aunt Mimi is delighted, and everyone, including the slightly reluctant Davis, agrees they now have an excellent track for the sampler.

---

9   "Past Jackson" is how Cash Money's Ron B. describes her on the phone to Mannie Fresh in season two's episode "Slip Away" (cf. footnote 6). The reference is to Garden District, which is past Jackson Avenue.

What makes this scene so enjoyable is that Katey gets to tell Davis off and is applauded for it. However, this scene also sheds light on the problems *Treme* has in addressing hip-hop. Throughout, *Treme* privileges the music that is performed – in the clubs, the streets, the schools, and in the studios of New Orleans – as authentic. The music that is produced and lacking 'proper' instrumentation, however, like hip-hop (but the argument could easily be extended to include house and disco), when it occurs, is presented – pun intended – as juvenile, as lacking in seriousness, as merely dance music.[10] The immediate impression is that the hip-hoppers are presented as irresponsible kid-artists who are merely interested in booty-shaking and who need to be reprimanded by Davis to take the recording session seriously. The first shot of the scene shows an unused writing pad. Then the camera zooms out to show Katey Red fiddling with her cell-phone. Davis, in the altercation quoted above, interprets this as her texting rather than writing. For all we know, however, Katey might be using her phone to write her songs, as Josh Jackson points out on NPR's blog on *Treme* (cf. Jackson/Jarenwattananon 2011). Probably, what Davis fails to grasp is that someone who does not enjoy the comforts of a home office or studio is likely to have a different approach to technology, work, and concentration. The association of bounce with immaturity is immediately established, though, and nothing in this scene tells you that Katey is a mother of at least two who supports her family by pursuing her career.

Before I conclude with a brief look at Davis's second strategy for hip-hop fame, I want to take a detour through a literary text that I consider pertinent to the historical context from which sissy bounce emerges in New Orleans. In the final part of his 1963 novel *City of Night*, John Rechy makes a striking case for New Orleans exceptionalism as a sexual exceptionalism the city holds in the American imagination. This semi-autobiographical account of a young hustler's journey through metropolitan America's "sexual underworlds" (blurb text) – most of the events fictionalized by Rechy occur in the second half of the fifties – ends in New Orleans for a specific reason. Come Mardi Gras, from all over America the denizens of these sexual underworlds travel to New Orleans. The nameless protagonist and narrator tells us how they come in waves: First, the hustlers, a "tattered army of young vagrants" (343), begin to hitchhike to New Orleans. Soon after come the street queens and drag queens[11] – often sexworkers, too, since Rechy's novel addresses the lives of poor queers – in whose socially abjected

---

10 I want to thank Charles Nero for alerting me to this dynamic at work in *Treme*.

11 Today we might say trans women, although it is not given that these categories overlap exactly.

position Rechy acknowledges a dignity in a manner unprecedented in American letters:

[T]he second wave of fugitives will have felt the stirring of this call to brief Freedom. New Orleans is now the Pied Piper playing a multikeyed tune to varikeyed ears. In those same darkcities equally restless queens, wringing from their exiled lives each drop of rebellion, will feel the strange excitement ('My dear, the Most Fabulous Drags in the world go there'). (344)

In a third wave, the people we are more likely to associate with tourism follow the allure New Orleans at Mardi Gras holds out:[12] "Like flotsam from the world's seas, the vagrants of America's blackcities are washed into New Orleans" (375). The queens play an important role for the social cohesion of the nightlife scenes of Time Square, New York, Pershing Square, Los Angeles, and similar places all over the United States, and the novel makes clear there is a very specific reason that attracts them to Mardi Gras New Orleans. At a time in the United States when ordinances on sartorial order regulate what people are allowed to wear – Rechy cites New York City's three garment rule, which held that at any given time you had to wear at least three gender-specific items of clothing – and provide police and society with a pretext to degrade and brutalize gender-nonconforming people at every turn, the Catholic tradition of Mardi Gras, of which New Orleans has the only relevant example in the U.S., provides the only time and place when cross-dressing in public is legal. As the novel shows, New Orleans police still manage to harass and humiliate the queens by forcing them to cut their hair, but there is no way to keep the queens from going in the parades in drag. Rechy's protagonist may be a tourist, but he is in a position to show us sites an imaginary Davis living in the fifties would be oblivious to.

Treme's lack of genuine interest in hip-hop is accompanied by a lack of interest in the sexual dissidence that, too, has been part of the city's history for so long. And it is worth pointing out that prostitution, present in Rechy's depiction of Mardi Gras in the middle of the last century in *City of Night*, as well as in Katey Red's comments on everyday life in the projects in "Melpomene Block Party," also has its place in the history of the established musical genres that the show

---

12 "Still later, the more comfortable wave of this exodus (the tired richmen, the tired richwomen, the not-so-rich but tired men and the not-so-rich but equally tired women – and the other Young men and women – equally curious but not as defiant as the vagrants of the first and second waves) will feel the call of Shrove Tuesday" (Rechy 1963: 284).

celebrates. Storyville, the area adjacent to Kongo Square designated as a site for legalized prostitution by city authorities between 1897 and 1917, was of great importance for the development of Jazz, for in an era of increasing segregations these were the venues that would hire black musicians. It is now part of Jazz mythology that Storyville is where Louis Armstrong first heard many of the musicians that influenced him. Until recently, the Iberville projects stood on the site of the former Storyville. But this is not the authenticity that *Treme* is looking for, when it presents musical performances as prime sites of male bonding. In its desire to present New Orleans music as authentic as well as respectable, it excludes the unwanted parts of its history just as it goes to exclude the contemporary bounce innovators. The series reduces its knowledge of the fact that sexuality, too, functions differently in New Orleans and indeed has an exceptional tradition, to police captain Terry Colson's admonition to his colleagues to "let Bourbon Street be Bourbon Street" ("Everything I Do," 04:55). Had *Treme* explored New Orleans' queerness to its full extent, it might have acknowledged that, for example, the wonderful video for "Iberville" by late sissy bounce rapper Messy Mya, which features a bunch of hip-hoppers of all genders twerking to the backdrop of the Iberville projects, has as much relation to the city's history as the show's celebrated heritage music.

 Davis's second strategy for hip-hop fame he pursues independently of Aunt Mimi. He starts his own band, The Brassy Knoll, which he envisions as "Bounce funk rap with a brass band twist" ("Feels Like Rain," 19:44). Davis considers it to be his prerogative to front this band, but since his flow as a rapper is far from overwhelming, his status as the band's frontman is soon challenged by the young rapper and spoken word performer Lil Calliope. A comparison of Davis's two projects reveals his inconsistent approach to hip-hop. Lil Calliope has a local hit with another project he is involved in. As *Treme* enacts Davis's failure at hip-hop stardom as comedy, in one of the funnier scenes Davis and Lil Calliope are in the car and Davis misinterprets Lil Calliope's delighted realization "I'm on the radio!" To his chagrin Davis soon realizes that it is not The Brassy Knoll, but Lil Calliope's second project that is played on the radio. Further on, in his desire to set his own band apart from Lil Calliope's side project (and from the tracks he himself has collected for his bounce sampler) he tells his unwanted co-rapper that "New Orleans has enough dance music" (14:14). Then he berates Lil Calliope on conscious rap. He hands him records by Public Enemy, and as examples of politically engaged music from other traditions, The Clash, and Woody Guthrie with the condescending words: "Beginning of a journey, brah" (13:55). As if Lil Calliope had not been on his journey for a long time already, as if he had no relevant past. Listening to these examples from music history is of course in itself interesting, but it is unclear why a young man from the projects would have to rely on Davis's input to find his anger and give voice to it. Thus, rather than lending him hip-hop credibility, the scene shows Davis as being out of touch with the hip-hop community whose recognition he seeks. As Thomas points out, in order to make its case of hip-hop as apolitical, *Treme* willfully ignores those bounce songs that feature lyrics with clear political intent.[13] While *Treme* paints Davis as a buffoon in these scenes, we already know that Lil Calliope is more successful than Davis both with The Brassy Knoll and with his own dance project, thus bringing to a crisis Davis's desire for hip-hop credibility, and, by extension, for blackness. And like Katey Red, Lil Calliope implodes any simplistic separation of dance and politics. To paraphrase Davis's study on the blues once more: pleasure is not without its critical dimension, and critique or research not without its pleasures (cf. 1998: xvii). This is, of course, the same, old conflict that prompted Emma Goldman to say "If I can't dance to it, it's not my revolution."[14]

But ultimately, the situation in which *Treme* places its hip-hop subjects is one of an insufferable paradox: In order to assert themselves they are forced to ridicule (Katey Red) or circumvent (Lil Calliope) the only protagonist interested in them, that is their only gateway into the show. Thus, their moment of agency is, at the same time, the moment of their obliteration, for the bounce storyline is discontinued in season three. Surprisingly, there is no release party for Davis's sampler, as one would expect within the logic of serial narration. But the bounce sampler is merely a McGuffin. And hip-hop resurfaces only briefly to provide the material for Davis's career as a one-hit-wonder. Thus, in its presentation of New Orleans music, rather than living up to the fullness of the city's musical landscape, and despite of its celebration of so much of its musical heritage, *Treme* continues contributing to the exclusion of those who have traditionally been considered juvenile: the black, the poor, the queer, and women.

---

13 Zenia Kish mentions a number of politically conscious rap songs by New Orleans rappers that Lil Calliope and Davis would have to be aware of are "Fuck Katrina (The Katrina Song)" by 5th Ward Weebie (2005), "My FEMA People" by Mia X (2006), "Get Ya Hustle On" by Juvenile (2006), and "Georgia Bush" by Lil Wayne (2006). Rappers from outside of Louisiana also addressed Hurricane Katrina and its aftermath, for example K-Otix, a group from Houston in their song "George Bush Doesn't Care about Black People" (2005). Houston was one of the main destinations for people fleeing New Orleans (Kish 679).

14 There is no source for this quote, of which there exist a number of variants, and which is attributed to Goldman. In her biography *Living My Life* (1931) she recounts being reprimanded for dancing by a fellow activist (56).

Bibliography

Big Freedia: Queen of Bounce, (2013-current). Produced by Fenton Bailey, Randy Barbato and Tom Campbell, February 24, 2015 (http://fuse.tv/shows/bigfreedia).

Davis, Angela (1998): *Blues Legacies and Black Feminism: Gertrude Ma Rainey, Bessie Smith, and Billie Holiday*, New York: Vintage.

Dennis, David (2013): "Cheeky Blakk: Queen Be Hustlin'." In: *OffBeat. Louisiana Music and Culture*, November 10, 2014 (http://www.offbeat.com/2013/03/01/cheeky-blakk-queen-be-hustlin/).

Eckstein, Barbara (2006): *Sustaining New Orleans. Literature, Local Memory, and the Fate of a City*, New York: Routledge.

Goldman, Emma (1931): *Living My Life*, Vol. 1. New York: Dover.

Jackson, Josh/Jarenwattananon, Partrick (2011): NPR blog on *Treme*, September 15, 2014 (http://www.npr.org/blogs/ablogsupreme /2011/05/16/136358303/treme-ep-14-christmas-blues).

Kish, Zenia (2009): "'My Fema People:' Hip-Hop as Disaster Recovery in the Katrina Diaspora." In: *American Quarterly* 61/3, pp. 671-692.

Kitwana, Bakari (2002): *The Hip Hop Generation: Young Blacks and the Crisis in African American Culture*, New York: Basic Books.

Levine, Lawrence W. (1977): *Black Culture and Black Consciousness*. New York: Oxford University Press.

Miller, Matt (2012): *Bounce. Rap Music and Local Identity in New Orleans*, Amherst: University of Massachusetts Press.

Miller, Matt (2006): "Bounce: Rap Music and Cultural Survival in New Orleans." In: *HypheNation: An Interdisciplinary Journal for the Study of Critical Moments Discourse* 1/1, October 6, 2013 (http://www.emory.edu/HypheNation/Articles%20page.htm), pp.15-31.

"NO Projects," November 10, 2014 (http://noprojects.blogspot.com).

Porter, Eric (2009): "Jazz and Revival." In: *American Quarterly* 61/3, pp. 593-613.

Rechy, John ([1963] 2013): *City of Night*, 50th anniversary edition, New York: Grove Press.

Reed Jr., Adolph (2011): "Three Tremés." In: *Nonsite*, November 10, 2014 (http://nonsite.org/editorial/three-tremes).

Thomas, Lynnell L. (2012): "'People Want to See What Happened': Treme, Televisual Tourism, and the Racial Remapping of Post-Katrina New Orleans." In: *Television & New Media* 13/3, pp. 213-224.

Treme, (2010-2013): Created by Eric Overmyer and David Simon. Burbank, CA: Warner Home Video. DVD.

———. Season 1, Episode 2 (2010): "Meet de Boys on de Battlefront," dir. by Jim McKay.

———. Season 1, Episode 5 (2010): "Shame, Shame, Shame," dir. by Christine Moore.

———. Season 2, Episode 1 (2011): "Accentuate the Positive," dir. by Anthony Hemingway.

———. Season 2, Episode 2 (2011): "Everything I Do Gonh Be Funky," dir. by Tim Robbins.

———. Season 2, Episode 4 (2011): "Santa Claus, Do You Ever Get the Blues?" dir. by Alex Zakrzewski.

———. Season 2, Episode 5 (2011): "Slip Away," dir. by Rob Bailey.

———. Season 2, Episode 06 (2011): "Feels Like Pain," dir. by Roxann Dawson.

———. Season 3, Episode 10 (2012): "Tipitina," dir. by Anthony Hemingway.

———. Season 4, Episode 1 (2012): "Yes We Can," dir. by Anthony Hemingway.

Vukadinović, Vojin Saša ([2011] 2013): "Boys in the Back." In: Katja Peglow/Jonas Engelmann (eds.), *Riot Grrrl Revisited. Geschichte und Gegenwart einer feministischen Bewegung*, Mainz: Ventil Verlag, pp. 109-112.

Lewis Watts: *Brass Band on Claiborne Ave.,* Tremé 2010

Being a musician is a strong tradition in New Orleans. It is a skill that is passed on from parents to their children. This brass band had just finished playing for a funeral in the Tremé. Before the 1960s, Claiborne Ave. had been a wide street lined with oak trees that were destroyed by the construction of the elevated I-10-freeway, which cut out the light and divided the community in half.

Dance Back From the Grave: Marc Cohn's and Jackson Browne's Musical Responses to Hurricane Katrina

CYPRIAN PISKUREK

THE CULTURE OF MUSICAL TRIBUTES

One of the most dominant associations with the city of New Orleans is in all likelihood that of a musical city: arguably, there is hardly a city in the United States, with the exception of maybe Nashville, whose fame and reputation rests so much on the symbiosis between place and musical scene (cf. Spera 2011: 2). From negro spirituals to the famous New Orleans jazz bands, but in genres like hip hop, rock or blues as well, artists from the city have influenced the musical world like few others. For that reason, it came as no surprise that musical artists from New Orleans, from other parts of Louisiana, from all over the U.S. and also other parts of the world, almost immediately responded to the devastation wrought by Hurricane Katrina and recorded or performed tributes for 'The Big Easy.'

The discourse around musical tributes has been clearly altered by September 11, 2001, because this watershed event of the 21st century brought about a new culture of public commemoration and public grief. New York City, a musical city like New Orleans after all (although not as uniquely dependent on its musical reputation), had seen an enormous output of tribute concerts, records or radio broadcasts after the attacks on the World Trade Center, with a telethon or the high-prestige *Concert for New York City* as just the main examples. When Hurricane Katrina hit four years later in what proved to be the next American disaster, it seemed obvious that the established pattern of telethon relief would be instituted again. The victims of the hurricane were thus publicly and televisually commemorated, among others, at NBC's *A Concert for Hurricane Relief*, MTV and VH1's joint show *ReAct Now: Music & Relief*, or at the multi-channel program *Shelter from the Storm: A Concert for the Gulf Coast*. When another devastating hurricane hit Haiti in 2010 and MTV hosted a major international telethon, or when on a much smaller scale Hurricane Sandy's victims were commemorated in a minor telethon in 2012, one could recognize a similar pattern; although the charity telethon as such has a much longer and more complex tradition, it seems safe to speak of a culture of catastrophe telethons that has developed over the past 13 years.

I would argue that three major reasons are responsible for the emergence of this telethon culture with its musical tribute performances after disaster has struck: first, it may sound clichéd that some things can be better said in music than in spoken words, but it probably rings true that musical artists feel a special duty and a special opportunity to work with the unspeakable. The long tradition within the musical world of requiems and funeral music is proof of this. Secondly, telethons and even many musical tributes outside such structured events are meant to produce financial benefits for the disaster-ridden citizens and communities; it is only logical that one of the biggest and financially most successful industries, the music industry, contributes in this way. *America: A Tribute for Heroes*, for example, is said to have made somewhere between 120 and 200 million dollars for a fund helping the families of 9/11 victims (cf. Melnick 2009: 52). Thirdly, and without wanting to question an ethical motivation in the first place, artists can cash in on their participation as well: if not with direct financial benefits then at least in terms of cultural capital and social prestige.

This is not only true for artists, but as most of these telethons are run by giant television networks, corporate business is involved as well. Even if in most cases these events are explicitly free of commercials, it seems difficult to see this involvement as a genuinely altruistic gesture. John Storey, in a ground-breaking essay, has laid bare the hegemonic relations between West Coast Rock and companies which financed the Vietnam War (cf. 1988); in a vaguely similar fashion does it appear complicated, to say the least, if television networks, which contribute to the widening of social injustice apparently address precisely these injustices. Moreover, the sentiments disseminated by these events certainly fulfill a hegemonic function: Jeffrey Melnick has called most messages conveyed by the aforementioned 9/11 telethon "one-dimensional reassurances" and a "first communal effort to define how 'we' felt" (2009: 63). This is achieved by "a powerful claim that would influence much post-9/11 art in the telethon that instructs audiences to receive it as natural, authentic, heartfelt, and without any motive outside of the eulogistic and patriotic" (ibid: 24).

Notwithstanding a general trend towards a monolithic telethon culture, one should not forget that 9/11 was no natural disaster, and that for that matter a more political discourse is called upon from the beginning. However, Hurricane Katrina is the sad, but perfect example that even natural disasters do not take place outside the realm of politics, as both the governmental reactions to disaster (evacuations, medical treatment, financial aid) and the prevention of disaster (ghettoization, insurances, financial support) made clear. Rapper and co-presenter Kanye West pointed this out when, during the NBC telethon, he implicitly accused the Bush government of racism manifest in the lack of help for hurricane victims: "George Bush doesn't care about black people." It is precisely this hint at the racial politics involved in disaster management (a discourse mostly absent in post-9/11 debates – at least with regard to the victims in the twin towers, the Pentagon and on the planes), which breaks with the conventions of a telethon, withdrawing from the patriotic and humanitarian unity on which these events rest. The scandalous nature of West's comment may have been exaggerated by the media, but his use of the uncritical framework of the telethon for his remarks certainly gave his thesis an edge.

As cynical as that may sound, the consequence of this telethon or tribute discourse is that works that publicly respond to disasters like Hurricane Katrina are often met with general suspicion. However, this does not keep us from studying how such works represent the disaster in question and shape our perception of human catastrophe. It may help in this context to call on a classical concept from British Cultural Studies, namely Raymond Williams's concept of structures of feeling developed in the 1960s. His theoretical approach how to get at the "felt sense" (1961: 63) of a certain culture at a certain historical moment has been criticized by some thinkers as too blurry, but it is precisely because of this that his concept is so well suited to study cultural meanings in flux. Assuming that a particular culture is always defined by the "meanings and values implicit in a particular way of life" (ibid: 57), and conveyed by all its cultural practices, Williams postulates that we should study the works of art of a historical moment if we want to derive either dominant, residual or emergent structures of feeling.

It is essential to note that Williams's feeling is a 'social' occurrence, not something as personal or individual as 'emotion'; it is precisely because a particular culture conveys its implicit values in works of art (in Williams's case mostly novels, but music, paintings, architecture etc. carry such values just as well) that feeling for Williams must be social. Nonetheless, and this is no paradox for Williams, do we obviously study individual voices to get at this felt sense of a historical moment in a particular culture; and it is by reading a multitude of such individual voices that such patterns or structures of feeling will show. These structures of feeling, on the one hand, reflect social reality, on the other hand they affect social reality in turn as they add something to a respective discourse.

A catastrophe as enormous as Hurricane Katrina will most certainly be represented and negotiated in works of art, be it in books, such as Dave Eggers's *Zeitoun*, films, such as Spike Lee's *When the Levees Broke* or the numerous musical responses to the hurricane. In the wake of a catastrophe like Katrina it is first and foremost the more prominent vignettes or individual tracks explicitly addressing what has happened which take the limelight. Green Day and U2's cover version of "The Saints are Coming," Juvenile's "Get Ya Hustle On" or some of the tribute covers performed at the benefit concerts were thus circulated as accompanying tracks to the pictures either commemorating the victims or later criticizing government response. Williams stresses that we need to read a multiplicity of texts to sharpen our understanding of structures of feeling, so we have to look beyond such more prominent tracks and put them into the context of other voices as well. For that matter I would like to suggest a reorientation towards an art form which, in recent years, has suffered from the music and television industry's focus on individual tracks and singles, and which is all too often neglected when Cultural Studies scholars study popular music: the album. In the days of iTunes and YouTube (some would claim since the launch of MTV in 1981), the shift towards particular songs and the neglect of the more extensive collection of songs on an album, has reached unforeseen heights. Single releases (formerly '45s) have certainly been an important feature of the rock and pop industries since the 1950s and 1960s, and critics have often somewhat derogatorily talked of 'album tracks' as songs not good enough to cut a hit single. Too tempting is the focus on individual songs, too arbitrary and heterogeneous the choice and quality of song material over the course of 35 to 75 minutes, to study a rock or pop album in detail, apparently. If, however, a range of short stories can tell us more about structures of feeling than an individual text (compare James Joyce's short stories in *Dubliners* to his novel *A Portrait of the Artist as a Young Man*), the same goes for a variety of songs on an album compared to individual tracks. From Tom Waits's *Closing Time* to the Beastie Boys's *Licensed to Ill*: one could think of numerous albums that tell us more in their entirety about the culture and historical moment they represent than individual tracks.

It seems fair to say that there are still genres which cherish the album more than others, and the retro trend for vinyl records is certainly a good example for a (sub)culture around the art form album. However, in the wider scheme of things the album has been moved towards the margins of popular music culture; still, especially when it comes to studying structures of feeling, this text form deserves closer scrutiny. For this purpose, the following discussion shall focus on two albums by befriended artists Marc Cohn and Jackson Browne, recorded and released a couple of years after the hurricane hit New Orleans, which capture and inform post-Katrina structures of feeling. Although both artists can be called household names in American music, I would claim that even the more prominent songs on both albums were not at the forefront of representing Katrina to wider audiences; moreover it is in the context of the even lesser known 'album tracks' that structures of feeling after the hurricane shimmer through. It would, however, be bold to claim that two albums by two different artists can inform us sufficiently about the structures of feeling shaped by Hurricane Katrina. Given that both albums, although different in their approach, are texts by white, middle-aged Americans, one can see that the perspective these texts offer is too narrow to allow us to capture a heterogeneous variety of voices. Still, both texts point us in a certain direction as to how the disaster contributed to the felt sense of post-Katrina times, especially since they favor different strategies: while Cohn takes a very personal and spiritual view on Katrina, certainly influenced by a near-death experience of his own, Browne's stance is clearly more political. Rather than opposing each other, these different takes on the event show how structures of feeling can accommodate and negotiate divergent ways of representation.

JOIN THE PARADE AND *TIME THE CONQUEROR*

In 2007, U.S. artist Cohn released his fourth studio album *Join the Parade*, with its central and programmatic song "Dance Back From the Grave." Cohn, interestingly enough, achieved his breakthrough with another homage to a musical town in his 1991 hit single "Walking in Memphis," but despite three critically acclaimed albums he was relegated to second rank among U.S. singers/songwriters in the eyes of the wider public. His fan base was severely shocked to learn in August 2005 that Cohn had been shot in the head in an attempted carjacking after a gig in Denver, Colorado (cf. CNN 2005). Cohn's skull was not penetrated by the bullet and he narrowly got away with his life. Only two weeks later, Hurricane Katrina hit the Gulf Coast and devastated New Orleans. Cohn – not personally, but professionally linked to the city – had to witness television images of this devastation while recovering from his own near-death experience.

It may sound a bit corny to some, but when Cohn released his album *Join The Parade*, he convincingly explained that it was a combination of his own trauma and the citizens of New Orleans' trauma that helped to end the songwriter's block from which he had been suffering (cf. Scott 2008); there had been no new album since 1998's *Burning the Daze*. The crucial trigger for his new inspiration came in the form of two sentences by Rick Bragg, published in an article about Katrina in the *Washington Post*: "But I have seen these people dance, laughing, to the edge of the grave. I believe that, now, they will dance back from it." (2005, n.p.) This quotation by the American writer, later named as co-author of Cohn's song "Dance Back From the Grave," is a reference to the special relationship between death and music in New Orleans. The jazz funerals in the city are one of the strongest and most impressive musical traditions, although for 'Western' eyes hard to understand at first glance. Bragg himself writes about these occasions:

What a place, so at ease here at the elbow of death, where I once marched and was almost compelled to dance in a jazz funeral for a street-corner conjurer named Chicken Man, who was carried to his resting place by a hot-stepping brass band and a procession of mourners who drank long-neck beers and laughed out loud as his hearse rolled past doorways filled with men and women who clapped in time. (ibid.)

The joyful note, which accompanies the sad occasion, the prototypical coupling of tears and laughter so prominent in the philosophy of jazz, seems hard to fathom for people accustomed to the somberness of funerals in other parts of the world. Medieval paintings of dead bodies dancing, or various *danses macabres* from classical music are especially employed in Western tradition to represent such a celebration of death as the Other, the non-civilized, the heathen; the liminality of death seems to be questioned in such instances. In New Orleans however, jazz funerals are an institution and a vital part of the black community. As Ellis Marsalis jr. has written in the introductory notes to Leo Touchet and Vernel Bagneris's photo collection *Rejoice When You Die*: "That this should be so says a great deal about that community and its uniqueness. [...] Only in New Orleans was a style of music so intertwined with daily life and death as to give not only its sound, but eventually its name, to a local funerary custom." (1998: 2) Fictionalized and satirized in the opening scene of the James Bond classic *Live And Let Die*, the funeral procession led by a jazz band is a very real and common occurrence in the streets of the Ninth Ward and surrounding areas. In Lee Friedlander's portrait collection of New Orleans musicians, photographs of brass bands accompanying a coffin to the cemetery stand next to pictures of brass bands at Mardi Gras (2013: 74-75); Touchet and Bagneris's abovementioned collection offers more fascinating insights into this tradition. Originally, funeral processions with music were reserved for fellow musicians, but this has more and more become a standard practice for other prominent members of the community, or when young people have died. It is characteristic for these processions to start out with somber marches and dirges, but they will then cathartically turn to upbeat numbers once the body is entombed: "the somber journey to the gravesite and the exuberant return from it" (Marsalis jr. 1998: 2).

Hurricane Katrina brought too much death to New Orleans and the city, especially the city's musical scene, which by way of its jazz funerals has a very special relation with death. For that matter, it is maybe not surprising that these two strands – music and death – should be coupled, which is precisely what Cohn does on *Join the Parade*. This happens explicitly when taking Bragg's description of the jazz funerals as a slogan for the central song on the record, but it also happens in more subtle ways. The coupling of music and death is certainly a striking motif throughout the whole album because Cohn is negotiating his own being alive against the background of so many victims in New Orleans. The lyrics often have a spiritual note: in "Live Out The String" Cohn wonders whether "life is curious to see what you would do with the gift of being left alive" (Cohn/Silverstone 2007), and shows deep humility with a nod to gospel in a 'call and response' that "sometimes you better get down on your knees" (ibid.). Cohn asks questions raised by the arbitrariness of the mere fact that he is still able to record an album: "Fate is kind, fate is cruel, fate is terminally cool / It's a random interruption in the middle of your groove" (ibid.). This is quite an explicit reference to his being shot in the head, as he "tries to find the meaning in beating the odds" (ibid.). When Cohn evokes fate and the odds of being alive, he implies that Hurricane Katrina is first and foremost a natural disaster – not the man-made political catastrophe which others (for example Jackson Browne) have taken the storm for. Read in this context of natural disaster, such words transcend the merely personal level, as the randomness of natural catastrophes always sparks questions of why someone beats the odds and someone else does not.

In another song on the record, "The Calling," Cohn has a jazz guitarist by the telling name of Charlie Christian hear a spiritual calling. This is the only song on the album which was written years earlier, but which fits the pattern of spiritual awakenings in the face of life and death (cf. Cohn 2007a). The final track on the album ties in with this, and is again torn between fatalism and hopefulness, as it is entitled "Life Goes On." Cohn muses that "without your sister or your brother / Life goes on […] Without Elvis / Without Jesus / Life goes on" (2007b), and that even "with all the undertakers / Life goes on" (ibid.). Even the album's titular track, "Join The Parade," quite literally referring to a musical parade, is in the New Orleans context trying to subtly reconcile life and death. The words "I know I'm finally home and dry / Please come and join the parade / Don't let it pass you by" (Cohn/Burn/Salem 2007) even employ a distant reference to the artist's narrow survival and the city's symbolic resurrection in standing its ground against the adversary forces of nature. All these exemplary passages from the lyrics of almost half the album's tracks would just be more than understandable personal musings about Cohn's narrow survival at the hands of the Denver carjacker, but in the course of the whole work these are further observations about the arbitrariness of death as experienced during Katrina.

Most central to the record is the aforementioned "Dance Back From the Grave," and it is this song, which influences a reading of the whole album as a post-Katrina text. What could be seen as a metaphor for Cohn's own dancing back from the grave intertwines his fate with that of the citizens of New Orleans. In the first stanza he muses about his own survival, saying that he "used to wake up every morning saying 'I must be getting away with something here' / Every day was like parole / Before the levees overflowed" (Cohn/Bragg 2007). A little later Cohn evokes the jazz funerals when he reminisces about having seen "the people laughin' / All the way down to the cemetery / Just to send another soul off on its way / I've seen them dancin' / Right up to the edge of it / But this time they're gonna dance back from the grave" (ibid.). This is a resurrection narrative, which works not along primary Christian motifs, but by referring to the musical representation of these ideas via the meeting point between Dixieland and Spirituals. This is highlighted when Cohn, in the chorus, calls on everybody to "get [their] tambourines and slide trombones and dance back from the grave" (ibid.). In the final stanza, the song even manages to give this resurrection dance the spooky air of a *danse macabre* when it speaks of the undead masses "as they circle and swoop and promenade / They're just carrying their torches / Marching in a heavenly parade" (ibid.). This slight uncanniness in his metaphysical chant against death is emphasized by the singer's hypnotic narration, reminiscent of various Tom Waits tracks,[1] and the compression on his voice in the chorus. As a further musical element, the brass section in the chorus rattles as if trying to scare death away; "Dance Back From the Grave" thus becomes musically as well as lyrically the most outspoken reference to New Orleans after Katrina.

The importance of this song for the record's track list becomes clear when looking at the album cover and the accompanying booklet. In the booklet there are five photographs, four usual portraits of the artist and one which is so different that it stands out: next to the lyrics of "Dance Back From the Grave" we encounter a 1963 photograph by Leonard Freed of a jazz funeral; five brass band musicians and the grand marshal (a 'master of ceremony' who leads funeral processions) march in front of a cemetery. On the album cover of Cohn's record, the same brass band is transferred from the cemetery, and is here pastiched against dark and

---

1   I am not mainly referring to the well-known Waits track "I Wish I Was in New Orleans," but rather to New Orleans' influences on his instrumentation and singing style; a fitting example is his 1985 "Anywhere I Lay My Head," which actually resembles a two-minute jazz funeral with its slow dirge turning into an exuberant but solemn march.

impending storm clouds in the background – the jazz band which in the original defies the finality of death by turning from the somber dirges to the joyful marches here defies a very specific death brought about by the storm. This is of course not just any storm, but Hurricane Katrina, as becomes more than obvious when studying the album's recording history and its lyrics. *Join The Parade* is not a concept album; still one might say that the other songs are grouped around "Dance Back From the Grave," as at least half of them negotiate this personal struggle over life and death, which was so close to Cohn when writing and recording the album. The accompanying artwork on the album cover and in its booklet emphasize these negotiations and visually anchor the musical and lyrical meanings.

A somewhat different take on Hurricane Katrina was pursued by Jackson Browne one year later. His song "Where Were You" was to become one of the central songs on his record *Time the Conqueror*, released in 2008, and stands out from the rest of the record in a similar way as "Dance Back From the Grave" stands out from Cohn's *Join the Parade*. "Where Were You" is the beginning of a whole array of rhetorical questions culminating in an attack on President George W. Bush and his administration for mismanaging the Katrina crisis. As Manfred Prisching has noted, the weather may be fate but everything around it is politics and economics (cf. 2006: 110), and it is with regard to the political management of the crisis, with long delays, or with discrimination between different parts of the city, that the government was accused of failing to react adequately to the disaster. The natural disaster is thus overwritten with an interpretation as manmade. The 'lyrical thou' of the song works on various levels: firstly, the general question about someone's whereabouts when an event of historical proportions occurred has by now become quite a standard practice of remembrance – where were you when the planes hit the Twin Towers, where were you when JFK was killed, etc. On the face of it, the various specific questions asked in the song are directed at people immediately affected by the hurricane: "Where were you when the sky cracked open? / Heading for shelter and barely coping / Thinking you could ride the storm out" (Browne et al. 2008b), or "Where were you in the social order? / The Lower Nine or a hotel in the Quarter / Which side of the border between rich and poor?" (ibid.). Over the course of the song it becomes clear that this question is more of an accusation against the absent president who took so long to acknowledge the catastrophe and to visit the city: "We hold the truth self-evident," Browne says, hinting at Bush's betrayal of the essence of American independence and democracy, "The photograph of the President / From Air Force One, he views the devastation / Shaved face, rested eyes / Looking down, he circles twice / On his way home from his vacation" (ibid.), leading to the double meaning of "Where were you, when you got the picture?" (ibid.). Thus, the more or less neutral questions about the victims' whereabouts turn into an accusing question of where those who should have helped were at the time they were needed. Earlier in the song, Browne asks "however strong, however wise / However true our leaders appear to be / When they talk about prosperity / However hard this country strives / If property is valued more than lives [...] How long do we imagine we'll be free?" (ibid.). This is a song which depends on the oppositions it establishes: on the one hand the poor and exhausted victims, on the other hand the "shaved" president with "rested eyes" and "the safety of the west bank" (ibid.) which many victims are not allowed to reach on the one hand, and on the other, the president circling over the flood. Browne thus describes the catastrophe and how it affects the citizens of New Orleans in various ways, but the song's message condenses in a critique of the way the government handled the crisis.

It is noteworthy that in "Where Were You" these attacks focus on a singular event, but already evoke questions about America's idea as a nation, which is called into question. References to self-evident truths or a rhetorical question like "How long do we imagine we'll be free?" (ibid.) point towards an essential crisis of the values of American democracy. This line of attack on the Bush administration runs through the album. Another monumental song, "The Drums of War," harshly criticizes the war cries and various military conflicts Bush engaged the U.S. in. In the same vein as the rhetorical questions in "Where Were You," Browne here delivers another list:

Who lies, then bombs, then calls it an error?
Who makes a fortune from fighting terror?
Who is the enemy trying to crush us?
Who is the enemy of truth and justice?
Who is the enemy of peace and freedom?
Where are the courts, now when we need them?
Why is impeachment not on the table? (Browne et al. 2008a)

Not only since Dave Eggers's account of the Zeitoun family (cf. 2009) do we know that Bush's War on Terror and the management of Katrina cannot be seen as separate entities, and this is what Jackson Browne's album underlines in many passages. In another, more subtle, attack, he criticizes the condemnation of all things Cuban in official U.S. discourses in "Going Down to Cuba": "They've got to deal with that embargo / Enough to drive any country insane / They might not know all the freedoms you and I know / But they do know what to do in a hurricane" (Browne 2008b). Even if U.S.-Cuban policy obviously reaches back a lot further than George W. Bush, we can observe how the mismanagement of Katrina triggers a general lyrical assault on U.S. politics. Especially the line, which praises Cuba for a more adequate hurricane management links the various fields of discontent that Browne addresses on his album. These concrete accusations then tie in with nostalgic and slightly self-ironic comments on the singer's younger years in the 1960s when Browne muses "Didn't we believe in love? / Didn't we believe in giving it away? / That didn't really leave us with the love / To find our way / After RFK and Martin Luther King" (Browne 2008a). And even if Browne's record only in a few instances references New Orleans in terms of musical arrangements (as Cohn's *Join the Parade* does), there is more than just a nod to Louisiana spirituals when he verbatim quotes the line "[l]et my people go" from "Go Down, Moses" in his song "Live Nude Cabaret" (cf. Browne 2008c).

It should have become clear by now that Browne's take on Hurricane Katrina is much more political than Cohn's. There are several explanations for this: on the one hand, Browne has been more politically active throughout his career, especially in the 1970s and 1980s when he became an activist against nuclear power, or in the 2000s when he campaigned for presidential candidate John Kerry. Classic songs like "For America" can almost be seen as predecessors of the mood that prevails on *Time the Conqueror*. On the other hand, it is not surprising that Cohn chooses a more personal or metaphysical representation of Katrina's impact because of his own near-demise two weeks before the storm hit. Then again, we also should not underestimate that Cohn's album was released a year before Browne's, which means that Browne's writing process was not as directly affected by the events as Cohn's; that reactions to disasters develop from personal to political with time passing is a long-established and much-observed phenomenon. While it would be too simple to just call Cohn's take 'personal' and Browne's approach 'political,' both certainly contribute in their own ways to a structure of feeling which blends the personal with the political.

This is a tendency that one can observe in representational discourses of tragic events over at least the past twenty years. Think of the death of Princess Diana in 1997, which developed from mourning the clarified humanitarian princess to condemning the modern media circus with its paparazzi, which chased her into death. Think of 9/11, which highlighted individual fates to make the unspeakable a bit more tangible, before ultimately leading towards the politics of death and terrorism. The tsunami of 2005, catastrophes in Haiti or the Philippines: mass deaths, in Anette Pankratz, Claus-Ulrich Viol and Ariane de Waal's words "virtually unrepresentable as such" (2012: 1) need to be personalized and individualized in order for us to grasp them; this is an unmistakable part of our structures of feeling surrounding such events. In the same vein, we cannot accept this inherent absurdity of death, which requires us to interpret death via a political dimension that explains these events as abnormal, putting the blame on some political actor and interpreting the event as man-made rather than natural. This is precisely what Cohn's *Join the Parade* and Browne's *Time the Conqueror* represent: a pairing of two sides of a coin. However, one should not lose sight of the two artists' position when representing Hurricane Katrina: as both are white men, racial difference is in their works only captured from the outside; especially in the case of New Orleans and Katrina, a thorough analysis of the corresponding structures of feeling would have to take other voices into account as well.

CONCLUSION: "THEY'RE TRYING TO WASH US AWAY…"

If the personal blends into the political, then the individual also blends into the social, and it is here that Williams's structures of feeling can be read off the works under scrutiny. In studying the two exemplary albums by Cohn and Browne, a pattern emerges over the multiplicity of individual songs. In Cohn's case, the experience of Katrina, alongside his personal fate, helps to structure a revaluation of mankind's mortality and the arbitrariness of death in natural disasters. With Browne, the individual and collective grief has already been permeated by bitterness and anger about the way that the crisis was officially handled. Two artists from the same genre (mainstream singer/songwriter) have thus derived very different though complementary meanings from the same event, which in my opinion tie in with bigger discourses about catastrophe and catharsis. Then again, these two albums as texts do not exist in a vacuum: even if Browne, for example, does not explicitly refer to racial difference in "Where Were You," his accusation of government inaction latches onto West's rant against racial inequality in the light of disaster management. In their emphasis on personal fate and inequality, the structures of feeling recur on the lived experience of a historical moment; but in turn they also add to the discourse about this specific catastrophe, interpreting the event in complementary ways.

On a related note, it seems all too sad that the quintessential song about Hurricane Katrina had already been written long before the storm hit the Gulf. In 1974, Randy Newman recorded a song entitled "Louisiana 1927," in which he paints a picture of the Great Mississippi Flood of 1927, both describing the fate of the poor victims and the inaction of the government. Here again, questions about the arbitrariness of falling victim to the flood are raised when the speaker in Newman's song states that "Some people got lost in the flood / Some people got away alright" (1974). All the same, the structural inequality within American society (always a big topic with Randy Newman) is addressed, and it is explicitly directed at the government. Here, President Calvin Coolidge pays a fictional visit to the area: "President Coolidge came down in a railroad train / With a little fat man with a note-pad in his hand / President say 'Little fat man, isn't it a shame / What the river has done to this poor cracker's land'" (ibid.). Newman's song is testament to the sad fact that Katrina was not a one-off event but that the devastation brought to the city of New Orleans, as well as the mismanagement on the government's behalf are instances of history repeating. The song was performed by various artists in the wake of Katrina and the chorus' repetitive lament – "They're trying to wash us away" – shows that Browne's reaction to the catastrophe in "Where Were You" is just a variation on Newman's verdict. In any case, it is an important reminder of the fragility both of the geographical position of New Orleans and of the – equally fragile – social contracts within American society.

BIBLIOGRAPHY

Bragg, Rick (2005): "This Isn't the Last Dance." In: *The Washington Post*, March 2, 2015 (http://www.washingtonpost.com/wp-dyn/content/article/2005/09/01/AR2005090101813.html).

CNN (2005): "'Walking in Memphis' Singer Shot in Head, Survives," March 2, 2015 (http://edition.cnn.com/2005/SHOWBIZ/Music/08/09/cohn.shot/index.html?s=PM:SHOWBIZ).

Eggers, Dave (2009): *Zeitoun*, New York: Vintage.

Friedlander, Lee (2013): *Playing for the Benefit of the Band: New Orleans Music Culture*, New Haven: Yale University Press.

Marsalis jr., Ellis (1998): "Introduction." In: Leo Touchet/Vernel Bagneris (eds.), *Rejoice When You Die: The New Orleans Jazz Funerals*, Baton Rouge: Louisiana State University Press, pp. ix-xi.

Melnick, Jeffrey (2009): *9/11 Culture*, Chichester: Wiley Blackwell.

Mervis, Scott (2008): "Music Preview: Near-death experience sparked Marc Cohn's 'Join the Parade.'" In: *Pittsburgh Post-Gazette*, March 2, 2015 (http://post-gazette.com/ae/2008/01/24/Music-Preview-Near-death-experience-sparked-Marc-Cohn-s-Join-the-Parade/stories/200801240517).

Pankratz, Anette/Viol, Claus-Ulrich/de Waal, Ariane (2012): "Introduction: Liminality, Power, and Performance." In: Anette Pankratz/Claus-Ulrich Viol/Ariane de Waal (eds.), *Birth and Death in British Culture: Liminality,*

Power, and Performance, Newcastle upon Tyne: Cambridge Scholars Publishing, pp. 1-15.

Prisching, Manfred (2006): *Good Bye New Orleans: Der Hurrikan Katrina und die amerikanische Gesellschaft*, Graz: Leykam.

Spera, Keith (2011): *Groove Interrupted: Loss, Renewal, and the Music of New Orleans*, New York: St. Martin's Press.

Storey, John (1988): "Rockin' Hegemony: West Coast Rock and Amerika's War in Vietnam." In: Alf Louvre/Jeffrey Walsh (eds.), *Tell Me Lies About Vietnam: Cultural Battles for the Meaning of the War*, Milton Keynes: Open University Press, pp. 181-197.

Touchet, Leo/Bagneris, Vernel (1998): *Rejoice When You Die: The New Orleans Jazz Funerals*, Baton Rouge: Louisiana State University Press.

Williams, Raymond (1961): *The Long Revolution*, London: Chatto & Windus.

Discography

Browne, Jackson (2008a): "Off of Wonderland," *Time the Conqueror*, Inside Recordings.

Browne, Jackson (2008b): "Going Down to Cuba," *Time the Conqueror*, Inside Recordings.

Browne, Jackson (2008c): "Live Nude Cabaret," *Time the Conqueror*, Inside Recordings.

Browne, Jackson/McCormick, Kevin/Goldenberg, Mark/Lewak, Mauricio/Young, Jeff (2008a): "The Drums of War," *Time the Conqueror*, Inside Recordings.

Browne, Jackson/McCormick, Kevin/Goldenberg, Mark/Lewak, Mauricio/Young, Jeff (2008b): "Where Were You," *Time the Conqueror*, Inside Recordings.

Cohn, Marc (2007a): "The Calling (Charlie Christian's Tune)," *Join The Parade*, Decca.

Cohn, Marc (2007b): "Life Goes On," *Join the Parade*, Decca.

Cohn, Marc/Bragg, Rick (2007): "Dance Back From the Grave," *Join The Parade*, Decca.

Cohn, Marc/Silverstone, Michael (2007): "Live Out The String," *Join The Parade*, Decca.

Newman, Randy (1974): "Louisiana 1927," *Good Old Boys*, Reprise.

Lewis Watts: *Ashton Ramsey*, Artist and Historian, Backstreet Museum, Mardi Gras Day, Tremé 2007

Every year for Carnival, Ashton Ramsey designs and wears a suit with symbols around a theme of New Orleans history and culture. In 2007, he used the names of people and places that no longer existed. His living sculpture is an elegant tribute to what had come before.

Revisiting Place, the Memorial, and the Historical in Tom Piazza's *Why New Orleans Matters* and Natasha Trethewey's *Beyond Katrina*

COURTNEY GEORGE

The South is a place created in our imaginations. Southern studies scholars have described the many ways that artists, historians, and observers have imagined the South through the years – from the "moonlight and magnolias" of plantation literature to the racist images of *Birth of a Nation,* to the social critiques of the Southern Renascence, to the strip malls and immigrant hubs of the post- and global-Souths. In fact, in 2008's *The Real South,* Scott Romine argues that the region is "increasingly sustained as a virtual, commodified, built, themed, invented, or otherwise artificial territory […] less imaginable as a 'natural' or 'organic' culture" (2008: 9). But when we begin to think about a "place" as wholly imagined, we begin to wonder whether the ground under our feet actually exists – until a natural disaster strikes, and through its destruction, makes us aware of the physical "space" we inhabit. Natural disasters and the recovery processes afterwards ask us to re-define what we mean by the terms "place" and "space." The introduction to the 2010 collection *Places of Public Memory* describes "place" and "space" as both distinct but also dependent on one another: "a *place* that is bordered, specified, and locatable by being named is seen as different from open, undifferentiated, undesignated *space* […] place as structured, bordered, or built locale depends in part for its character on how it deploys space" (Dickinson/Blair/Ott 2010: 23, emphasis original). In this definition, while place is determined by space, place is viewed not only as a physical construct but also as a social construct while space is viewed as the land itself.

When Hurricane Katrina made landfall in the Gulf Coast region on August 29, 2005, suddenly, the imagined South (the constructed "place") – with its poverty, prejudices, and diverse cultures – became again a physical "space," where the realities, made clear in the storm's aftermath, were worse than anyone could have imagined. In order not only to make sense of Katrina and its aftermath but also to provide a sort of access to the physical space itself, writers and artists continue to imagine the place: the Gulf Coast region as a part of the South. However, in these portrayals, the social and physical impacts of Hurricane Katrina also significantly impact the way we consider connections between the larger concepts of history/memory, space/place, and local/global, which have for so long stymied our southern imaginations. In discussions of two book-length personal narratives, Tom Piazza's *Why New Orleans Matters* (2005) and Natasha Trethewey's *Beyond Katrina: A Meditation on the Mississippi Gulf Coast* (2009), I argue that those previously imagined and contested binaries in southern studies – between history and memory, the local and the global – collapse in multiple ways as we try to rebuild and preserve both "place" and "space" in Katrina's aftermath. Both authors construct their visions of "place" from their personal biographies and their individual experiences, which ask readers to further understand "place" as inauthentic – as created from not only cultural and historical perspectives but also from the individual's perspective. Because both Piazza's and Trethewey's narratives also reflect on the physical space of the Gulf Coast before the storm and during the process of rebuilding, these works offer a good starting point for reconsidering the seeming binaries of history/memory, space/place, and local/global.

In my discussions of *Why New Orleans Matters* and *Beyond Katrina*, I argue that Katrina's impact calls for us to rethink how we define "place" (and more specifically our constructs of the South), suggesting that the concept of place is tied not only to concepts of identity, memory, and history but also to physical spaces that must be continually preserved and restored. However, gaining access to specific physical spaces is often difficult during and after a natural disaster, and so we rely on representations of that space to reach a wide audience. For both Gulf Coast residents and the general public, reliance on representations increased in the days leading up to and the weeks following Katrina because very few people were allowed to visit the physical space; the *only* access was provided by television, radio, and the written word. In this way, we relied on and continue to rely on representations of "place" to gain access to the physical space of the Gulf Coast and its people. For instance, beyond the initial television, radio, and newspaper reports immediately following the storm, written works like Piazza's and Trethewey's, along with televisual representations like Spike Lee's two HBO documentaries or David Simon's fictional series *Treme*, continue to depict Katrina and the aftermath for those unable to return to the region.

French theorist Pierre Nora would call these subsequent popular representations "sites of memory," traces of living history which have replaced more objective or tangible historical evidence. The writers that contributed to *Places of Public Memory* depart from Nora's important work in memory studies to suggest that meaningfulness can be achieved through the rhetorical strategies located in physical memorials, in actual physical spaces. Our constructions of histories and our memories, whether in physical memorials and museums or other cultural representations like written memoirs or documentary films, are born out of both place and space – the way we construct culture and the land (place) and the perception of the physical land before human development (space). As stated above, these imagined constructions of place become especially significant for those unable to travel to the physical space itself.

While the contributors to *Places of Public Memory* focus on the way we construct physical memorials, for my purposes, I apply these definitions to written memorials, which address the destruction of the physical space and its proposed redevelopment after Hurricane Katrina. Most popular accounts or reflections about Katrina are necessarily focused on space and place.[1] Notably, the proliferation of fictional or scholarly texts about the failure of the manmade levees in New Orleans has led to a debate about whether to call Katrina a natural or manmade disaster. Specifically, Mississippi residents were incensed by the lack of attention given to their plight, which led to a public outcry for acknowledgement of the effects of Katrina as a natural disaster. As James Patterson Smith argues in *Hurricane Katrina: The Mississippi Story*:

On the Mississippi coast, homes, schools, and public buildings not only flooded, but were collapsed and literally swept away by the thousands in a powerful 30-foot surge of swirling water that pushed straight in from the sea. But for the calamities that befell New Orleans, the fate of almost 40.000 people of the Mississippi Gulf Coast would have stood forth on its own as an unparalleled national disaster epic. (2012: xi)

---

1 For instance, both Douglas Brinkley's history *The Great Deluge: Hurricane Katrina, New Orleans, and the Mississippi Gulf Coast* (2006) and Jed Horne's *Breach of Faith: Hurricane Katrina and the Near Death of an American City* (2006) open with a detailed map of the area to orient readers to both space and place, showing readers the destruction of the physical space that is followed by narrative accounts of the cultural places. Even in Chris Rose's *1 Dead in Attic* (2006), which opts for photographs instead of maps, the references to physical places are detailed and specific.

Those who argue that Katrina is a manmade disaster focus mostly on those "calamities that befell New Orleans." As grassroots organizer Jordan Flaherty writes, "New Orleans was not devastated by a hurricane. The damage came from decades of brutal negligence, and from a stunningly slow response on the part of a local, state, and federal government that didn't care about the people of New Orleans, and still doesn't." (2007: 100) Beyond debating the storm's gruesome effects by state – whether in Louisiana or Mississippi – the environmental community continues to engage in the debate over whether to call Katrina a natural or manmade disaster, with some activists suggesting that "Katrina's real name is global warming" (Gelbspan 2007: 23). In confronting these debates, we must acknowledge that how we treat our land affects how we treat each other, which invites an ecocritical perspective on place and space combined with the previous definitions drawn from memory and cultural studies.

In my analysis of Piazza and Trethewey's texts, I suggest an approach that brings together cultural and memory studies with the ecocritical study of bioregionalism to investigate how popular representations of Katrina after the storm call attention to the way an imagined place – with its borders and restrictions – is consistently tied to the way we use physical space. Bioregionalism makes a useful companion lens for my argument because it moves beyond local environmental movements and concerns to encompass a larger region shaped by similarities in landscape (including watersheds, ecosystems, and significant landforms). As the editors to *The Bioregional Imagination* explain,

[b]y foregrounding natural factors as a way to envision place, bioregionalism proposes that human identity may be constituted by our residence in a larger community of natural beings – our local bioregion – rather than, or at least supplementary to, national, state, ethnic or other more common bases of identity. (Lynch/Glotfelty/Armbruster 2012: 4)

Concepts of bioregionalism encourage sustainable living and direct, deep engagement with the environment in contrast to the way we engage with imagined, or constructed, places: "Bioregions can be seen as more phenomenologically real than politically constructed places" (ibid: 5). For a bioregional analysis, instead of focusing solely on New Orleans as manmade disaster or on Mississippi as natural disaster, it is important to focus on how the entire Gulf Coast continues to be affected after the storm. However, in considering the Gulf Coast as a larger bioregion, I am not suggesting that other culturally constructed identity markers – like those of race, gender, or class – be excluded or supplanted. Instead, I investigate how Piazza and Trethewey bring place and space together, or rather how viewing Piazza's observations about New Orleans alongside Trethewey's observations about the Mississippi Coast contributes to both a cultural and bioregional exploration of the post-Katrina Gulf South through written memorials.

Hurricane Katrina and its consequences, as Piazza and Trethewey show, call on us to think about constructed (i.e. imagined) places and physical spaces as inextricably tied, which is, surprisingly, rather new to humanities scholars in southern studies.[2] However, the nature and even the very definition of physical space have long been a focus in literature about the American South, from the earliest travelogues by explorers who described both the wealth of natural resources and the savageness of non-white peoples (whether Native Americans or African slaves).[3] Subsequent meditations on the South continue to mirror these early narratives: an admiration for the physical space and resources alongside an oppression of its non-white peoples, which morphs into a romanticized view of place as seen in popular plantation novels. In the years following the Civil War, fought over that same oppressive history so deeply connected to the exploited landscape, the South was defined more by the morals, customs, and traditions of the ruling classes than physical space, as represented in works like the Fugitive Agrarians' 1930 collection, *I'll Take My Stand*. Still, this definition of the South was firmly rooted in place and lines drawn on physical spaces (the "agrarian" South versus the "industrial" North).[4] More psychological depictions of the South emerged in the 1940s with writers like W.J. Cash and Lillian Smith.[5] Discussions of physical space were traded for analyses of social customs (including the oppression of women and people of color), along with the beginnings of dismantling the imagined "moonlight and magnolias" South of plantation literature. In more recent scholarship about place in the South, the line of discussion has been, in some ways, to erase the idea of physical space as a

---

[2] In terms of literary studies, Anthony Wilson's *Shadow and Shelter: The Swamp in Southern Culture* (2006), Chris Reiger's *Clear-Cutting Eden: Ecology and the Pastoral in Southern Literature* (2009), and Rob Nixon's *Slow Violence and the Environmentalism of the Poor* (2011) offer three recent, excellent book-length studies employing an ecocritical lens to discuss southern literature and culture.

[3] For instance, Thomas Jefferson's *Notes on the State of Virginia* (1787) is a clear example of travel writing of this sort.

[4] As a starting point, see *I'll Take My Stand: The South and the Agrarian Tradition by 12 Southerners* (1930).

[5] See Lillian Smith's *Killers of the Dream* (1949), W.J. Cash's *The Mind of the South* (1941), and even the later Bertram Wyatt Brown's *Honor and Violence in the Old South* (1982), which begin to uncover the socio-psychological justification for slavery, segregation, gender, and class oppression.

significant identifier of regional identity in order to discuss the post-South or the Global South.[6] Literary and cultural studies scholars have slowly brought ecocritical and bioregional analysis into southern studies, but these writers and scholars remain in the minority to those who continue discussions of "place" as imagined, as a sort of transportable identity marker not clearly tied to a physical space. Contemporary authors like Wendell Berry, Alice Walker, and bell hooks steadfastly connect the way we treat the land to the way we treat each other.[7] Like these authors, both Piazza and Trethewey engage with how the Gulf South has been imagined as a place, and both works, in different degrees of effectiveness, also call for the way we imagine place to inform how we restore and memorialize physical spaces after Katrina.

Published in November of 2005, Tom Piazza's *Why New Orleans Matters* was one of the first books about New Orleans to appear after Hurricane Katrina ravaged the Gulf Coast earlier that August. Piazza, a New Yorker who came to call New Orleans home in the early 1990s, wrote his treatise during conservative political discussions that called for the city to be nearly condemned or completely reshaped into a landscape of casinos and theme parks. This short narrative about Piazza's love affair with the city is written in two parts, the first which details Piazza's initiation into New Orleans culture, and the second which describes his experiences after evacuating for Katrina. In its intensely personal and largely conceptual ruminations on New Orleans and Katrina's effects on the city, Piazza's work is decidedly different from the more historical or journalistic books that would follow in 2006. While Piazza admits that history influences his memoir, he also warns that "this isn't a history book. It is a book about the things that have evolved parallel to the city's history [...] history is what has passed, and this is a book about what is and must continue to be" (2005: 7, 9). In his plea for the restoration of New Orleans, Piazza distinguishes between his definition of history – the "hard and sad facts" – and the collective memories and mythologies that

---

6   See Michael Kreyling's *Inventing Southern Literature* (1998), Richard Gray's *Southern Aberrations: Writers of the American South and the Problems of Regionalism* (2000), Martyn Bone's *The Postsouthern Sense of Place in Contemporary Fiction* (2005), James C. Cobb and William Stueck's collection *Globalization and the American South* (2005), Scott Romine's *The Real South: Southern Narrative in the Age of Cultural Reproduction* (2008), Jon Smith's *Finding Purple America: The South and the Future of American Cultural Studies* (2013).

7   See *The World Has Changed: Conversations with Alice Walker* (2010), bell hooks's *Belonging: A Culture of Place* (2008), and Wendell Berry's *The Unsettling of America* (1977) and *Imagination in Place* (2010) (for a starting point).

develop alongside history (ibid: 9). Unlike Douglas Brinkley or Michael Eric Dyson, Piazza shifts focus from historical and political analyses to his memories of the city; unlike Jed Horne or Chris Rose, Piazza refrains from journalistic accounts that target a localized audience. Because Piazza was writing at a time when few were granted access to the physical space, the book attempts to transport a general, popular reading audience to New Orleans and to convince readers to rebuild the city in a way that recreates its previous spirit as described through his memories. It is both a written memorial to the place and a call to action to restore the physical space responsibly.

In his pathos-inflected plea for the preservation of New Orleans, Piazza frequently uses the somewhat indefinable catch phrase, "the spirit of place," which he describes as emanating from the generations of families who live in the city. Piazza describes this spirit as existing

between the lines. New Orleans is not just a list of attractions or restaurants or ceremonies, no matter how sublime and subtle. New Orleans is the interaction among all those things, and countless more. It gains its character from the spirit that is summoned, like a hologram, in the midst of all these elements, and that comes, ultimately, from the people who live there – those who have chosen to live there, and those whose parents and grandparents and ancestors lived there. (ibid: xxii)

Piazza's descriptions represent the people as intimately connected to the physical space, so much so that Piazza personifies New Orleans: the city "has a mythology, a personality, a *soul*, that is large, and that has touched people around the world. It has its own music (many of its own musics), its own cuisine, its own way of talking, its own architecture, its own smell, its own look and feel" (ibid: xviii-xix, emphasis original). This is the definition of place – specifically of New Orleans – that Piazza wants to depict and to salvage from the destruction of Katrina.

Although Piazza wants his narrative to impart more than a tourist guide, the book often reads like one, bringing the reader into the best-known and most-loved cultural elements of New Orleans: the food, the music, and the parade culture. While Piazza dedicates one chapter to a meditation on the race and class inequalities and the political underpinnings of such inequalities, his narrative asks readers not to dwell on the anger and the sadness. Instead, as disturbing as his descriptions of violence, poverty, police and political corruption may be, we are to understand that this is all part of the larger New Orleans spirit, specifically living with and/or overcoming hardship. In his descriptions of jazz funerals, Piazza points to the spirit of endurance that the city embraces, an especially significant spirit after Katrina's destruction: the participants "wear officially sorrowful expressions, and some of them are no doubt sorrowful inside as well, but in the most profound sense it is a masque of grief that is being staged here, in which the fact of mortality is being given its due" through the music and dancing of the procession (ibid: 29-30). As Piazza understands,

[t]his isn't escapism, or denial of grief; it is acceptance of the facts of life, the map of a profound relationship to the grief that is a part of life, and it will tell you something about why the real New Orleans spirit is never silly, or never just silly, in celebration, and never maudlin in grief. (ibid: 32)

Piazza's descriptions of jazz funerals capture what he seeks to describe as "the spirit of place" – the romantic idea that culture triumphs over tragedy. Piazza's memoir insists that the people's customs emanate from the physical space itself: "New Orleanians are attached to tradition, which is fused to a sense of place, to the ground itself, and that, too, is something to remember in the aftermath of Hurricane Katrina." (ibid: 104)[8] Piazza directly relates the "spirit of place" to a "sense" of the physical space and landscape ("the ground itself"), suggesting that the city must be physically rebuilt in a responsible manner if the "spirit of place" is also to remain intact.

Piazza's frequent nods to the physical rebuilding of the city become more direct in the second section of the book in order to clarify how the "spirit of place" connects to the physical space. In the second section, place becomes specified: "Two weeks after Hurricane Katrina, I went back to New Orleans for the first time, to see what was left of *my place*, of *my partner Mary's place*, of the city." (ibid: 113, emphasis mine) Place refers to the physical spaces of his and Mary's homes but also the cultural place – the spirit of the city – that Piazza earlier recounts for us. Through images that dramatically contrast those in the first section, readers are made to see the specific damage to Mary's home, the debris in the streets, the quiet

---

8   This passage refers specifically to the continued tradition of the Wild Magnolias Mardi Gras Indian tribe, which meets at the H&R Bar, despite the fact that the bar itself burned several years ago. Piazza's concept of place depends on the cultural traditions of New Orleans' residents along with the preservation of cultural landmarks associated with those traditions. In this way, Piazza's definition of place incorporates the aforementioned definitions of place and space, where the metaphorical construction of place is dependent on the physical construction of space. Piazza strategically champions certain cultural aspects of place – like the Mardi Gras Indian tradition – in order to convince his general reading audience that pre-Katrina New Orleans is worth preserving and rebuilding.

in the city. When describing Mary's ruined home, Piazza draws in the reader more fully by suggesting an experiment that involves drowning the very book we are reading "in a mixture of water, urine, spoiled food, feces, weed killer, and perhaps your beloved cat, preferably drowned and bloated" (ibid: 129). However, while Piazza admits to briefly losing his sanity after visiting Mary's home, he is soon cheered by the survivor mentality in New Orleans as witnessed in the visiting troops and a party at a local store where the owners give out free food and drinks. While Piazza shows the ruination of a specific physical space, he also suggests that the spirit is still intact. However, he argues that this "spirit of place" cannot survive without the conscientious physical rebuilding of the city, which will require not only the participation of those displaced residents but also the national and global communities who care about New Orleans – the readers who have been convinced by Piazza's narrative to save the wrecked city.

For Piazza, this literal rebuilding involves returning the poor African American population to New Orleans. Piazza rails against what he calls the top-down approach, which involves creating a theme park-like landscape full of casinos built for the moneyed elite. He imagines a postmodern plantation landscape:

New Orleans will be...a big gaudy façade for all the high-rollers, controlled by mobsters and businessmen...a playground decorated and populated with grotesque caricatures of everything that made New Orleans real and beautiful in the first place, and behind the façade the endless tract of housing where the help lives. (ibid: 155)

While this newly imagined New Orleans is as exaggerated as Piazza's romantic vision of the pre-Katrina city, these were real threats in the months after the storm, with a large displaced population who had little power in the decision-making. In Piazza's suggestion of a "bottom-up approach" that rebuilds existing landmarks and revitalizes the housing constructions in neighborhoods like the Lower Ninth Ward, he calls on readers to responsibly rebuild: "Give people a sense that they have a stake in rebuilding their own lives, a collective project that can make everyone feel proud instead of cheap. That will be in the spirit of New Orleans, and it will pay dividends for the entire country." (ibid: 163) Piazza longs for a physical rebuilding that restores the previous "spirit of place," which he views as collective and culturally rich, and he calls on his readers to help enact this rebuilding, so we may all someday meet again at Mardi Gras (ibid: 163).

While Piazza's work places responsibility with the reading public, any reader who knows something about environmental injustice will question his statement that "collective" rebuilding has been historically in the "spirit" of New Orleans.

As Robert D. Bullard and Beverly Wright argue in the introduction to *Race, Place, and Environmental Justice after Katrina*:

In the real world, all communities are not created equal. If a community is poor, black, or on the wrong side of the tracks, it receives less protection than suburbs inhabited by affluent whites. Generally, rich people take land on higher elevations, leaving the poor and working class more vulnerable to flooding and environmental pestilence. Race tracks closely with social vulnerability and the geography of environmental risks. (2009: 1)

Echoing these ideas in his essay on "Katrina and the Myth of Self-Sufficiency," David Dante Troutt compares the rise of the mostly-white suburbs in New Orleans to Jim Crow segregation, arguing that the mythological "racial exceptionalism" of New Orleans is "belied by its racial geography" (2010: 186). Similarly, Karen O'Neill has argued in "Who Sank New Orleans? How Engineering the River Created Environmental Injustice," that the very beginnings of the levee systems were founded on profit, not social equality (2010: 9). While Piazza's attempt to imagine his romantic New Orleans into a real space of equality is ennobling, it is flawed due to his desire to return to the imagined New Orleans of his memory.

In contrast, Natasha Trethewey's *Beyond Katrina: A Meditation on the Mississippi Gulf Coast* calls for readers to rebuild in a way that addresses the social and ecological landscapes in overtly critical and reflective terms. While Piazza's connections between the "spirit of place" and the physical space of New Orleans are somewhat romantic and implied, Trethewey steadfastly connects cultural constructs of history and memory with the physical landscape of coastal Mississippi. *Beyond Katrina*, Trethewey's foray into non-fiction structured in two sections labeled 2007 and 2009, was published five years after the storm. Trethewey tells the story of the Mississippi Gulf Coast from the perspective of a mixed race woman who grew up there post-integration, and, at one point, she proclaims herself to *be* the Gulf Coast (2010: 66). Trethewey, who identifies as part of the African American community in coastal Mississippi, lends an insider's view to the historical race and class prejudices that Piazza can only acknowledge as part of the spirit of place in New Orleans. Trethewey's book is different from Piazza's in author's perspective and her focus on Mississippi, but perhaps the biggest difference between the two narratives is that, while Piazza targets a popular audience, *Beyond Katrina*, published by UGA Press, is more cerebral – a meditation not only on Trethewey's individual and familial experiences in Mississippi but also a larger meditation on what it means to rebuild both place and space. Almost immediately, Trethewey asks readers to consider how "space" and "place" are related to concepts of memory and history after Katrina: "This too is a story about a story – how it will be inscribed on the physical landscape as well as the landscape of our cultural memory. I wonder at the competing narratives: What will be remembered, what forgotten? What dominant narrative is now emerging?" (ibid: 11)

As Piazza attempts to do, Trethewey ties how we build place in cultural memory to how we will rebuild physical space. She emphasizes the physical and natural elements of the Gulf Coast in the remaining live oaks, which she describes as "monuments" and "witness[es] to history" that "suggest a narrative of survival and resilience. In the years after the storm, as the leaves have begun to return, the trees seem a monument to the very idea of recovery. Such natural monuments remind us of the presence of the past, our connection to it" (ibid: 55). In her invocation of a historical past represented in the live oaks, Trethewey clarifies the ties between the physical space and the way we construct the place in our memories, collapsing concepts of history/memory and space/place.

Although the natural monuments seem immovable even in the wake of Katrina, Trethewey describes how the *manmade* landscape continually changes. Intertwining memory and history, she wraps the story of her family in historical narratives about the Mississippi Gulf Coast, specifically in the ways that the physical and social landscapes were changed by the casinos, the development of the beaches, and the processes of segregation and desegregation. While the manmade landscape changes with development, the natural landscape – the coastal wetlands – erodes, as does the social landscape, with further diminishing opportunities for minorities. As Trethewey describes, the history of the physical space, as well as the opportunities for its people, are tied to profit and commercialization, which continues in the post-Katrina landscape. This becomes evident in the way the storm is memorialized by a plexi-glass box filled with found objects placed in the central town green of Biloxi:

Even more telling is the dedication [of the box]: not for whom but *by* whom the monument was commissioned. A gift donated to the city of Biloxi by *ABC's Extreme Makeover: Home Edition*, the memorial not only remembers the storm and the people but also inscribes on the landscape a narrative of the commercialization of memory. (ibid: 57, emphasis original)

Trethewey also describes the giant glowing guitar sculpture that heralds the new Hard Rock Café that has opened post-Katrina, revealing how mostly upper class whites have profited from the storm and the rebuilding process. She warns about the dangers of rebuilding not only the physical landscape but also the memorial landscape because the two are inextricably tied – how we remember the land and its history influences how we will rebuild. Whereas Piazza calls for a rebuilding of his imagined New Orleans with little change to the culture or space that existed before the storm, Trethewey cautions that omissions in or revisions of memory will lead to a repeated neglect of the physical landscape and the people who live on the Mississippi Coast.

As Trethewey explains, while the individual memories may vary, the overall collective memory about the storm begins to take narrative shape. After she relays the story of her brother's girlfriend, Aesha, and the struggles Aesha faced when she was unlawfully evicted from her apartment after Katrina, Trethewey notes that Aesha willfully erases these struggles from her memories. As Aesha tells Trethewey about the unity and friendly attitudes after Katrina, Trethewey stops herself from reminding Aesha about her trouble with her landlord:

> I know that a preferred narrative is one of the common bond between people in a time of crisis. This is often the way collective, cultural memory works, full of omissions, partial remembering, and purposeful forgetting. People on both sides of a story look better in a version that leaves out certain things. It is another way that rebuilding is also about remembering—that is, not just rebuilding the physical structures and economy of the coast but also rebuilding, revising, the memory of Katrina and its aftermath. (ibid: 20-1)

Trethewey is careful not to romanticize the effects of the storm, perhaps most significantly in the story of her brother Joe, who ends up in prison for trafficking cocaine after Katrina. In her recording and analysis of Aesha's memories, along with the memories of her brother, her grandmother, and the casino workers and others she interviews, Trethewey emphasizes the significance of revising memory to the rebuilding of a physical space. As the wetlands and social landscape of minorities were neglected in the original commercial development of the coast, now these same processes threaten the post-Katrina landscape – unless we are willing to fully embrace and reflect on the ways that memory shapes not only historical narratives but also the very real process of recovery and development.

The way that Aesha revises her memories to showcase unity after Katrina reminds readers of another historical substitution in constructions of the South as a whole – of the fictional "moonlight and magnolias" South substituted for a region haunted by violence, segregation, and oppression. In her exploration of the way Katrina is remembered, Trethewey subtly emphasizes how the development of the physical space also undergirds the memories and histories of the South as a region. For instance, when Trethewey muses over a photograph of her grandmother, Leretta, standing on the newly-developed Gulf Coast beach in the 1950s, the social history also comes into focus: "In a photograph, my grandmother stands on the small part of the beach designated for 'colored' people. She is smiling, although it will not be until 1968, four years after the passage of the Civil Rights Act, that the beaches are fully integrated" (ibid: 42). The physical space of the beach, as built and revised by human development, remains segregated, evincing the historical tie between social exploitations of the land and its people.

Trethewey points to similar inequalities during the rebuilding after Katrina. While she provides a statistical and factual progress report of the blighted areas in North Gulfport, she also remarks on the narratives presented about recovery, from narratives angry in tone about the misuse of federal dollars when the poor still suffer to nostalgic narratives that view Mississippi's story as more triumphant than that of Louisiana. As Trethewey explains, both narratives are flawed, and the "racial tensions" beneath those narratives run deep (ibid: 89-90). Specifically, she describes the rebuilding of Confederate President Jefferson Davis's former home, Beauvoir, where local leaders used federal funds for a grand re-opening complete with champagne toasts to the Confederacy (ibid: 90). While the symbolic home of Davis was restored (and, as Trethewey suggests, with it a history of racial oppression), the poorer residents in North Gulfport still struggled with rebuilding, often due to the lack of state and federal support provided them (ibid). In examples such as this, Trethewey shows readers how the social histories of a place are shaped by the un-equal recovery and rebuilding of the physical space itself.

But if Trethewey's narrative about Katrina reveals the still existent racism and poverty in the South, her varied stories of recovery also reveal the coast to be a historic space of diversity, somewhat collapsing the binary of local/global. In fact, her brother Joe finds the influx of diverse peoples to be the most positive aspect of Katrina's aftermath:

Still, as much as Joe worries about the impact of the decisions of 'out-of-towners,' he points to the coast's growing diversity – its influx of newcomers – as one of the best outcomes of the rebuilding effort. I can see his point; in a region where the vestiges of racism hang on, played out in debates about 'heritage' and the Confederate flag [...] the arrival of newcomers must also signal a new coast, a new Mississippi [...] immigrants from Jamaica and Mexico are helping to inscribe a more multiethnic narrative, as did the Vietnamese immigrants of the 1970s and the Slovenian and Yugoslavian immigrants – and others of European and African descent – more than a century before that. (ibid: 60)

Because Trethewey is invested in remembering the history of racism that occludes the Coast and the South more generally, she carefully negotiates the idea of diversity in the region – hoping for progress and acknowledging the building and rebuilding of the past. As she writes, "one hope we can have for the future, beyond the necessities with which we must concern ourselves – environmentally sound rebuilding, fair and equal recovery – is the continuity of culture and heritage fostered by ongoing change and honest, inclusive remembrance of the past" (ibid: 61). The way we remember and revise our pasts impacts future visions and reconstructions of place and space.

In a broader sense, the ways these texts address the aftermath of Hurricane Katrina should significantly impact studies of southern culture, particularly with current scholarship that privileges an imagined global South often not grounded in physical spaces. As much as scholars have deemed "place" and "southernness" constructs, we must also work to understand the dangers of constructing new Souths, which deflect attention from bioregional spaces. The very real consequences of Katrina, while mediated for a larger audience by representation, force us to think about the concepts of history/memory, space/place, and local/global as in conversation with, rather than in opposition to one another. This will undoubtedly require a further collapsing of disciplines where memory studies and bioregionalism meet, where ecology, the humanities, and popular culture interact more fully, where the history of physical space collides with the way people remember and imagine it. As evinced in both Piazza's and Trethewey's work, we must continue to disassemble binaries which have plagued southern studies, paving the way for tangible action that physically restores and responsibly remembers the local in order to fully understand our impact in the global arena and vice versa. Perhaps then we can build the South of our imaginations, whatever that may be.

BIBLIOGRAPHY

Berry, Wendell (1977): *The Unsettling of America*, New York: Avon.
Berry, Wendell (2010): *Imagination in Place*, Berkeley: Counterpoint.
Bone, Martyn (2005): *The Postsouthern Sense of Place in Contemporary Fiction*, Baton Rouge: Louisiana State University Press.
Brinkley, Douglas (2006): *The Great Deluge: Hurricane Katrina, New Orleans, and the Mississippi Gulf Coast,* New York: Harper Perennial.
Bullard, Robert D./Wright, Beverly (2009): "Introduction." In: Robert D. Bullard/Beverly Wright/Jeffrey Dowd (eds.), *Race, Place, and Environmental Justice after Hurricane Katrina: Struggles to Reclaim, Rebuild, and Revitalize New Orleans and the Gulf Coast,* New York: Westview Press, pp. 1-18.
Cash, W.J. ([1941] 1991): *The Mind of the South*, New York: Vintage Books.
Cobb, James C./Stueck, William (eds.) (2005): *Globalization and the American South*, Athens: University of Georgia Press.

Dickinson, Greg/Blair, Carole Blair/Ott, Brian L. (2010): "Introduction: Rhetoric/Memory/Place." In: Greg Dickinson/Carole Blair/Brian L. Ott (eds.), *Places of Public Memory: The Rhetoric of Museums and Memorials*, Tuscaloosa: University of Alabama Press, pp. 1-56.

Dyson, Michael Eric (2005): *Come Hell or High Water: Hurricane Katrina and the Color of Disaster*, New York: Basic Civitas.

Flaherty, Jordan (2007): "Corporate Reconstruction and Grassroots Resistance." In: The South End Press Collective (eds.), *What Lies Beneath: Katrina, Race, and the State of the Nation*, Cambridge, MA: South End Press, pp.100-119.

Gelbspan, Ross (2007): "Nature Fights Back." In: The South End Press Collective (eds.), *What Lies Beneath: Katrina, Race, and the State of the Nation*, Cambridge, MA: South End Press, pp. 15-27.

Gray, Richard (2000): *Southern Aberrations: Writers of the American South and the Problems of Regionalism*, Baton Rouge: Louisiana State University Press.

hooks, bell (2009): *Belonging: a Culture of Place*, NY, London: Routledge.

Horne, Jed (2006): *Breach of Faith: Hurricane Katrina and the Near Death of a Great American City*, New York: Random House.

Jefferson, Thomas ([1787] 1994): *Notes on the State of Virginia*. In: Merrill D. Peterson (ed.), *Thomas Jefferson: Writings: Autobiography/Notes on the State of Virginia/Public and Private Papers/Addresses*, New York: Library of America.

Kreyling, Michael (1998): *Inventing Southern Literature*, Jackson: University Press of Mississippi.

Lynch, Tom/Gotfelty, Cheryll/Armbruster, Karla (2012): "Introduction." In: Tom Lynch Cheryll Gotfelty/Karla Armbruster (eds.), *The Bioregional Imagination,* Athens: University of Georgia Press, pp. 1-32.

O'Neill, Karen M (2010): "Who Sank New Orleans? How Engineering the River Created Environmental Injustice." In: Keith Wailoo/Karen M. O'Neill/Jeffrey Dowd/Ronald Anglin (eds.), *Katrina's Imprint: Race and Vulnerability in America*, New Brunswick: Rutgers University Press, pp. 9-20.

Nixon, Rob. (2011): *Slow Violence and the Environmentalism of the Poor*. Cambridge: Harvard University Press.

Nora, Pierre. (1996): *Realms of Memory*. Trans. Arthur Goldhammer. NY: Columbia University Press.

Piazza, Tom (2005): *Why New Orleans Matters,* New York: Regan Books.

Reiger, Christopher (2009): *Clear-Cutting Eden: Ecology and the Pastoral in Southern Literature*, Tuscaloosa: University of Alabama Press.

Romine, Scott (2008): *The Real South: Southern Narrative in the Age of Cultural Reproduction*, Baton Rouge: Louisiana State University Press.

Rose, Chris (2006): *1 Dead in Attic,* New Orleans: Chris Rose Books.
Smith, James Patterson (2012): *Hurricane Katrina: The Mississippi Story,* Jackson: University Press of Mississippi.
Smith, Jon (2013): *Finding Purple America: The South and the Future of American Cultural Studies,* Athens: University of Georgia Press.
Smith, Lillian ([1949, 1961] 1978): *Killers of the Dream,* New York and London: Norton.
Trethewey, Natasha (2010): *Beyond Katrina: A Meditation on the Mississippi Gulf Coast.* Athens, University of Georgia Press.
Troutt, David Dante (2010): "Katrina and the Myth of Self-Sufficiency." In: Keith Wailoo/Karen M. O'Neill/Jeffrey Dowd/Ronald Anglin (eds.), *Katrina's Imprint: Race and Vulnerability in America,* New Brunswick: Rutgers University Press, pp. 183-191.
Walker, Alice (2010): *The World Has Changed: Conversations with Alice Walker,* Rudolph P. Byrd (ed.), New York and London: The New Press.
Wilson, Anthony (2006): *Shadow and Shelter: The Swamp in Southern Culture,* Jackson: University Press of Mississippi.
Wyatt-Brown, Bertram ([1982] 1986): *Honor and Violence in the Old South,* New York and Oxford: Oxford University Press.
12 Southerners ([1930] 1962): *I'll Take My Stand: The South and the Agrarian Tradition,* New York: Harper Torchbooks/The Academy Library.

Lewis Watts: *St Claude Ave.*, 9th Ward 2005

Six weeks after Hurricane Katrina, most of the water was gone, but there was still strong evidence of the storm and the people's reaction to it. There was much graffiti, which presented a powerful narrative. The phrase "the fire next time" is a quotation from the Spiritual "Mary Don't You Weep," in which it says "God gave Noah the rainbow sign, no more water, the fire next time." This is, of course, an allusion to the Old Testament. James Baldwin has used the phrase "the fire next time" as the title of his 1963 essay collection.

Natural Hazards, Human Vulnerability: Teaching Hurricane Katrina Through Literary Nonfiction

PHILIPP SIEPMANN

With regard to Hurricane Katrina, the American geographer Neil Smith claims that "there is no such thing as a natural disaster" (2006: n.p.). His statement seems controversial, if not even cynical, in the light of the destruction the Category 5 hurricane left behind in late August 2005. In total, Katrina took more than 1800 lives, injured thousands, damaged or destroyed more than 800.000 houses and caused overall costs of 160 billion USD (cf. URI 2014). What else could Hurricane Katrina be but a natural disaster? Smith, however, explains that "[i]n every phase and aspect of a disaster – the contours of disaster and the difference between who lives and who dies is to a greater or lesser extent a social calculus" (ibid.). Indeed, the impact of Hurricane Katrina affected the lower-class population of New Orleans and the state of Louisiana much more severely than the middle and upper classes, and once more revealed the deep-rooted racial disparities in the southeastern United States.

Hurricane Katrina is a powerful reminder that even industrialized societies are vulnerable to humanitarian crises triggered by natural events, and serves as an example of how today's ecological challenges are interconnected with social and cultural concerns. As environmental issues like meteorological hazards become a core element of the cross-curricular pedagogical agenda of global education in schools across the world (cf. Cates 2002), teaching Hurricane Katrina can foster students' awareness of the human dimension of apparently 'natural' disasters. Approaching the topic of this volume from a pedagogical vantage point, I will propose a concept for teaching the sociocultural implications of Hurricane Katrina which links environmental education to cultural studies. This concept was originally developed for EFL (English as a foreign language) and geography classrooms. However, due to its interdisciplinary scope, it can be adapted to a variety of other school subjects, such as literature, social sciences, and history.

To foster students' critical awareness of how certain sociocultural factors determined the population's vulnerability to Hurricane Katrina, I will argue that works of literary nonfiction have a great didactic potential. In the years that followed Hurricane Katrina, a wide array of fictional and nonfictional texts was published. Among these publications were many texts that combine elements of nonfictional and fictional writing. They use the narrative techniques of fiction to reconstruct the events in New Orleans as they were experienced by eyewitnesses of the storm. Thus, they foreground the personal dimension of Hurricane Katrina and allow for case studies of how race and class rendered some parts of the city's population more vulnerable to disaster than others. At the same time, they can be read in class to analyze how a particular historical event is represented and fictionalized in literature and popular culture, and thus 'made sense of.' Therefore, teaching the sociocultural implications of Hurricane Katrina through literary nonfiction can, on the one hand, sensitize students for the interrelation of global ecological and social challenges, and, on the other hand, contribute to their critical (inter-)cultural and text/media competences. In this essay, I will focus on a selection of three texts that I read as literary nonfiction: the oral history project *Voices from the Storm* (2008), Josh Neufeld's graphic novel *A.D.: New Orleans After the Deluge* (2009), and Dave Eggers's biographical novel *Zeitoun* (2009).

TEACHING HURRICANE KATRINA: A DIDACTIC FRAMEWORK

The approach to teaching Hurricane Katrina in the EFL classroom proposed here links environmental education to cultural studies. It has been developed for and taught in EFL and geography classes at a German secondary school (*Gymnasium*) in grades 10 and 11. For students of these classes, Hurricane Katrina obviously is a topic both historically and geographically remote. After all, today's 16-year-olds still went to primary school when Katrina struck. In addition, New Orleans is an American city which is rarely dealt with in the German EFL classroom (apart from the occasional reading of Tennessee Williams). Nevertheless, Hurricane Katrina has not lost any of its currency and exemplarity. Teaching Hurricane Katrina can foster students' understanding of the interrelation between nature and culture in a globalizing world, and raise their awareness of the role that social and racial inequalities play in dealing with natural hazards.

In the following, I will refer to this approach as 'ecocritical cultural studies.' I define ecocritical cultural studies as the study of the interrelation of environmental processes, society, and culture, and its representation in cultural texts and practices. It uses a variety of methods deriving from disciplines such as geography, social sciences, as well as from cultural and literary studies. I understand 'ecocritical' in the sense of the German literary scholars Cathrin Gersdorf and Silvia Mayer, who define ecocriticism as

a methodology that re-examines the history of ideologically, aesthetically, and ethically motivated conceptualizations of nature, of the function of its constructions and metaphorizations in literary and other cultural practices, and of the potential effects these discursive, imaginative constructions have on our bodies as well as on our natural and cultural environment. (2006: 10)

Cultural studies in the EFL classroom, according to the German scholar of English studies Doris Teske (2006), aims at a complex analysis of cultural phenomena, in contrast to the widespread methodology of intercultural learning, which often presents a superficial and simplified view of the foreign culture. Like its academic counterpart, Teske's didactic approach to cultural studies relies on exemplary case studies and focuses on the social construction of categories such as gender, race, or class. It uses a variety of methodological instruments, like semiotics, text/media analysis, and social sciences (cf. Teske 2006: 27).

In the context of teaching the sociocultural implications of the Katrina disaster, ecocritical cultural studies aims to challenge the idea of Katrina as a natural disaster and to critically examine how race and class influenced the impact of Hurricane Katrina on particular social groups within the population of New Orleans. Methodologically, text analysis (of literary nonfiction) is complemented by methods deriving from sociology (conducting case studies) and geography (working with maps, applying the concept of vulnerability).

UNDERSTANDING THE SOCIOCULTURAL DIMENSION OF NATURAL DISASTER: THE CASE OF HURRICANE KATRINA

As I have pointed out, the primary aim of teaching Hurricane Katrina is to raise students' awareness of the human dimension of what appears to be an entirely 'natural' disaster. The first step to approaching this aim is to raise critical awareness of the term 'natural disaster,' which suggests that the causes of disaster lie outside of human reach. A possible entry point for such a discussion is provided by Smith's claim that "[t]here is no such thing as a natural disaster." The students may comment on Smith's statement and make suggestions about its meaning with regard to Hurricane Katrina: What was Hurricane Katrina but a natural disaster? What role does the population or the government have in preventing disaster? Which sociocultural factors determine whether a hurricane results in a humanitarian disaster or not? In a next step, the geographical concepts of 'natural hazard' and 'vulnerability' are introduced, which allow for an analysis of the significance of particular sociocultural factors.

In the following, I will briefly discuss the concept of vulnerability in the context of Hurricane Katrina. In geography and other geosciences, Smith's position on the concept of 'natural disaster' is widely accepted. From a scientific view, hurricanes are natural events that occur more or less regularly and are predictable to some extent. Natural events, however, may trigger humanitarian disasters, as they may cause injury and death, damage public infrastructure as well as personal belongings. The British geographers Ben Wisner, Piers Blaikie, Terry Cannon, and Ian Davis criticize a one-sided view of disasters which either "emphasises the 'trigger' role of geo-tectonics, climate or biological factors arising in nature" or "focus[es] on the human response, psychosocial and physical trauma, economic, legal and political consequences" (Wisner et al. 2003: 10). The authors therefore propose an alternative approach, which seeks the causes of disaster both in natural events, and in the specific socio-economic and political circumstances under which these events occur. Thus, the authors intend to prevent a deterministic view of 'disaster' and to highlight human agency in disaster mitigation.

According to such a view of disaster, hurricanes and other forces of nature are understood as natural hazards to human societies. A hazard is defined as the (chance of the) sudden occurrence of a natural event that destabilizes the structure of the society of a larger region, causes injury or death and destroys goods (cf. Dikau/Pohl 2011: 1117). The term covers both the objective probability by which a natural event occurs, and the subjective perception and evaluation of the possibility of its occurrence (cf. ibid.). The impact of a natural hazard on a society or a particular part of it is determined by its vulnerability. Vulnerability, again, is defined as

[t]he characteristics of a person or group and their situation that influence their capacity to anticipate, cope with, resist and recover from the impact of a natural hazard [...]. It involves a combination of factors that determine the degree to which someone's life, livelihood, property and other assets are put at risk by a discrete and identifiable event [...] in nature and society. (Wisner et al. 2003: 11)

The population of New Orleans is vulnerable to the natural hazards of hurricanes and floods due to the city's geographical location alone. To all sides, it is surrounded by water: Lake Pontchartrain in the North, the Mississippi River and the Gulf of Mexico in the South, 17th Street Canal in the West, and the Industrial Canal in the East. What adds to the city's vulnerability is that most of its neighborhoods are located below sea level. Some of the city's canals are only fenced off from residential areas by relatively thin walls. However, not all parts of the population are equally vulnerable to these hazards. Many of the poorer neighborhoods are located lower than the suburbs with primarily middle- or upper-class residents. Therefore, they were more exposed to incoming floods after the levees broke. One of the neighborhoods which suffered the most severe damage by the incoming floods was the Lower 9th Ward. The suffering of its inhabitants, which was televised across the world in the aftermath of Katrina, made the enormous structural problems and the poverty of the predominantly black neighborhood visible at once. As Michael Eric Dyson points out in his analysis of the racial implications of Hurricane Katrina, "[t]he faces of the Lower 9's residents – though forgotten by their government and overlooked by their fellow citizens – looked out from their watery wasteland and for a moment focused the eyes of the world on their desperate plight" (2007: 12). Reinforcing Kanye West's statement on television that George Bush did not care about black people, Dyson maintains that race is a key to understanding the failed efforts of New Orleans to fully recover from Hurricane Katrina:

Katrina's fury may have been race neutral, but not in its effect: 80 percent of New Orleans's minority households lived in the flooded area, while the same was true for only 54 percent of the city's white population. The average household income of those in the flooded area trailed those who lived on New Orleans's higher ground by $17,000. Concentrated poverty rendered poor blacks much more vulnerable to the effects of natural disaster. (ibid: 31-32)

For Dyson, the notion of a 'natural disaster' is misleading: "When a disaster like Katrina strikes – a natural disaster not directly caused by human failure –, it frees us to be aware of, and angered by, the catastrophe. After all, it does not directly implicate us; it was an act of God." (ibid: 3-4) From his point of view, the term obscures the fact that much of the disaster that unfolded after Hurricane Katrina made landfall at the coast of Louisiana was man-made and resulted from long-standing social and racial disparities in the United States and particularly in New Orleans.

Hurricane Katrina is exemplary of how the notion of a 'natural disaster' glosses over human responsibility for and agency in preventing disaster. The geographical concepts of 'hazard' and 'vulnerability' can be used as an analytical instrument in an examination of the sociocultural implications of the Katrina disaster. They may draw attention to how social factors such as location, mobility or cultural issues such as racial disparities determined Katrina's impact on the population of New Orleans and the U.S. Gulf Coast. Thus, they help understand that dealing with global environmental issues is first and foremost a social and political challenge.

COUNTERACTING 'NATURAL DISASTER': REPRESENTATIONS OF HURRICANE KATRINA IN NONFICTIONAL LITERATURE

Reading and discussing literary nonfictional texts on Hurricane Katrina in class can contribute to understanding the complex relationship between race, class, and vulnerability to natural hazards. In the following, I will briefly analyze how *Voices*, *A.D.* and *Zeitoun* approach the sociocultural dimension of Hurricane Katrina and point out the different narrative strategies they employ to fictionalize the true stories of eyewitnesses from New Orleans. These theoretical considerations will serve as a basis for an analysis of the didactic potential of these texts for teaching Hurricane Katrina.

My understanding of literary nonfiction is informed by Peter Bruck (1986) and David Schmid (2011). According to Bruck, the genre emerged from the realist novel and was strongly influenced by the advent of postmodern writing. Rejecting realism's "belief in an integrated and objective rendering of reality" (336), literary nonfiction foregrounds subjectivity. Yet it makes a claim to authenticity that "derives from the fact that the writers either did careful research on the events they relate [...] or as participant observers minutely recorded the actions and events they participated in and were witness to" (ibid.). Acknowledging that there is no objective reality, literary nonfiction can be defined very broadly as an account of a factual event as it was experienced by one, or a number of individuals. Besides subjectivity, another characteristic of literary nonfiction is its exemplarity. In his examination of the American nonfiction novel, Schmid notes that nonfictional writing aims to narrate American reality "through attempts to give narrative form to what is violent and/or traumatic" (986). He adds that the genre is not primarily interested in the nature of a particular act of violence or traumatic event, but rather in their "cultural representativeness [...], in other words, [their] ability to throw light on American culture" (ibid: 989). Far from providing matter-of-fact accounts, these texts combine the "authority of nonfiction" with the "emotive power of fiction" (ibid: 990). Thus, they fictionalize a factual event to a greater or lesser extent to arouse their readers' sympathy for the victims or survivors of the depicted event.

Hurricane Katrina was traumatic on various levels. Especially from the point of view of the poor African-American population, Katrina's impact goes far beyond the immediate effect of the storm. The media coverage was dominated by a one-sided representation of those stranded in the city center as looters or even criminals. They were thus victimized in a double sense: not only were they more vulnerable to the natural hazard of a hurricane, they were also indirectly accused of having caused the anarchy and violence in New Orleans. Counteracting the biased coverage of the media, *A.D.*, *Voices*, and *Zeitoun* aim at drawing a more differentiated picture of the events during and after Hurricane Katrina. Neufeld, author of *A.D.: New Orleans After the Deluge* (2009), in the afterword to the graphic novel writes that he "felt it was important to tell the story from the perspectives of a range of people who had lived through the storm: well-off and poor, black and white, young and old, gay and straight, male and female" (191). Similarly, the primary aim of the *Voice of Witness* series in which *Voices from the Storm* was published is to "amplify the voices of men and women most closely affected by injustice" (2014: n.p.).

Reconstructing the events during and after Hurricane Katrina, as experienced by various New Orleanians, *Voices*, *A.D.* and *Zeitoun* emphasize how certain sociocultural factors made the difference in whether or not the hurricane resulted in a personal disaster. However, to narrate their subjects' experiences of Hurricane Katrina, these texts follow different strategies. While the authors of all three texts underline that they set great value on accurate research, they chose different narrative techniques, resulting in a different extent of fictionalization of the depicted events. Of all three texts, *Zeitoun* is the only novel in a traditional sense. Eggers weaves Abdulrahman's and Kathy's accounts into a dense plot and puts great effort into developing the family's history. Quite differently, *Voices from the Storm* is based on oral history, a methodology used, for example, in social sciences to get a first-hand account of a historically or culturally significant event. *A.D.* links journalistic research to the narrative techniques of the graphic novel. Using two levels of narration, verbal and visual, the graphic novel is based on eyewitness interviews and photographs of New Orleans after the hurricane. Neufeld insists that "[t]he places and details are real too – down to the DVDs and comics on Leo's shelves and the contents of Abbas's store" (2009: 191). However, despite his journalistic attention to detail, he uses color, perspective, and panel layout to draw attention to the protagonists' individual perception of and emotional response to the events in New Orleans, and to emphasize human vulnerability to the forces of nature as well as the arbitrariness of the authorities. Moreover, the narrative is structured in a way that shifts the focus from the seemingly natural causes and the inevitability of disaster to the more tangible, human implications of it. Finally, the eyewitnesses do not simply recount their experiences, but reflect on them and comment on the public discourse about Hurricane Katrina.

The introductory chapter of *A.D.* summarizes the events from August 22 to 31. Held in sober, green and grey colors, the panels zoom into New Orleans from outer space and alternate between satellite images of the evolving hurricane, aerial views of the Hurricane towering behind the skyline of the city, and street scenes showing the population's reactions to the approaching storm. These images, which are based on photographs and television images, suggest a straightforward interpretation of the causes of disaster as outside of human reach. Such a view, however, glosses over the social and cultural implications of 'disaster' that lie beyond the surface of media images. The following chapters of *A.D.* therefore present the same events from a different angle, as they were experienced by Kwame, son of a pastor from New Orleans East, Abbas, owner of a shop in Uptown, the Doctor, a well-off resident of the French Quarter, Denise, a counselor from Mid-City, and Leo and Michelle, a young couple, also from Mid-City. Seen from their point of view, it becomes discernible what made some citizens more vulnerable to the impact of the hurricane and the floods than others.

Rather than simply recounting the events in different parts of New Orleans from their memory, the protagonists of *A.D.* and *Voices* comment on their experiences. These moments of reflection play an important role in the graphic novel. They serve as a critique of the media coverage of, and the public discourse about Hurricane Katrina, which, from their point of view, drew a distorted image of the actual events. For Leo, the loss of his comic collection seems tragic at first. However, he and his girlfriend Michelle decide to evacuate right on time and reach Oklahoma safely. Listening to the news report on the radio, they realize their privilege of owning a car. When a caller in a radio show asks what was wrong with the people seeking shelter in the Superdome that they did not "just leave the city before the storm" (Neufeld 2009: 147), Leo is infuriated by the inherent ignorance of this remark. He pinpoints the dilemma of many of those who had to stay in town: "What these idiots don't realize is that when the evacuations were called, it was only the 26th. If someone was waiting for a paycheck slated to come today – the first of the month – they weren't going to see it." (ibid.) Very obviously, Leo's remark refers to the depiction of the so-called refugees in the provisional shelters predominant in the mainstream media. Unaware of how social factors such as location, mobility or income influenced their capacity to evacuate town or to withstand the forces of nature, the public blamed the victims for their situation or even criminalized them as looters. As Leo puts it, "when you take for granted you can hop on a computer and make a reservation at a Hilton five hundred miles away, it's pretty easy to forget what it's like to be a have-not" (ibid: 148).

While the consequences of the hurricane for the middle and upper class were by and large limited to material loss, its impact on many lower-class citizens, who had no chance to leave New Orleans, was existential. Inside and outside the provisional shelter of the Convention Center, the situation for the people became increasingly tense. Desperate, Denise exclaims: "How can this be happening? Don't the authorities know about us?" (cf. fig. 1)

Figure 1: Panel from A.D.: New Orleans After the Deluge

(Neufeld 2009: 146)

This panel illustrates Neufeld's use of visual strategies to narrate the eyewitnesses' accounts. In the background, the panel shows a scene from the Convention Center: a young mother comforting her crying daughter, and an elderly woman offering help. In the foreground, Denise seems to directly address the reader – or, more generally, the American public –, when she expresses her despair and disbelief. In this panel, Neufeld indicates two levels of action as Denise's silhouette overlaps the panel outlines. While the background conveys Denise's memory of the situation in the Convention Center, the foreground adds a level of reflection and commentary.

Quite similarly to the subjects of *A.D.*, the narrators of *Voices from the Storm* reflect on the causes of the chaotic situation in the city center and the evolving disaster. Renee Martin, a nursing assistant from the West Bank who stayed in the

Superdome during the storm, describes the situation in the shelter and the people's anger at the authorities' lack of support as follows:

Everybody in the Dome was mad. The mayor wanted people to evacuate, but a lot of us couldn't evacuate. I mean, everybody don't own a car. Everybody didn't have means for transportation, no money to travel. But the city of New Orleans has cabs. They have schoolbuses, charters. They have public-service buses. They have planes, trains, boats. If it is mandatory, and he knew the city of New Orleans is under a Category 5, he should have thought about all those transportations, and let those people out. *You* got out, so you should've helped us out. (Vollen/Ying 2008: 124, emphasis original)

Martin realizes that the Katrina disaster was not natural, but man-made: "It's a horror story, really. It goes from being a storm by Mother Nature, or an act of God, into a horror. To me, it's a combination of having an act of Mother Nature and then an act of man." (ibid.) The oral history approach of *Voices from the Storm* creates an aura of authenticity. This is supported by the word-by-word transcription which even pays attention to dialectical and sociolectical peculiarities of the book's subjects.

In this aspect, *Zeitoun* differs significantly from *Voices from the Storm*. Inspired by Abdulrahman Zeitoun's part in the latter, Eggers uses his story to stylize him as a Muslim-American hero in a period of anti-Muslim sentiments. While Zeitoun's story in *Voices* demonstrates how human rights were suspended in the aftermath of Hurricane Katrina, Eggers's novel uses his case as an example of how the civil rights of Muslim Americans were restricted in the U.S. after the terror attacks of September 11, 2001, and of how their precarious situation increased their vulnerability to crisis and disaster. Looking back at his incarceration, Zeitoun, in *Voices*, figures that his arrest resulted from individual failure: "I can't blame somebody because somebody did mistake. I got in wrong hands, with the wrong guy. The timing. I feel that we're in wrong time." (ibid: 240) Only through this addition at the end of the quote, Zeitoun establishes a connection between his case and the situation for Muslims in post-9/11 American society. Eggers, in his version of Zeitoun's story, takes a different perspective on the case, reading it as a failure of the American society rather than an individual. The novel elaborates on Abdulrahman's and his family's background at great length and portrays him as a Muslim-American idol. After he is released from prison, Zeitoun first feels at odds with his fate:

How could he have been guilty of such hubris? He had put himself in harm's way, and by doing so had put his family in danger. How could he not have known that staying in New

Orleans [...] would endanger him. He knew better. He had been careful for so many years. He had kept his head low. He had been a model citizen. But in the wake of the storm, he'd come to believe that he was meant to help the stranded. He believed that the damned canoe had given him the right to serve as a shepherd and savior. He had lost perspective. (Eggers 2009: 262)

Only later Zeitoun realizes that it was not his, but the country's hubris that brought him there:

This country was not unique. This country was fallible. Mistakes were being made. He was a mistake. In the grand scheme of the country's blind, grasping fight against threats seen and unseen, there would be mistakes made. Innocents would be suspected. Innocents would be imprisoned. (ibid: 263)

By inscribing Zeitoun's story into the discourse of the War on Terror, the nonfictional novel does not simply recount it. In the weeks and months after the book's publication, the public took increasing interest in Zeitoun's story. In a tragic turn of events however, the family's breakup, following scenes of domestic violence and Zeitoun's alleged attempt to kill his wife were instrumentalized to cast doubt about the Syrian-American's integrity and the credibility of his story.

Zeitoun thus shows that literary nonfiction does not simply represent reality, but fictionalizes it to a degree at which it actively interferes with it. Using literary nonfiction in a classroom sequence on Hurricane Katrina therefore requires sensitizing students for the fictionalization of factual events in texts which are labeled 'nonfiction,' and which thereby make a strong claim to authenticity.

THREE LEVELS OF CULTURAL ANALYSIS IN THE CLASSROOM

So far, I have discussed some theoretical aspects of teaching the human dimension of the Katrina disaster through literary nonfiction. As a final step, I will now turn to some practical aspects. I will propose three levels of analyzing the sociocultural implications of Hurricane Katrina, which I call the empirical level, the level of representation and the level of exemplarity. I will illustrate these levels of analysis, giving practical examples based on one of the texts discussed in this essay.

The empirical level of analysis aims at understanding how class and race determined Katrina's impact on particular social groups within the population of

New Orleans. *Voices, A.D.* and *Zeitoun* reveal aspects of the disaster, which official statistics or damage reports alone cannot provide. *Voices from the Storm*, for example, allows for an in-depth analysis of the influence that geographical factors (e.g. location of residence, elevation of a neighborhood) and sociocultural factors (class, race, age, gender, etc.) had on the vulnerability of a particular social group or an individual. In the book, the eyewitness accounts are supplemented by statistical data on Katrina's impact on various social groups as well as maps of the eyewitnesses' location before and after the storm. The students form groups, each of which reads excerpts from one eyewitness's account and analyzes what, from their point of view, turned the hurricane from a natural into a man-made disaster. The following guiding questions may help:

- Gather as much background information as possible about the subject (age, gender, social background, ethnicity, profession, location of residence in New Orleans, etc.)
- How did the eyewitness experience the hurricane?
- What problems did the eyewitness encounter after the hurricane?
- What, from the eyewitnesses' point of view, turned Hurricane Katrina into a disaster?

The groups then prepare to take the subjects' role in a 'talk show' on the topic "Hurricane Katrina: An (Un-)Natural Disaster?" This step is especially important in the foreign language classroom, which aims at fostering communicative skills and intercultural learning (which includes a change of perspective). During the talk show, only one student per group is taking part in the discussion, while the rest of the class takes the role of an active audience. Their task is to collect as much information as they can about the eyewitnesses' background and their experiences during and after the hurricane. One or two students may also take the role of the host. They prepare questions, lead the debate and moderate when necessary. After the debate, the information collected by the audience is used to discuss the influence of geography, race, and class on the impact Hurricane Katrina had on different social groups. In a final step, the findings are related to Smith's statement that "the contours of disaster and the difference between who lives and who dies is to a greater or lesser extent a social calculus" (2006: n.p.).[1] A similar approach can be taken to discuss *A.D.* When reading *Zeitoun*, a comparison between the experiences of eyewitnesses from different social groups is, of course, not possible. Here, the analysis may concentrate on the question to

---

1 For teaching materials and more information, cf. Siepmann 2015.

what extent his Arab-American identity made Zeitoun especially vulnerable in the context of Hurricane Katrina and, more generally, to natural and man-made hazards in post-9/11 America.

The second level of cultural analysis, the level of representation, focuses on how literary nonfiction reconstructs and thus fictionalizes the events around the hurricane, and which textual strategies these texts use to highlight the sociocultural causes of the Katrina disaster. *A.D.*, as I have mentioned, conveys a very complex sociopolitical issue in only few images and words. It is necessarily elusive and presents aspects of the eyewitnesses' experiences of Katrina in a very bold and striking manner. The label 'nonfiction' therefore needs to be carefully reflected: While it may contribute to students' motivation that the graphic novel is based on the true stories of survivors, they should be sensitized for the textual strategies the author/illustrator uses to achieve a particular effect. The effect that Neufeld's use of color, perspective, panel layout etc. has on the reader hence should be carefully reflected. In a first step, a single panel or a short sequence of panels should be analyzed in detail, focusing on its composition and its various elements. In the next step, the visual and narrative strategies are discussed with regard to their intended effect. If, for example, the panel shown in fig. 1 is examined, the question is, whom does Denise address: the government, the American people, or even the reader? This aspect may lead to the more general question about the role literature and popular culture play in making sense of a historically significant or traumatic event, and in restoring social justice.

While the first and second levels may sensitize students for the sociocultural complexity of a particular 'natural' disaster, they do not satisfyingly answer the question of Katrina's exemplarity of global environmental and social challenges. The third level of analysis, the level of exemplarity, considers Hurricane Katrina in a wider context of post-9/11 America and the problem of global warming. *Zeitoun* offers an opportunity to reflect on the interplay of seemingly independent developments. On the one hand, Katrina's size and impact is unprecedented in American history. According to the latest report by the International Panel on Climate Change (IPCC), Hurricane Katrina is exemplary of the increasing frequency and strength of tropical storms as a consequence of anthropogenic climate change.[2] On the other hand, Zeitoun's case can only be understood in the historical context of post-9/11 America and the 'War on Terror.' Notwithstanding that Zeitoun's arrest in the days after the hurricane may have been completely

---

2 Scientists from various disciplines are "virtually certain that the frequency and intensity of the strongest tropical cyclones in the North Atlantic has increased since the 1970s" (IPCC 2014: 162).

coincidental, his outward appearance that identified him to the authorities as Arab-American made him vulnerable to the deficient disaster management of FEMA. Understanding the interrelation between environmental challenges on a global level, and sociocultural issues on a local or national level, enables students to analyze what sociocultural factors might influence the population's vulnerability to natural hazards in their country or region, and to develop possible solutions.

In this essay, I proposed a concept of teaching the sociocultural implications of Hurricane Katrina to high school students, which aims at raising their awareness of the interrelation between ecological and social challenges in the globalizing world. I have argued for literary nonfiction as the main source for a classroom sequence on Katrina, as it can both be used as a basis for empirical case studies and for an analysis of the textual strategies used to reconstruct the events in New Orleans during and after the hurricane. As I have shown, Hurricane Katrina can teach us more than one lesson about social inequality and justice, about the role that class and race play in preventing disaster, and about the local implications of global environmental challenges. School education can certainly contribute to preparing future citizens for the social and ecological challenges of a globalizing world. Some questions, however, remain: What is society's responsibility in disaster mitigation? What actions can even individuals take to prevent future disasters? Teaching Katrina may not answer these questions, but understanding the interrelations between the forces of nature and the sociocultural structures and power relations will help develop solutions.

BIBLIOGRAPHY

Bruck, Peter (1986): "Facts and Events as Fabulated Realities: The Epistemological Basis of Literary Nonfiction." In: Hedwig Bock/Albert Wertheim (eds.), *The Contemporary American Novel*, München: Hueber, pp. 335-354.

Cates, Kip (2002): "Teaching for a Better World: Global Issues and Language Education." In: *Human Rights Education in Asian Schools* 5, pp. 41-52.

Climate Change 2014: Impact, Adaptation, and Vulnerability, International Panel on Climate Change (IPCC), January 14, 2015 (http://ipcc.ch/).

Dikau, Richard/Pohl, Jürgen Pohl (2011): "Hazards: Naturgefahren und Naturrisiken." In: Hans Gebhardt et al. (eds.), *Geographie: Physische Geographie und Humangeographie*, Heidelberg: Spektrum, pp. 1115-1170.

Dyson, Michael Eric (2007): *Come Hell or High Water. Hurricane Katrina and the Color of Disaster*, New York: Basic Civitas Books.

Eggers, Dave (2009): *Zeitoun*, New York: Vintage Books.

Gersdorf, Cathrin/Mayer, Sylvia (2006): "Nature in Literary and Cultural Studies: Defining the Subject of Ecocriticism – an Introduction." In: *Nature in Literary and Cultural Studies: Transatlantic Conversations on Ecocriticism*, Amsterdam: Rodopi, pp. 9-24.

"Katrina Meteorology and Forecasting," January 14, 2015 (http://hurricanescience.org/history/studies/katrinacase/storm/).

Neufeld, Josh (2009): *A.D.: New Orleans After the Deluge*, New York: Pantheon Books.

Schmid, David (2011): "The Nonfiction Novel." In: Leonard Cassuto/Claire Eby/Benjamin Reiss (eds.), *The Cambridge History of the American Novel*, Cambridge: University Press, pp. 986-1001.

Siepmann, Philipp (2015): "There is No Such Thing as a Natural Disaster. Hurrikan Katrina in Augenzeugenberichten." In: *Praxis Englisch* 1, pp. 39-44.

Smith, Neil (2006): "There is no such thing as a natural disaster," 11 June 2006 (http://understandingkatrina.ssrc.org/Smith/).

Teske, Doris (2006): "Cultural Studies: Key Issues and Approaches." In: Werner Delanoy/Laurenz Volkmann (eds.), *Cultural Studies in the EFL Classroom*, Heidelberg: Winter, pp. 23-36.

"Our mission," *Voice of Witness*, January 14, 2015 (http://voiceofwitness.org/about/).

Vollen, Lola/Ying, Chris Ying (2008): *Voices from the Storm. The People of New Orleans on Hurricane Katrina and Its Aftermath*, San Francisco: McSweeney's Books.

Wisner, Ben et al. (2003): *At Risk: Natural Hazards, People's Vulnerability and Disasters*, New York: Routledge.

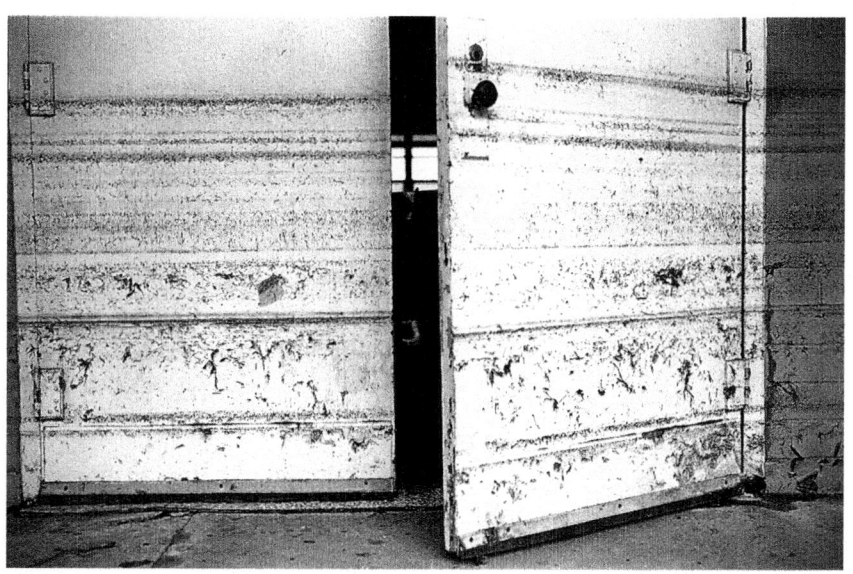

Lewis Watts: *Abandoned School with Multiple Flood Lines*, Central City 2006

The water lines taken a year after Hurricane Katrina, show that there was multiple flooding during and after the storm in various parts of the city. Because most of New Orleans is situated below sea level, the amount of damage from flooding was variable. Central City is away from the Lower 9th Ward, which sustained a great deal of flood damage and loss of life after the hurricane hit. The French Quarter, which is the highest ground in the city, sustained mostly wind damage and relatively little flooding.

Where Y'at Since the Storm?: Linguistic Effects of Hurricane Katrina

KATIE CARMICHAEL

New Orleans is known for its distinctive cultural, culinary, and linguistic heritage – a result of the unique mixture of influences in this southern metropolis. Linguistically speaking, the local varieties of English have developed due to the particular immigrant groups that settled in New Orleans over time, as waves of French, African, Irish, Italian, and German arrivals made their home in this port city. One of the most commonly remarked-upon language varieties in New Orleans is the traditional white, working-class dialect, often referred to as Yat after the common New Orleanian greeting "where y'at?" (cf. Mucciaccio 2009; Eble 2003). This dialect closely resembles New York City English in its pronunciations such as "cah" for "car" and "cawfee" for "coffee" (cf. Labov 2007; Lyman 1978). John Kennedy Toole characterizes its distinctly Northeastern sound in his New Orleans-based novel *A Confederacy of Dunces*, writing that Yat is an "accent that occurs south of New Jersey only in New Orleans, that Hoboken near the Gulf of Mexico" (1980: 4). Though the Yat way of speaking is widely cited by locals as an essential component of New Orleans' heritage, many of its most distinctive features appear to have been on the decline in the latter portion of the twentieth century, as numerous speakers of this language variety departed city limits following the integration of schools in the 1960s (cf. Brennan 1983; Coles 2001; Labov 2007; Mucciaccio 2009; Schoux Casey 2013). In 2005, the area with the heaviest concentration of Yat speakers – the New Orleans suburb of Chalmette in St. Bernard Parish – was inundated by Hurricane Katrina's storm surge, thereby further threatening this speech variety, and calling into question its future vitality.

In the wake of a natural disaster, one consequence may be the temporary or permanent displacement of residents. In the case of Hurricane Katrina, there has been a diaspora of New Orleanians throughout the United States and beyond – although a remarkable number of locals have returned to Greater New Orleans, whether rebuilding their original homes or settling in a new area of the metropolitan region. The upheaval has changed the fabric of the city geographically and demographically, with potential concomitant cultural and linguistic effects.

This study examines how linguistic identity is maintained or lost following a natural disaster, as individuals pick up the pieces in the aftermath. My analysis focuses on St. Bernard Parish, which before Hurricane Katrina consisted of a collection of suburban towns to the east of New Orleans, predominantly populated by white, working-class residents. Though some residents returned to St. Bernard after the storm to rebuild, many others were unwilling or unable to do so, choosing to relocate. A large concentration of St. Bernardians relocated to the Northshore of Lake Pontchartrain, to towns like Mandeville, Covington, and Slidell (cf. Lasley 2012). To determine the linguistic effects of the reshuffling that occurred post-Katrina, I conducted interviews in 2012 with 57 returners and relocators, examining their speech for local linguistic markers such as r-lessness (pronouncing *car* as "cah") and vowel quality (pronouncing *bought* as "bawt" or *bad* as "byad"). If relocation post-Katrina has had an effect on the linguistic landscape, as relocators attempted to fit in with speech patterns in their new homes, I would expect to see fewer local linguistic markers in their speech than in that of returners. As my analysis reveals, however, this is not the case, thereby suggesting that many linguistic features are being retained despite external linguistic pressures – the possible reasons for which this paper will detail.

A SOCIO-HISTORICAL LOOK AT GREATER NEW ORLEANS

New Orleans is known as the "Crescent City" because of the distinct crescent shape the Mississippi River carves into the land between the river and Lake Pontchartrain. Despite this moniker, outsiders' knowledge of the city's geographic characteristics – for example that it is the only major city below sea level in the United States (cf. Leavitt 1982) – had traditionally been surpassed by New Orleans' cultural reputation, until Hurricane Katrina made landfall in 2005 inundating this low-lying city.

Established in 1718 by Jean-Baptiste Le Moyne, Sieur de Bienville, New Orleans was plagued by disease and floods throughout its early colonial years. However, its crucial role as a port city situated on the Mississippi river delta ensured that it would be a valuable site of trade for whoever could retain power in the region, which changed hands between the French and Spanish several times before famously being purchased by the United States, along with the rest of the Louisiana territory. Throughout its history, New Orleans was the center of immigration for many Europeans – in particular, French, Italian, Irish, and German immigrant groups (cf. Campanella 2005). As one of the major centers of the slave trade in the South up until Reconstruction, New Orleans was also home to a large quantity of Africans and Afro-Caribbeans (cf. Brasseaux 2005). This particular mixing of ethnic groups would have a profound effect on the sociocultural and linguistic landscape of this port city, especially as New Orleans advanced throughout the nineteenth and twentieth centuries.

Racial tensions mounted during the Civil Rights movement of the 1960s, which enforced the desegregation of schools in Orleans Parish. As a result, many white New Orleanians fled to surrounding suburbs, in an attempt to enact de facto segregation. The Western towns of Metairie and Kenner in Jefferson Parish and the Eastern towns of Arabi and Chalmette in St. Bernard Parish became the sites of this "white flight," with the latter developing a distinctly white, working-class identity as a result of this influx of workers from working class neighborhoods in the Ninth Ward.

Aided by the construction of the Causeway Bridge, which spanned the length of Lake Pontchartrain, in the 1960s the metropolitan area also began to expand beyond the surrounding areas to the East, West, and South of the city. Throughout the latter portion of the twentieth century, areas to the North of the lake – commonly referred to as "The Northshore" – began to see large population increases, as "southshore" New Orleanians moved to the burgeoning suburban towns in previously rural St. Tammany Parish (cf. Lasley 2012).

As mentioned, in the time preceding Hurricane Katrina, St. Bernard Parish was known as a white, working-class community, in which many of the residents worked at the factories or refineries located therein. As a later site of "white flight," St. Tammany Parish was ethnically similar to St. Bernard Parish, though distinctly upper middle class. These patterns of movement by different subsets of the population have affected the perceptions of which social and linguistic groups inhabit different areas of Greater New Orleans, as the following section will explore.

PRE-KATRINA LINGUISTIC LANDSCAPE

Linguistic research on pre-Katrina Greater New Orleans is sparse, though local ideological associations placed linguistic boundaries around neighborhoods and wards within the city, roughly mapping onto race- and class-based neighborhood divisions (cf. Kolker/Alvarez 1984). Recent research identifies the following dialects of English within the Greater New Orleans region (cf. Carmichael 2014; White-Sustaíta 2012):

- **Yat English**: The traditional white, working-class dialect; primarily spoken downtown and in the suburban outskirts (such as St. Bernard Parish).
- **Southern White English**: A version of Coastal Southern English was historically spoken Uptown; another version of Southern White English can be heard in the Florida Parishes of the Northshore.
- **African American English/Creole English**: Although it is likely there are dialectal divisions within these varieties, many researchers have treated African American/Creole Englishes as a single variety.
- **Mainstream U.S. English**: Commonly spoken by post-Katrina arrivals from elsewhere, but also by middle- to upper-class New Orleanians who feature fewer local linguistic markers.

Note in these descriptions how race and class divisions are salient categories even in how language varieties are identified and distinguished from one another. Such race- and class-based divisions extend out to the suburban towns on the outskirts: Metairie and Kenner to the West, Arabi and Chalmette to the East, and Algiers across the river. Before the storm, these suburban towns were the locus for the distinctive local speech variety, linked to the white, working-class residents that populate these areas. Just as race relations – in particular "white flight" in the 1960s following the integration of schools – have determined settlement patterns in Greater New Orleans, they have also affected the language varieties associated with different locations. While African American and Creole English dialects are more strongly associated with the urban core, the white, working-class vernacular is associated with nearby suburbs, and more standard diction is associated with far suburbs such as the Northshore, or pockets of wealthy areas within the city (such as Uptown).

The language variety being examined in this study is the white, working-class dialect spoken by St. Bernardians. The features of this variety that I chose to examine are those most studied and documented within Greater New Orleans, with the added caveat, of course, that there are only a handful of previous linguistic studies documenting this variety:

- **R-lessness** (Reinecke 1951; Rubrecht 1971; Brennan 1983; Schoux Casey 2013; Carmichael 2014)
- **Raised BOUGHT** (Labov 2007; Carmichael 2014)
- **Split short-a system** (Labov 2007; Carmichael 2014)

R-lessness represents a consonantal feature under examination. R-lessness is the term used to describe the variable absence of /r/ following vowels – for example, pronouncing "water" as "watuh" or "market" as "mahket." This feature has been studied extensively both throughout the United States (cf. Nagy/Irwin 2010; Feagin 1990; Labov [1966] 2006) and within New Orleans specifically (cf. Reinecke 1951; Rubrecht 1971; Brennan 1983; Schoux Casey 2013; Carmichael 2014). The results of past research indicate that over time, r-lessness is losing ground within New Orleans, with many speakers shifting to the exclusively r-ful pronunciations common throughout much of the U.S. Thus r-lessness represents a crucial indicator of the relative "health" of the local dialect.

In contrast with r-lessness, raised BOUGHT represents a vocalic, or vowel-related, feature. The vowel sound in words like "caught," "walk," and "coffee" is often represented linguistically through the word BOUGHT, which stands in as a lexical indicator of the vowel under discussion. In New Orleans, BOUGHT may be pronounced with the tongue positioned slightly higher in the mouth – which linguists refer to as "raising." Raised BOUGHT is also a feature of New York City English (cf. Becker 2010; Labov [1966] 2006), often parodied as in the *Saturday Night Live* skit "coffee talk" (pronounced with raised BOUGHT in the first syllable of "coffee" as well as in "talk"). By examining tongue position in pronunciation of words with the BOUGHT vowel, it can be determined whether speakers are adopting the more common non-local pronunciation of BOUGHT, without tongue-raising.

The split short-a system is another vocalic feature being analyzed. Short-a is the vowel in words like "cat," "basket," or "damage." For many speakers of U.S. English, these first two words – "cat" and "basket," – feature a similar-sounding version of short-a, while the last word – "damage" – features a raised tongue, rendering a slightly different quality to the vowel. This particular system of pronunciations is generally called a "nasal" short-a system, since the tongue remains lax (or unraised) when pronouncing short-a before all sounds except nasal consonants like /m/ or /n/. Thus speakers with a nasal short-a system produce a slightly different vowel for the words "cat" versus "can." This constraint on pronunciation is fairly straightforward; in contrast, speakers with a split short-a system feature a complex system of constraints governing whether short-a will be produced with the tongue raised or not. In New Orleans' split short-a system, for example, the pronunciation of short-a in "cat" and "damage" are similar, while "basket" differs (cf. Labov 2007; Carmichael 2014). Split short-a systems are also present in New York City (cf. Becker 2010; Labov [1966] 2006), Cincinnati (cf. Boberg/Strassel 2000), and Philadelphia (cf. Labov 1989), however each locale features slightly different constraints that determine tongue-raising – meaning the split short-a system in New Orleans is distinctive to this area. Whether speakers in the current study feature split short-a systems, nasal systems, or something in between (usually called a "continuous" system) may indicate whether speakers are shifting away from the traditional split short-a system in New Orleans.

POPULATION SHIFTS POST-KATRINA

Hurricane Katrina made landfall on August 29, 2005, devastating the city of New Orleans and the surrounding areas. Many residents of Greater New Orleans had evacuated the city, watching the destruction on motel televisions, and bearing witness to the misfortune of those who were not able or not willing to leave – and indeed, both returners and relocators in the current study recounted such experiences. In the weeks and months following the storm, locals battled to secure the essentials: income, shelter, and a plan for moving forward. Located downriver of New Orleans, St. Bernard Parish in particular received the brunt of Katrina's storm surge. When all was said and done, there were only six structures in the entire parish that did not take water (cf. Lasley 2012). For this reason, much of the parish was uninhabitable, prompting a number of St. Bernardians – even those who initially planned to return to their pre-Katrina homes – to secure long-term housing elsewhere.

The Northshore of Lake Pontchartrain, which comprises the towns of Mandeville, Covington, and Slidell in St. Tammany Parish, received only minor flooding and wind damage. Thus Northshore towns quickly became a site of relocation for "southshore" New Orleanians, including St. Bernardians. Figure 1 demonstrates that a quarter of St. Bernard Parish residents relocated to the Northshore following Katrina.

Figure 1: Census estimate for sites of St. Bernardian relocation following Hurricane Katrina

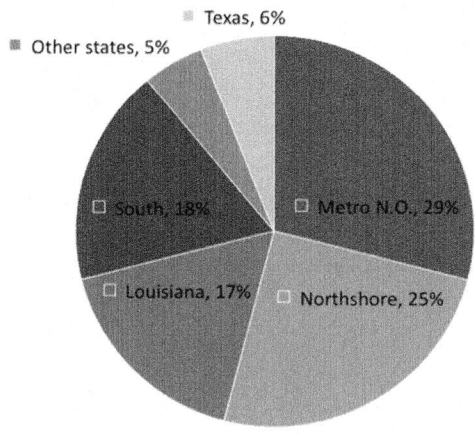

(Adapted from Lasley 2012)

The Northshore did not readily receive this influx of outsiders, who dressed and talked differently, and generally did not fit into the upper middle-class landscape. As mentioned, before Katrina, St. Bernard Parish was a stigmatized, working-class community while St. Tammany Parish was the wealthiest parish in Louisiana, with the highest median income in the state (U.S. Census 2000). A search of online forums post-Katrina revealed reams of negative commentary about the "St. Tammanards" (a derogatory blend of St. Tammany and St. Bernard), and interviewees themselves revealed the negative response they got on the Northshore. Relocator Benjamin explained, "there was a lot of hatred – genuine hatred, it seemed like – from these people [on the Northshore] trying to keep the people from St. Bernard out.[1] Returner Bella recounted the experiences of her relocator friends, asserting that "people actually said stuff like, 'you need to go back home where you came from.'" Returner Sugar Magnolia summarized the situation, saying, "As a whole St. Tammany was very, very bitter, because they had this influx of the St. Bernard people. Be like a ghetto taking over, you know, it really was very – no matter how much money you had, you were still from St. Bernard." Thus the unwelcoming nature of the Northshore residents made a clear division between pre-Katrina St. Tammany residents and post-Katrina relocators.

---

1 All names used in this paper are pseudonyms selected by the interviewee.

This relocation process also created a schism between those St. Bernardians who left, and those who returned. As relocator Maria explained, "Katrina really separated us, that broke our hearts." Relocator Margaret described her detachment from her friends who returned after the storm, saying, "there's this, like, invisible curtain. With a lot of people, I sense that, 'oh we're back and you're not.'" There was also a sense of bitterness from the returners towards the relocators, who had made a new life for themselves away from the recovery process, and away from their working-class roots. Many returners reported that those individuals who relocated had changed in a number of ways – culturally, as well as linguistically. Returner Bella commented, "you move to Mandeville [on the Northshore] and you think you're high and mighty." Returner Savannah added, "[some people] even changed the way they say it, they say, 'Mahndeville...I want to live in Mahndeville.'" As Savannah's observation suggests, the movement away from St. Bernard to St. Tammany was characterized by locals as triggering changes in demeanor and self-presentation, including linguistic changes.

In addition to these local perceptions of difference between returners and relocators, past research has demonstrated that when speakers move to an area with different dialect features, they accommodate to some extent to the new dialect (Munro et al. 1999; Straw/Patrick 2007; Hazen/Hamilton 2008; Nycz 2011). Thus, there is reason to believe that the large-scale relocation following Hurricane Katrina might affect speech patterns, with relocators featuring lower rates of local dialectal features than returners if they have adapted to non-local norms. In the following section, I report on linguistic analyses of speakers from these two groups, in order to determine the linguistic effects of post-storm relocation.

LINGUISTIC EFFECTS OF HURRICANE KATRINA

I conducted one to three hour-long recorded interviews with each interviewee, asking about their experiences living in St. Bernard before the storm, and their lives since Hurricane Katrina. At the end of interviews, each individual was asked about their perceptions of language varieties within Greater New Orleans, though they were not told initially that I was studying language patterns. The recordings were then transcribed and coded for linguistic variables. Vowel quality was examined acoustically, through the use of the analysis software Praat (cf. Boersma 2001).

Interviewees were all classified as returners or relocators based on their residence at the time of the interview in 2012. Most interviews took place in the homes of participants, meaning on the Northshore in the case of relocators, and in

St. Bernard in the case of returners. It is worth noting that even returners spent some time out of St. Bernard following the hurricane, as the parish was closed to residents for a period of time after the storm. Furthermore, some returners spent several years in other locations before being able to return and rebuild in St. Bernard. The ideologically charged nature of being a returner versus a relocator in this situation, however, validates the classification of participants into these two groups based on their final location, regardless of how long it took them to reach this point after the post-storm upheaval.

R-lessness was analyzed by going through the data and noting every instance of post-vocalic /r/, recording whether /r/ was fully pronounced or not. Thus in a word like "car," where the /r/ sound occurs following a vowel (post-vocalically), I noted simply whether I heard the /r/ pronounced or not ("car" vs. "cah"). My coding was checked by two other independent coders; we featured over 80% agreement across a sample of the data set. Figure 2 presents rates of r-lessness, or non-pronunciation of /r/, for returners and relocators.

Figure 2: Rates of r-lessness for relocators and returners

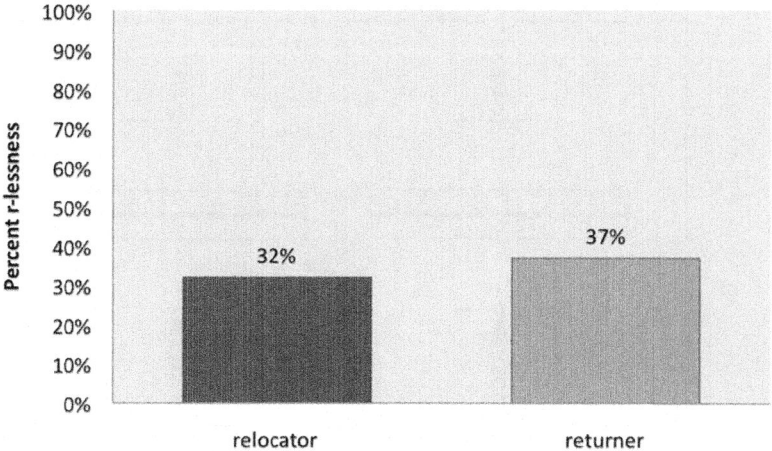

Relocators dropped /r/ 32% of the time and returners dropped it 37% of the time. Though this means that relocators pronounce /r/ somewhat more than returners, this difference is very small. I interpret these data as suggesting that St. Bernardians who relocated to the Northshore were no more likely to produce r-ful pronunciations than those who returned to St. Bernard after the storm. This finding is surprising in light of the fact that this feature is commonly remarked upon or mocked as being a feature of the stigmatized local St. Bernardian accent throughout Greater New Orleans. In spite of the stigma attached to r-lessness throughout Greater New Orleans, the physical movement of these speakers away from their predominantly r-less hometown does not seem to have had an effect on their use of this linguistic feature.

Raising of BOUGHT – or the vowel in words like "bought," "caught," and "caution" – was measured according to the height of the first formant (F1), which indicates raising and lowering of the tongue within the vowel space. F1 values for all speakers were normalized using a z-score transformation, which places all pronunciations on the same scale so that pronunciations of BOUGHT are comparable across speakers. Figure 3 presents boxplots of returners' and relocators' pronunciations of BOUGHT in terms of the normalized F1. Since there is an inverse relationship between F1 and tongue height, data points located *lower* along the y-axis in Figure 3 indicate *raising* of BOUGHT. In other words, the lower the data point along the y-axis, the more local-sounding an individual token of BOUGHT is.

Figure 3: BOUGHT *vowel height for relocators and returners*

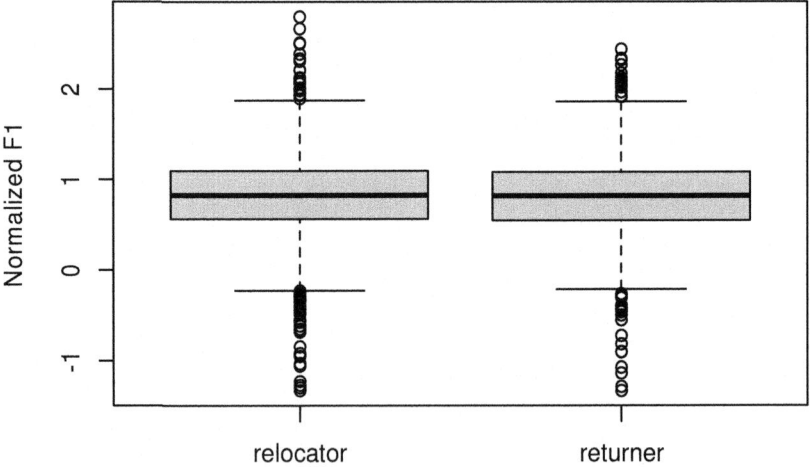

As was the case with r-lessness, there is no discernible difference between the returner and relocator groups in terms of their pronunciation of BOUGHT. Thus I conclude that relocation to the Northshore following Hurricane Katrina does not affect this particular linguistic variable, either.

For short-a systems, speakers were classified into three groups along a continuum from nasal to split short-a systems, according to visual analysis of their vowel spaces. Speakers who appeared to feature neither a clear nasal nor a clear split short-a system were classified as featuring "continuous" short-a systems. Table 1 presents the patterning of short-a system types across returner and relocator groups, according to these classifications.

Table 1: Short-a system types across speakers

	Nasal	Continuous	Split
Relocator	6	10	12
Returner	6	11	12

Once again, it is clear that there is little difference between returner and relocator groups in terms of distribution of short-a system types, with almost identical distribution across the three system types for both returner and relocators. As was the case with r-lessness and BOUGHT raising, the short-a system type does not appear to have been affected by whether speakers relocated post-Katrina.

DISCUSSION & CONCLUSIONS

Results indicated that there was no great difference between the speech of returners and relocators, in terms of the distinctive local features r-lessness, raised BOUGHT, and a split short-a system. Such patterning suggests that relocation following the hurricane does not necessarily produce a loss of linguistic heritage – at least not in a single generation. Worth noting as a caveat to this interpretation, though, is the fact that all three variables also patterned according to age, with younger speakers displaying lower rates of these local features (cf. Carmichael 2014 for a detailed analysis). That is, even though relocation does not appear to cause speakers to alter their language use, the features under examination in this study may disappear regardless of the storm, since younger speakers – both returners and relocators – are using them less and less. As relocator Frank explained, "[my kids] have good educations so they want to speak proper [...] especially my son. He's an English major type, so he wants to enunciate."

Despite the loss of certain language patterns over time in the region, we may still conclude that on some level, the distinctive local linguistic heritage of Greater New Orleans has remained a presence even in the face of discrimination and devaluing. This linguistic result may be interpreted in light of other "local pride" movements post-Katrina, for example the commodification of localness by way of tee shirts, coffee mugs, and other images bearing "local knowledge" – and local linguistic features – as a badge of honor. Tee shirts and coffee mugs emblazoned with the New Orleans-specific phrase "making groceries" or the word "heart" spelled "hawt" (reflecting a local r-less pronunciation) use language as a symbol of being a "true" New Orleanian. This commodification thereby links linguistic features to local status, which is newly revalorized and available for purchase. Schoux Casey writes of this meaning making process:

The mediated experience of Katrina, together with the disappearance of the city and its residents, has caused a valorization of the city. Former associations between New Orleans culture, including language, and negative or nonexistent social meanings have been subordinated to newer associations of everything New Orleans as local, authentic, sentimental, threatened and valuable. (2013: 129)

It is perhaps this selfsame pride in all things distinctive to the city of New Orleans that is protecting, in a way, the linguistic heritage of the city. Indeed, many interviewees characterized their speech as part of their cultural identity, which they carried forward after the storm as a badge of honor, as survivors. Thus it is possible that, despite some previous evidence that local linguistic features are being lost across generations (cf. Brennan 1983; Labov 2007; Carmichael 2014), the post-Katrina nostalgia movement will motivate future retention of New Orleans' distinctive linguistic identity.

To summarize, despite large-scale relocation following Hurricane Katrina, many of the linguistic features specific to the white, working-class areas of Greater New Orleans have remained intact. While such a finding seems to imply that there is hope for the future of this distinctive dialect even after the massive upheaval caused by Hurricane Katrina, the fact that younger speakers in both groups (returners and relocators alike) are eschewing these linguistic features suggests otherwise. The New Orleans nostalgia movement that has taken place since Katrina, however, may provide the impetus for speakers previously stigmatized for local speech patterns to hold onto locally distinctive forms as a point of pride. Longitudinal research on the returner and relocator communities in this study should shed light on the direction of linguistic changes, in particular as the younger generation matures in the post-Katrina landscape.

BIBLIOGRAPHY

Becker, Kara (2010): *Regional Dialect Features on the Lower East Side of New York City: Sociophonetics, Ethnicity, and Identity*, Unpublished New York University Dissertation.

Boberg, Charles/Strassel, Stephanie (2000): "Short-a in Cincinnati: A Change in Progress." In: *Journal of English Linguistics* 28, pp. 108-126.

Boersma, Paul (2001): "Praat, A System for Doing Phonetics by Computer." In: *Glot International* 5/9-10, pp. 341-345.

Brasseaux, Carl A. (2005): *French, Cajun, Creole, Houma: A Primer on Francophone Louisiana*, Baton Rouge: Louisiana University Press.

Brennan, Pamela (1983): *Postvocalic /r/ in New Orleans*, Unpublished University of New Orleans Master Thesis.

Campanella, Richard (2006): *Geographies of New Orleans: Urban Fabrics Before the Storm*, Lafayette: Center for Louisiana Studies (University of Louisiana at Lafayette).

Carmichael, Katie (2014): *"I Never Thought I Had an Accent Until the Hurricane": Sociolinguistic Variation in Post-Katrina Greater New Orleans*, Unpublished Ohio State University Dissertation.

Coles, Felice Anne (1997): "Solidarity Cues in New Orleans English." In: Cynthia Bernstein/Thomas Nunnally/Robin Sabino (eds.), *Language Variety in the South Revisited*, Tuscaloosa: University of Alabama Press, pp. 219-224.

Coles, Felice Anne (2001): "The Authenticity of Yat: A 'Real' New Orleans Dialect." In: *Southern Journal of Linguistics* 25 (1/2), pp. 74-86.

Coles, Felice Anne (2004): "The Authenticity of Dialect: Real Isleños Speak Yat, Too." Unpublished Presentation at Language Variation in the South (LAVIS) III in Tuscaloosa, Alabama.

Eble, Connie (2003): "The Englishes of Southern Louisiana." In: Stephen Nagle/Sara Sanders (eds.), *English in the Southern United States*, Malden: Blackwell, pp. 173-188.

Eble, Connie (2006): "Speaking the Big Easy." In: Walt Wolfram/Ben Ward (eds.), *American Voices: How Dialects Differ from Coast to Coast*, Malden: Blackwell.

Feagin, Crawford (1990): "Dynamics of Sound Change in Southern States English: From r-less to r-ful in three generations." In: Jerold A. Edmondson/Crawford Feagin/Peter Mülhausler (eds.), *Development and Diversity: Language Variation Across Time and Space: A Festschrift for Charles-James N. Bailey*, Arlington: SIL/University of Texas at Arlington, pp. 129-146.

Hazen, Kirk/Hamilton, Sarah (2008): "A Dialect Turned Inside Out: Migration and the Appalachian Diaspora." In: *Journal of English Linguistics* 36, pp. 102-128.

Kolker, Andy/Alvarez, Louie (1984): *Yeah, You Rite!* New York: Center for New American Media.

Labov, William (1989): "Exact Description of the Speech Community: Short A in Philadelphia." In: Ralph W. Fasold/Deborah Schiffrin (eds.), *Language Change and Variation*, Amsterdam/Philadelphia: John Benjamins Publishing Company, pp. 1-57.

Labov, William ([1966] 2006): *The Social Stratification of English in New York City*, Washington, D.C.: Center for Applied Linguistics/Second Edition: Cambridge, United Kingdom: Cambridge University Press.

Labov, William (2007): "Transmission and Diffusion." In: *Language* 83/2, pp. 344-387.

Lasley, Carrie Beth (2012): *Catastrophes and the Role of Social Networks in Recovery: A Case Study of St. Bernard Parish, LA, Residents After Hurricane Katrina*, Unpublished University of New Orleans Dissertation.

Leavitt, Mel (1982): *A Short History of New Orleans*, San Francisco: Lexikos.

Lyman, Tim (1978): "An Introduction." In: Bunny Matthews (ed.), *F'Sure! Actual Dialogue Heard on the Streets of New Orleans*. New Orleans: Neetof Press, pp. i-x.

Mucciaccio, Francesca (2009): *"A Gaggle a' Y'ats" and Other Stories: Tracing the Effects of Ideology on Language Change Through Indexical Formation in Y'at*, Unpublished Reed College Honors Thesis.

Munro, Murray J./Derwing Tracey M./Flege, James E. (1999): "Canadians in Alabama: A Perceptual Study of Dialect Acquisition in Adults." In: *Journal of Phonetics* 27, pp. 385-403.

Nagy, Naomi/Irwin, Patricia (2010): "Boston (r): Neighbo(r)s Nea(r) and Fa(r)." In: *Language Variation and Change* 22/2, pp. 241-278.

Nycz, Jennifer R. (2011): *Second Dialect Acquisition: Implications for Theories of Phonological Representation*, Unpublished New York University Dissertation.

Reinecke, George F. (1951): *New Orleans Pronunciation Among School Children and Educated Adults*, Unpublished Tulane University Master Thesis.

Rubrecht, August (1971): *Regional Phonological Variants in Louisiana Speech*, Unpublished University of Florida Dissertation.

Schoux Casey, Christina (2013): *Postvocalic /r/ in New Orleans: Language, Place, and Commodification*, Unpublished University of Pittsburgh Dissertation.

Straw, Michelle/Patrick, Peter L. (2007): "Dialect Acquisition of Glottal Variation in /t/: Barbadians in Ipswich." In: *Language Sciences* 29, pp. 385-407.
Toole, John Kennedy (1980): *A Confederacy of Dunces*, New York: Grove Press.
White-Sustaíta, Jessica (2012): "Socio-historical Perspectives on Black and White Speech Relations in New Orleans." In: *Southern Journal of Linguistics* 36/1, pp. 45-60.

Lewis Watts: *Uptown New Orleans Carrollton Neighborhood* 2011

This gentleman reflects New Orleans style and presence. This legacy has endured and migrated to other parts of the country and the world along with music, culture, and cuisine.

Life and Luck after Katrina: African American Men, Oral History, and Mentoring in New Orleans, 2010 to 2014

NIKKI BROWN

At the height of the chaos following Hurricane Katrina at the end of August 2005, the scenes of destruction, abandonment, and human misery at the New Orleans Superdome and Convention Center were so shocking that they became seared into American national memory. There were accounts, seemingly first-hand, of murder and rapes – all of which melded into a picture of nightmarish turmoil. Soon after the full measure of the cataclysm was revealed, the national media centered on the human destruction that followed. More reports filled the nightly newscasts of African American men looting, shooting, and other criminal acts across the city of New Orleans. The problem was that very few of these reports were true. As New Orleans *Times-Picayune* metro editor Jed Horne summed up, the central conflict of the national media coverage of the storm was that the repeated image of the roving bands of African American hoodlums bore little resemblance to actual events: "The aggregate portrait was of a city gone mad, a black city, a city of depraved men and women who would walk away from asthmatic children, and leave them to die, if they didn't violate them first." (2006: 108-109)

This essay joins the discussion on the representation of African American men and youth in post-Hurricane Katrina New Orleans. Although the media coverage of the storm affirmed and reinforced one of the oldest American cultural tropes, the Black Menace, nevertheless the reconstruction of New Orleans relies heavily on the engagement of African American men working with each other to address neighborhood and community troubles – youth violence, drugs, poor education, lack of after school programs, for example. This community activism offers a significant contrast to the reports of black criminality overtaking the city after the storm. However, these efforts span several communities, but they lacked a documentary trail.

Beginning in 2010, I embarked on a photography project that sought to counterpose the images of black criminality with alternative views of black authenticity and cultural production in New Orleans. The photography project became an extended collection, entitled "Ordinary Lives, Extraordinary Times: African American Men in New Orleans after Hurricane Katrina, 2010-2014." The images were on display at Leopold Franzens University in Innsbruck, Austria and Karl Franzens University in Graz Austria in late 2012. As the project came to a close, the photographs were displayed at the McKenna Museum of African American Culture in New Orleans from December 2013 through March 2014. The oral histories that accompany the photographs focus on African American men's work in the reconstruction of New Orleans.

The project immediately took shape in the most recognizable and cherished gathering space for African American men – the barbershop. The barbershop photographs produced one of the most evocative portraits of the series, of four-year old Marquis receiving his first ever haircut from barber-in-training Calvin Johnson. "Rites 1 – Marquis's First Haircut" (cf. fig. 1) represents the spirit of the project.

Figure 1: "Rites 1 – Marquis's First Haircut"

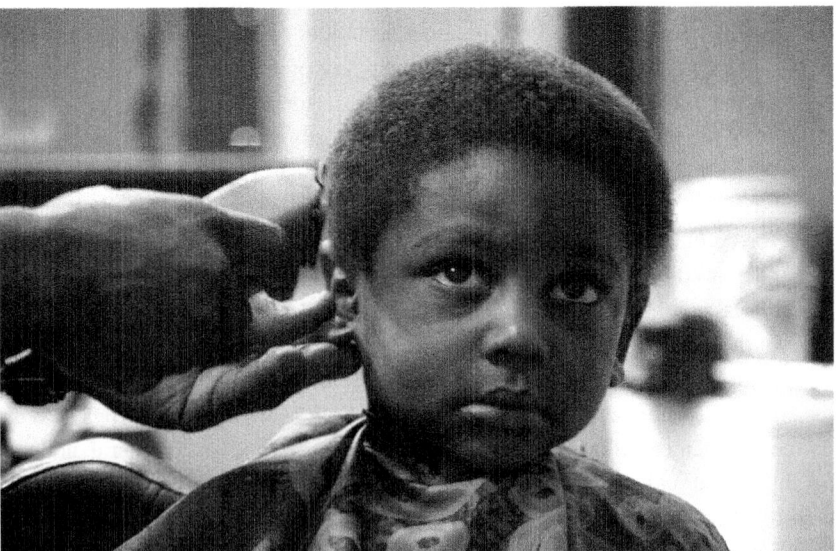

As I took more photographs of African American men in post-Katrina New Orleans, the project's perspective sharpened around the act of formal and informal mentoring. As much as I wanted to dispel the myths of widespread black criminality, I wanted even more to photograph African American men's inner lives and intimate interactions, the parts that are not meant for romanticized touristic consumption or short-sighted national media attention. For the next four years I photographed and conducted interviews with African American men in New Orleans. In all, I took about 50 portraits and conducted 20 interviews. Cultural critic and historian Michele Wallace has written that "the first job of Afro-American mass culture (or any 'minority' cultural production in which 'race' is an issue) should be to 'uplift the race' or to salvage the denigrated image of blacks in the white American imagination" (1990: 1).

Admittedly, my initial impulse was to challenge directly the image of black criminality with a more positive image of black community engagement. As a historian of twentieth century African American politics and visual culture, I am interested in the ways by which African Americans, particularly African American organizations addressing poverty, move between public and private masks of identity. Hurricane Katrina presented an opportunity for exploration. I had a nagging sense that the untold stories of the majority of working- and middle-class African Americans were going to be lost in the noise of the media onslaught. When the 2005 catastrophe unfolded, my interest was anxiously piqued on how African Americans would be portrayed, especially the black middle class – the civil servants, teachers, nurses, lawyers, social workers, and accountants – whose principal investment, their homes, were wiped out.

But there is more to this project. As the photographs and interviews grew in number, it crafted its own voice. A vitally important story of the cultural history of post-Katrina emerged – the private and public successes of African American men during the recovery of New Orleans. The photography and oral history project challenges the stereotype of the absent African American male parent, mentor, or father figure. Instead, my goal is to show African American men in socially intimate relationships, underscoring how formal and informal mentoring groups have contributed to the recovery of New Orleans while criticizing its transformation.

A methodology to document mentoring quickly emerged. I looked for places where African American men socialized. Obvious sites were barbershops, social aid and pleasure clubs, and second line parades. However, other, less visible places – the junior league football field, the convenience store, horseback riding stables, the dining area at Whole Foods market, busy kitchens at popular local restaurants, and gay bars on Bourbon Street – offered even more insight. Once I developed an eye for finding the places of congregation, the mentoring and care-taking – a gentle caress as a father teaches his son to tie a tie, or a teenager's confidence in handling his own horse – became more noticeable and palpable gestures. These images of African American men's nurturing offered a rich discourse on post-Katrina reconstruction, because the image of protective guidance and affection has too often been denied in the representation of African American men. As scholar Khalil Muhammad has found, black criminality occupies an essential space in the history of modern urban centers. By equating the growth of black populations with the perception of increased activity of law-breaking, the story of the rise of the black middle class in American urban areas has been supplanted effectively in the 21st century (2010: 267-274).

One example is the experience of chef Joe Smith of New Orleans Louisiana. "Chef Joe," as he likes to be called, is a culinary instructor at Café Reconcile in New Orleans. Chef Joe ran the "life skills" class for the incoming interns at the restaurant for several years when Hurricane Katrina hit. In late August 2005, like many residents, Chef Joe was unsure of the path of the storm or its level of intensity; however, his wife and mother were adamant about leaving as soon as possible. On Saturday August 30, at 1:30am, Chef Joe and his family drove out of the city and stayed in Forest City Arkansas for the next several months. Within two months of the storm, Café Reconcile re-opened, and Chef Joe was back to teaching and mentoring at-risk youth (Café Reconcile 2014: n.p.).

Passionate about mentoring, Chef Joe explained in an interview the reason he led the life skills class for Café Reconcile. The students, aged 12 to 18 years, came of age in low-income neighborhoods in New Orleans, which were the communities most devastated by the storm: "What I'm trying to get them to understand is, you don't have to behave as society dictates your culture should have you behave. There's ways of behaving that is across the board that all people, [...] no matter what their race or nationality or culture, [...] all have to learn." (Interview Smith 2013) Later, Chef Joe said that mentoring students helped him rebuild his life after the storm: "When [teachers] are teaching, you hear them all relate what they're teaching to something that's happened in their life. And that's how you pass on the message. Because you relate it to your experience in life. Yes, you're teaching, but you're actually mentoring. You're actually grooming someone to be better." (ibid.) Moreover, he had an educational agenda in his class, code-switching for African American teenagers: "[O]ne of the things we talk about in the life skills class is code-switching. And what we're referring to is: you don't talk, act, and behave the same way on the job as you do when you're on the block. Your vocabulary has to change. Your way of carrying yourself has to change." (ibid.)

Noticeably, African American men's social institutions in New Orleans maintained a strong connection to the language and visual culture of masculinity – how to be a man, a protector, a provider, a father, a silverback. Nearly all of the programs and organizations were for men and boys only; there were hardly any provisions made for the membership of women and girls. In fact, women were rarely the subject of conversation. Some of the leaders felt an urgent responsibility to rescue African American young men; they argued that the intervention of a patient male mentor had the power to save lives immediately. For the most part, older, heterosexual African American men were more eager to share than younger, gay men. Middle-class men were the most talkative. Yet, all the interviewees acknowledged my gender as a woman and my status as a professor of History at the University of New Orleans; some of the subjects refrained from cursing or drinking as I spoke with them. Given the different gendered perspectives, I found the advice of historian and photographer Lewis Watts very helpful in calibrating my expectations for the interviews. Watts writes that the work of representing race and gender in New Orleans,

does so in part because of the participation of the subjects who inhabit the frame: men, women, and children who gaze back at the lens and at us with looks that appeal, scold, calm, love, and satirize. In other words, there is a dialogue between photographers and their subjects – people who craft their humanity through action and reaction. (2013: xi)

The interviews further illuminated the cultural context of the photographs. At first, the questions followed a script: how long have the subjects lived in New Orleans; how were they affected by Hurricane Katrina; when did they return; did they live in New Orleans before the storm; were they comfortable talking about politics; were they married; did they have children; were they personally affected by violent crime in the last few years; and finally, how would they like to be pictured or remembered in the photograph? Though some of the subjects did not want to be interviewed, those who contributed spoke as if they had been waiting for a long time for someone to ask their opinion. Very quickly the interviews departed from the script, as we talked about the most urgent concerns in the current state of affairs in New Orleans – crime, education, jobs, and their personal safety. When we talked in abstractions, their conversations did not yield many results. However, when I asked them to detail personal stories – had they been robbed recently, did they know someone who had been shot, when did they join the marching band, how is the church in their neighborhood doing – their recollections drew a stark contrast between their work to restore their communities and the national media's depiction of the mainly white-led reconstruction of New Orleans.

In this regard, Chef Joe's commitment to mentoring at Café Reconcile revealed a side of New Orleans not often depicted in post-Katrina coverage – the emergence of double consciousness among the city's African American middle and working classes. For African American men, a delicate balance emerged, and it was one that they constantly negotiated. There was the public face of service work – waiters, valets, gardeners, cooks, and janitors – that proliferated after the storm that existed in conjunction with the private face of African American community networks – social aid and pleasure clubs, brass bands, and barbershops – that persevered despite the storm. When asked how he wanted the photographs of Café Reconcile to reflect his work and his mentees, Chef Joe summed up his interview in this way: "[I want people] to see growth and change. To understand that this is a picture of now, but look past the picture. You know. I think each picture says something. And I would want them to wonder where did this person come from? Where did he evolve from? Like I tell my students, I wasn't always 'Chef Joe.'" (Interview Smith 2013)

Beyond the practical importance of the life skills class, Chef Joe's work was central to the historical post-Katrina narrative. The life skills class specifically tackled the rising poverty and violent crime in New Orleans, and it was successful without engaging the racial mythologies in the reconstruction narrative. For example, criminologist Peter Scharf estimated that nearly 800 murders were committed in New Orleans between August 2005 and August 2010, and many of Chef Joe's students had encountered violent crime personally, usually in the death or injury of a loved one in New Orleans (Scharf 2010: n.p.). Though Scharf's report contributed to the national imagination about violence in New Orleans since the storm, Chef Joe's work, replicated around New Orleans, remained a local interest story until January 2007, when the restaurant was visited by former First Lady Laura Bush (Loven 2007: n.p.). The popularity of Café Reconcile and the success of similar efforts effectively reconfigured the reconstruction narrative, by taking the focus off of the story of the white savior, typified by Brad Pitt's Make It Right Foundation, and instead giving attention to African American grassroots, community-driven civil rights activism. Walter Umrani, a field coordinator for an anti-violence group called The Peace Keepers, described the role of race in the narrative this way: "There's a different breed of black people in New Orleans. We really do think that white folks will come to our communities and solve this problem. We have to do it ourselves. We have to tell them something they've never heard of before." (Interview Umrani 2013) Nearly all the interviewees shared Umrani's opinion.

By the early 2000s, despite a twenty-year run of community-focused African American mayors, New Orleans was still living down claims from the 1990s as having "one of the most brutal, incompetent, and corrupt police forces in the United States" (Moore 2010: 5). The state of Louisiana had had a string of bad luck with corruption in the legislature and governor's office (Hendrix Wright 1991: 175). African American neighborhoods, like St. Claude, the Tremé and Gentilly, though close in proximity to the French Quarter, were far distant culturally and economically from the tourist center. The city of New Orleans, a politically left-leaning island in a sea of statewide conservatism, had become the victim of legislative neglect. African Americans fiercely protected their cultural roots in the city's history. But, as they remained long and faithful supporters of the Democratic Party, African Americans and a city with a 67% African American population were left behind as Louisiana fully embraced the Republican Party in its state legislature by the year 2000 (U.S. Census Bureau 2000: n.p.).

In the immediate aftermath of Hurricane Katrina in 2005, the national media outlets repeatedly broadcast images of droves of black looters vandalizing the city. The *New York Times*, in an article about racial bias and Hurricane Katrina news coverage, noted how Fox News anchor John Gibson claimed that thugs, "looting, fires and violence," had overtaken the city. Further, the *New York Times* found that even on the politically progressive MSNBC cable news channel, an announcer reported without verification, "[p]eople are being raped. People are being murdered. People are being shot. Police officers being shot." (Carlson qtd. in Carr 2005: n.p.) On August 30, 2005, NBC News, echoing the coverage of other national media outlets, reported that the looting was the result of "people who are oppressed all their lives [taking] an opportunity to get back at society" (Carr 2005: n.p.). As scholar Steve Classen has argued, the journalists on the scene in New Orleans were stripped of the basic modes of objectivity as the storm unfolded and "lacking the supports of their conventional technical infrastructure, frequently ignored local racial, cultural and political history" (2009: 3).

In its haste to report the terrible details of the storm's impact, mainstream media coverage failed to accurately represent the African American victims of Hurricane Katrina at the time. Ultimately, middle- and working-class African American residents suffered disproportionately higher losses of wealth, income, and property due to the storm. Many families lost everything. In the weeks and months following the hurricane, whites were rarely labeled as criminals and there was little discussion of white criminality. Most famously (or infamously), the days after the storm, the Associated Press released photographs of African Americans, captioned as "looters," wading through chest-deep water with bags of "stolen" materials, while photographs of white persons navigating through the same muck depicted "survivors" who "found" food and clothing (Jones 2005: n.p.).

It was not difficult for Michael Eric Dyson to find individuals who were dismayed at the national media's portrayal of the city. Dyson recounted a telling interview with Dwayne Woodfox about New Orleans during the catastrophe: "My only challenge is with the news media. Because they're making blacks look [bad with] the few thugs and knuckleheads they've shown at the Astrodome and the Superdome. And that's not a correct portrayal of the majority of the black people that are here from New Orleans." (2006: 140) Woodfox's observation was remarkably prescient. Black criminality has always occupied an essential space in the narrative history of the making of modern urban centers. Khalil Muhammad writes: "By illuminating the idea of black criminality in the making of modern America, it becomes clear that there are options in how we choose to use and interpret crime statistics. They may tell us something about the world we live in and about the people we label 'criminals.'" (2010: 277) The prevailing racial mythology of black criminality was already deeply embedded in the national media discourse. It offered an easy, yet false analysis to use when describing poverty, inequality and disenfranchisement, presenting deeply biased images and stories as fair and balanced. If Hurricane Katrina showed anything, it was that one of the most powerful tropes in American popular culture was the image of the black man as a menace and perpetrator of violence, which ran concurrent with the news of the wreckage of the city.

Beginning in 2009 several non-profit organizations compiled and produced reports that focused on quality of life in New Orleans after the storm. The measurements of the African American quality of life also showed that race-based economic and social inequalities, which were highly disruptive before the storm, had widespread negative consequences for the recovery of African American men after the storm. African American men and boys stood as the most vulnerable population groups. Though poverty in New Orleans has always acted as a handmaiden to racial segregation, myriad, interwoven factors, coming to fruition long after the end of Jim Crow, produced the tremendous violence that gripped the city after the storm. Decades of economic inequality and political disenfranchisement had taken a considerable toll on the state's African American population. Natural disasters are just another way for disenfranchised groups to experience and see inequality. Historian Kent Germany has argued that the economic downturn in the 1980s in New Orleans was still felt some thirty years later. He continues, "Katrina dramatically exposed this fragile state of race and poverty and highlighted a complicated political bargain made by leaders responsible for cities at every level – and by implication, most other Americans. They had made peace with poverty." (2007: 748) Leroy Robinson, a retired truck driver, underscored Germany's point, when he described the impact of gun violence on his middle-class community and church, the New Hope Baptist Church: "Our church is in ... well, I call it the 'hood.' [...] Last night [December 2012], three people got shot, two died. Right across the street from our church! A woman and a man died." When asked why the church-members continued to attend after the shootings, Robinson responded: "We've been there so long ... we own the building. And then we have a couple of houses down there too. The Pastor doesn't want to leave. See, the Pastor tries to talk to these people." (Interview Robinson 2012)

Echoing Robinson's sentiment about ties to the community, *A Portrait of Louisiana: the Human Development Report*, commissioned by Oxfam America and written by the American Human Development Project of the Social Science Research Council, offered one of the most revealing analyses of quality of life for Louisianans in 2009. *A Portrait of Louisiana* stands out for its innovative way of defining and measuring quality of life by "emphasizing the everyday experiences of everyday people" (Burd-Sharps/Lewis/Martins 2009: 10). Prior to 2005, Louisiana's human development index ranked poorly among the 50 states and Washington, D.C., coming in 49th and followed by West Virginia and Mississippi (ibid: 6). After the storm, Louisiana came in last in the country in the human development index. In fact, Louisiana came in last in almost all indicators.

The hardest hit population was African American men and boys. *A Portrait of Louisiana* came to this conclusion by viewing income, education, and life expectancy through the filters of race, class, and gender. The report found that the hurricane had set back African American men and boys by *decades*. For white men in New Orleans, the quality of life ranked very highly, on par with Connecticut or New York in 2009. In contrast, for African American men living in Louisiana, the quality of life was much lower, on par with Louisiana in 1990. That is, an African American man, born and raised in Louisiana, might as well had been living in 1990, in terms of income, life expectancy, or education. In fact, white Americans in Louisiana with the lowest income still earned more and were vastly better off than the majority of African Americans in Louisiana in 2009. The median earnings for white men in Louisiana in 2007 were $37.034. Comparatively, African American men in Louisiana earned a median wage of $20.905, and African American women earned even less, about $15.000. Overall, the human development index for African American men in Louisiana is 2.01, on a scale of 0 to 10. For African American women, the index number is a little bit higher at 2.82 (ibid: 6, 29).

Furthermore, a contributing factor to the low quality of life for African American men was the immense growth of the private prison industry in the 1990s and early 2000s. In 2012, the New Orleans *Times-Picayune*, the once daily, Pulitzer Prize winning newspaper, undertook an eight-part investigation of the growth of the prison industry in the state. Entitled "Louisiana Incarcerated: How We Built the World's Prison Capital," the series' findings were astonishing. One in fourteen African American men was incarcerated in Louisiana in 2012. One in seven was in prison, on parole, or on probation. Louisiana's incarceration rate was nearly five times Iran's, thirteen times China's, and twenty times Germany's (cf. Chang/Threlkeld/Smith 2012: n.p.). The growth of the private prison industry has been the subject of many recent inquiries, most of which document how Louisiana experienced a tremendous surge in incarceration after the storm, due to the closing of mental health facilities and the transfer of mentally ill inmates to the local jails and state prison (Kotey 2009: 105-131).

In 2012, New Orleans reached a murder rate of 53 per 100.000 residents, higher than Chicago, New York, or Los Angeles, and second only to Detroit and Flint, Michigan (cf. Federal Bureau of Investigation 2014). The high number of murders in New Orleans confounded city and state officials, especially after the May 2012 murder of Brianna Allen and Shawanna Pierce, victims of a drug-related drive-by shooting in the Central City neighborhood. Yet, the city-wide problems of poverty and violent crime in New Orleans were treated as failures of culture, particularly when the victims and perpetrators were African American.

After 2011 and 2012, when nearly 200 people were killed in each year, the office of Mayor Mitch Landrieu devised new local policy initiatives, emphasizing "life management" skills and training over increased disaster aid, housing relief, and training programs for greater employment (Vargas/Martin 2012: n.p.). The most visible program, *NOLA for Life*, was inaugurated in 2012 to great fanfare, and was supported by donations from director Spike Lee, who made the documentary *When the Levees Broke* (2006) and who also produced the billboard campaign for *NOLA for Life* dotting the city. However, *NOLA for Life* got off to a slow start, and it lacked a concrete agenda. In 2014, *NOLA for Life* was awarded a $250.000 grant from the Robert Wood Johnson Foundation for public health, for a reduction in murders to "a 30-year low" (Daley 2014: n.p.). The connection between *NOLA for Life* and a lower murder rate was tenuous at best, however. What was clear was that, by spring 2014, New Orleans had a population of 86% of its pre-Katrina levels, and that the city's population had been in a gradual decline since the 1960s (cf. Rainey 2014).

In 2013, Hurricane Katrina was no longer on the forefront of the minds of New Orleanians, but it dominated the background. Wilbert "Chill" Wilson, owner of Mr. Chill's First Class Cuts Barber Shop, in an interview, enunciated clearly the intersection of poverty, crime, violence, and gender after Katrina:

First of all, we're going to talk about young men after Hurricane Katrina, young black men... They've been left on an island of their own [for] too long. And they have to find their own way home. No child can find their own way home. And as they grow up they're going to be lost. And a lot of African American kids that grow up in the United States without strong backgrounds are lost. [They are] lost to the ideas of education and religion. ... Lost to the idea of, "who am I?" (Interview Wilson 2013)

The answer to Wilson's question is found in popular African American vernacular, namely in the expression "flipping the script." By reversing the oft-heard racial mythologies about Hurricane Katrina, the photography project, "Ordinary Lives, Extraordinary Times" challenges the stereotypical image of the black male criminal by stressing community involvement and mentoring. The project's point was not to upend the black macho icons of Shaft and Lil Wayne. Indeed, the national television coverage had heavily invested in taking extreme examples of criminality, racializing them, and presenting them as ordinary African American life in New Orleans. Instead, "Ordinary Lives, Extraordinary Times" and the accompanying interviews spent several years capturing African American men and youth engaging in work that addressed the difficult, yet meaningful and altogether ordinary work of reconstructing African American neighborhoods and institutions.

Historian Lynnell L. Thomas has added tremendously to the historical literature of New Orleans history with her penetrating investigations of tourism in New Orleans, before and after Hurricane Katrina. Indeed, Thomas has reinforced the importance of photography projects such as "Ordinary Lives, Extraordinary Times," writing, "What is at stake in this battle over the historical memory of Hurricane Katrina is the very future of black New Orleans and its place in the nation." (2009: 750) It is ironic that many private tours of New Orleans start with the Reconstruction period of 1867, because these tours "sentimentalize slavery, and that ultimately sustains and propagates a racialized image of the city that ultimately diminishes and distorts African American history and culture" (ibid: 748). As Thomas continues, current-day tours continue to exoticize African American neighborhoods and cultures, in a way that emphasizes, ultimately, otherness and subjugation. Before the hurricane, in tours of the predominantly white French Quarter or Garden District there was a concerted effort to portray African Americans as faithful and compliant slaves, while avoiding mostly black neighborhoods as too dangerous. There was no middle ground. In "Ordinary Lives, Extraordinary Times" the centrality of stability of African American life after the storm is reinforced, by constructing ordinariness as both a central aspect of African American life and a privilege that was denied in the national media coverage.

Moreover, "Ordinary Lives, Extraordinary Times" carves out a space in the visual culture of New Orleans that rejects racist cultural categories sentimentalizing segregation and Jim Crow. Its initial goal was to depart significantly from the most common form of African American portraiture, the police mug shot. Over the years, the photographs in the documentary project neither exoticized African American men, as often happened with documentary work of the Mardi Gras Indians, nor did the photographs romanticize African American life in the city, given the long and complicated history of slavery and segregation in New Orleans. Instead, they seek to resolve the question posed by Chef Joe quoted at the beginning of this essay – how does one take a picture of progress? Furthermore, what is the privilege of ordinariness, and how does one photograph it?

By engaging the language of visual culture, "Ordinary Lives, Extraordinary Times" shows another perspective of the New Orleans reconstruction at a time when the face of the new New Orleans was of white benefactors and largesse. In many cases throughout the city, small organizations and businesses led by African American men presented the most viable option for stabilizing a struggling neighborhood. Returning to the image of a boy's first haircut, Marquis sat with a resignation felt by many who knew that a possibly difficult and probably unpleasant task lay before them. It is a matter of great importance that his haircut is at JuJu Bag Café and Barbershop in New Orleans, one of the first businesses to return to the black middle-class neighborhood of Gentilly after the storm. Phyllis Johnson, the co-owner of the JuJu Bag, said that she worked so hard to establish the business in the largely ruined area of Gentilly, because "we said that we would do something at that time that the community needed – which was to have a barber shop, have a little snack bar, a little coffee shop, a little something where people could get away from the devastation of it all, because there was nothing here" (Interview Johnson 2012).

As the documentary project evolved, mentoring between working and middle class African American men and African American youth took a much larger role in the series. Mentoring was a frequent topic of conversation in the oral interviews, and the interviewees most often expressed their hopes for the city in mentoring. "Ordinary Lives, Extraordinary Times" documents other powerful relationships, including peewee football coaching, brass band performances, social aid and pleasure club parades, and the construction of costumes for the Mardi Gras Indians. For instance, Billy Ray Bridges, a member of the Dirty South Riderz Horse Club, a group of African American horse enthusiasts and cowboys, explained that the reason he teaches horseback riding to African American boys was because, "I didn't know about black cowboys in school. I'm doing this to educate people about the black cowboys, especially younger folks." (Interview

Bridges 2012) In the photograph, "Cowboy-in-Training," (cf. fig. 2) the important legacy of Buffalo soldiers has been instilled in an African American teenager who holds his own horse. African American horsemanship has a long and storied history in Louisiana, signifying an authentic narrative and relationship to Louisiana's rural African American culture. The success of the black cowboys was well-known locally, but, despite their survival and success after the storm, was completely overlooked nationally.

Figure 2: "Cowboy-in-Training"

Other mentoring groups envisioned a long relationship with their mentees and maintained high expectations. When talking about mentoring African American youth at middle and high schools, D'Juan Hernandez, partner in the Chafee McCall law firm and co-founder of the Silverback Society, described in detail the process of African American mentoring:

As a reasonably intelligent black man with some level of influence in my community, I needed to get involved and find out what was going on. So I did… What we have not taught some of our [young] teachers is how to identify when some of our young brothers are actually struggling with something. They've got a problem! They've got an issue at home or somewhere in their lives that have led them to what you may think is a disciplinary problem. What we find in the Silverback Society is that when we identify that young brother, we're going to talk to them. And we want to know what's going on with them. (Interview Hernandez 2013)

One photograph, "Mentoring and the Art of Tie-Tying," (cf. fig. 3) depicts this precise moment. The photograph shows a professional African American man, whose class and status have afforded him the resources to buy and wear comfortable, well-made suits. The tie embodies the structure of the suit and the personality of the man wearing it. Mr. Chill, who earlier spoke of "young black boys' social isolation," hosted a tie-tying workshop called "Mr. Chill's Tie Tying on a New Tradition." He specifically intended the workshop to be a transfer of confidence and self-direction from an older, established generation of African American men to a younger one. He concludes, "[t]his tie tying event is really showing them [African American teenagers] that you are a king. You are a prince. You can look your best. Looking your best helps you feel great. Helping you feel great helps you achieve." (Interview Wilson 2013) Mayor Mitch Landrieu attended the event, as did other major public figures in the city, including professors, lawyers, judges, and journalists.

Figure 3: "Mentoring and the Art of Tie-Tying"

The photography project captures the transition from the old story of Hurricane Katrina – the losses of property and employment, lack of resources to rebuild – to the new story of the post-Katrina era, one in which African American men are determined not to be left out of discussions to bring back New Orleans. As the city nears its ten year anniversary of the storm, as government services continue to woefully under-serve black neighborhoods in the city, particularly, in public health and criminal justice, African American men's social groups have taken up the challenge of doing the work state and communal entities have stopped doing. The Silverback Society, a mentoring group connecting professional African American men to black teenagers in middle school, is a fitting example of this new story. D'Juan Hernandez, co-founder of the Silverback Society, offered a resolution to this narrative in this way:

I will never forget, Lloyd [Allen, also a co-founder of the Silverback Society] and I walking into a school on the west bank of the city. And as we walk into the school, there is a mother and a son sitting on the sofa. [He] had already been kicked out. ... [But] one of the basic tenets of what we do for this young brothers is we promise to be there. And so if I say that I'm going to be there on Wednesday at 12:00, every Wednesday at 12:00 I'm there. They need that stability in their lives. They need to trust that. With this guy, because we were there, because it was clear that we loved him, he actually turned around. That young man went from being kicked out and flunking to now being an A/B student in his new school, in the band, doing remarkably well. (Interview Hernandez 2013)

Yet, this story of the cultural politics of Hurricane Katrina is also one of redemption. A reinterpretation of African American visual culture rejects the criminality trope, and it also places the lived experiences of New Orleans' African American men within the larger narrative of the long civil rights movement. Hurricane Katrina showed that the war to eliminate poverty, particularly race-based poverty, remains unfinished. Historian Lawrence Powell tellingly writes that "the tension between capitalism and democracy has also driven politics in this country – the yin and yang of our national creed" (2007: 864). African Americans were failed by both. The successful redefinition of New Orleans for all African Americans – working and middle class, men and women, young and old – will depend on *how* well the counter-narrative of African American reconstruction challenges and prevails over the dominant discourse. "Ordinary Lives, Extraordinary Times" revealed that the renewal of African American New Orleans is not only possible, but highly probable when African American voices and communities form an equal partnership with a good and responsive government, turning the images of a broken charismatic city into faded pictures in a dusty history book.

Bibliography

Books and Articles

Burd-Sharps, Sarah/Lewis, Kristen/Borges Martins, Eduardo (2009): *A Portrait of Louisiana: Louisiana Human Development Report 2009*, New York: American Human Development Project.

Chang, Cindy/Threlkeld, Scott/Smith, Ryan (2012): "Louisiana Incarcerated: How We Built the World's Prison Capital." In: *New Orleans Times-Picayune*, pp. 13-20.

Classen, Steve (2009): "Reporters Gone Wild: Reporters and Their Critics on Hurricane Katrina, Gender, Race, & Place." In: *Journal of e-Media Studies* 2/1, pp.1-11.

Dyson, Michael Eric (2006): *Come Hell or High Water: Hurricane Katrina and the Color of Disaster*, New York: Basic Civitas.

Hendrix Wright, Beverly (1991): "New Orleans: The City That Care Forgot." In: Robert Bullard (ed.), *In Search of the New South: The Black Urban Experience in the 1970s and 1980s*, Tuscaloosa: University Alabama Press, pp.173-198.

Horne, Jed (2006): *Breach of Faith: Hurricane Katrina and the Near Death of a Great American City*, New York: Random House.

Kotey, Phyllis (2009): "Judging Under Disaster: The Effect of Hurricane Katrina on the Criminal Justice System." In: Jeremy Levitt/Mathew Whitaker (eds.), *Hurricane Katrina: America's Unnatural Disaster*, Omaha: University of Nebraska Press, pp.105-113.

Loven, Jennifer (2007): "New Orleans Not Part of Bush's Speech." In: *Washington Post*, March 2, 2015 (http://www.washingtonpost.com/wp-dyn/content/article/2007/01/23/AR2007012301449.html).

Luft, Rachel E. (2009): "Beyond Disaster Exceptionalism: Social Movement Developments in New Orleans after Hurricane Katrina." In: *American Quarterly* 61/3, pp. 499-527.

Mann, Nicola and Victoria Pass (2011): "Introduction: The Cultural Visualization of Hurricane Katrina." In: *Invisible Culture: An Electronic Journal for Visual Culture* 16, (https://www.rochester.edu/in_visible_culture/Issue_16/articles/mann%20and%20pass/mann_pass_intro.html).

Moore, Leonard (2010): *Black Rage in New Orleans: Police Brutality and African American Activism from World War II to Hurricane Katrina*, Baton Rouge: Louisiana State University Press.

Muhammad, Khalil Gibran (2010): *The Condemnation of Blackness: Race, Crime, and the Making of Modern America*, Cambridge: Harvard University Press.

Thomas, Lynnell L. (2009): "'Roots Run Deep Here': The Construction of Black New Orleans in Post-Katrina Tourism Narratives." In: *American Quarterly* 61/3, pp. 749-768.

Wallace, Michele (1990): *Invisibility Blues: From Pop to Theory*, London: Verso.

Watts, Lewis and Eric Porter (2013): *New Orleans Suite: Music and Culture in Transition*, Berkeley: University of California Press.

Online Sources

Café Reconcile (2014): "Katrina and Response." September 20, 2014 (http://cafe reconcile.org/about/history).

Carr, David (2005): "More Horrible Than Truth: News Reports." In: *New York Times*, September 20, 2014 (http://www.nytimes.com/2005/09/19/business/media/19carr.html?pagewanted=all&_r=0).

Daley, Ken (2014) "NOLA for Life awarded $250,000 Grant from New Jersey-based Public Health Foundation." In: *New Orleans Times-Picayune*, September 20, 2014 (http://nola.com/crime/index.ssf/2014/04/nola_for_life_awarded_250000_g.html).

Federal Bureau of Investigation (2012): "Crime in the United States 2012," February 24, 2015 (http://www.fbi.gov/about-us/cjis/ucr/crime-in-the-u.s/2012/crime-in-the-u.s.-2012/cius_home).

Germany, Kent (2007): "The Politics of Poverty and History: Racial Inequality and the Long Prelude to the Katrina." In: *Journal of American History* 94, September 20, 2014 (http://www.journalofamericanhistory.org/projects/katrina/Germany.html), pp.743-751.

Jones, Van (2005): "Black People 'Loot' Food … White People 'Find' Food." May 25, 2011 (http://www.huffingtonpost.com/van-jones/black-people-loot-food-wh_b_6614.html).

"Looters take advantage of New Orleans Mess," September 19, 2014 (http://www.nbcnews.com/id/9131493/ns/us_news-katrina_the_long_road_back/t/looters-take-advantage-new-orleans-mess/#.U2o1oIGSw8d).

"Mrs. Laura Bush meets with Teenagers and Staff during a Lunch and Roundtable Discussion at the Café Reconcile," September 19, 2014 (http://www.georgewbush-whitehouse.archives.gov/news/releases/2007/01/images/20070109-1_p010906sc-0388-1-515h.html).

Otte, Marline (2007): "The Mourning After: Languages of Loss and Grief in Post-Katrina New Orleans." In: *Journal of American History* 94, September 20, 2014 (http://www.journalofamericanhistory.org/projects/katrina/Otte.html), pp. 828-836.

Powell, Lawrence (2007): "What Does American History Tell Us about Katrina and Vice Versa?" In: *Journal of American History* 94, September 20, 2014 (http://www.journalofamericanhistory.org/projects/katrina/Powell.html), pp. 863-876.

Rainey, Richard (2014): "Fewer buses, longer wait times hamper New Orleans' growth, report says." In: *New Orleans Times-Picayune,* September 20, 2014 (http://www.nola.com/politics/index.ssf/2014/07/longer_wait_times_fewer_bus_ro.html).

Scharf, Peter (2010): "The 'Mundane Murders of Post-Katrina New Orleans," February 24, 2015 (http://pbs.org/wnet/tavissmiley/tsr/new-orleans-been-in-the-storm-too-long/the-mundane-murders-of-post-katrina-new-orleans/).

United States Census Bureau American Factfinder (2010): "Profile of General Demographic Characteristics, New Orleans in 2000," September 19, 2014 (http://factfinder2.census.gov/faces/tableservices/jsf/pages/productview.xhtml?pid=DEC_00_SF1_DP1).

Vargas, Ramon Antonia /Naomi Martin (2012): "Murders in New Orleans were slightly fewer in 2012 than in 2011." In: *New Orleans Times-Picayune,* March 2, 2015 (http://nola.com/crime/index.ssf/2012/12/murders_in_new_orleans_were_sl.html).

Interviews

Hernandez, D'Juan and Lloyd Allen, New Orleans, Louisiana, November 2013.
Bridges, Billy Ray, New Orleans, Louisiana, June 2012.
Johnson, Phyllis, New Orleans, Louisiana, July 2012
Robinson, Leroy, New Orleans, Louisiana, September 2012.
Smith, Joe, New Orleans, Louisiana, August 2013
Umrani, Walter, New Orleans, Louisiana, July 2013
Wilson, Wilbert "Chill," New Orleans, Louisiana, September 2013.

Exhibitions

Brown, Nikki (2014): "Ordinary Lives, Extraordinary Times: African American Men in New Orleans After Katrina." McKenna Museum of African American Art, New Orleans, Louisiana.

Lewis Watts: *Baptism Bath in Gutted Church*, Lower 9th Ward 2006

Even a year after the storm, most buildings had not been touched or at the least had only had the mold removed.

The Landscapes of *Man*: Ecological and Cultural Change Before Hurricane Katrina[1]

DEMETRIUS L. EUDELL

> The earth belongs always to the living generation. They may manage it then, and what proceeds from it, as they please, during their usufruct. They are masters too of their own persons, and consequently may govern them as they please.
> — THOMAS JEFFERSON, "LETTER TO JAMES MADISON"

> Human influence has been detected in the warming of the atmosphere and the ocean, in changes in the global water cycle, in reductions in snow and ice, in global mean sea level rise, and in changes in some climate extremes. [...] It is extremely likely that the human influence has been the dominant cause of the observed warming since the mid-20th century.
> — IPCC, 2013 "SUMMARY FOR POLICYMAKERS"

Taking a relatively short chronological sample within a restricted geographical area – European culture since the sixteenth century – one can be certain that Man is a recent invention within it.

---

[1] The article has been reprinted with permission of Brill publishers and originates from: Sommer, Bernd (2015): *Cultural Dynamics of Climate Change and the Environment in Northern America*, Leiden: Brill.

> [...] And that appearance was not the liberation of an old anxiety, the transition into luminous consciousness of an age-old concern, the entry into objectivity of something that had long remained trapped within beliefs and philosophies: it was the effect of a change in the fundamental arrangements of knowledge.
>
> — MICHEL FOUCAULT, THE ORDER OF THINGS

> In consequence, where the Other to the *True Christian Self* of medieval Europe had been the *Untrue Christian Self* (with the external Others being Idolaters and/or Infidels), with the invention of *Man* in two forms (one during the Renaissance in the context of the intellectual revolution of civic humanism, the other in the context of that of Liberal or economic humanism which took place at the end of the eighteenth and during the nineteenth century), Europe was to invent the Other to Man in two parallel forms. And, because *Man* was now posited as a supracultural universal, its Other had logically to be defined as the Human Other.
>
> — SYLVIA WYNTER, "TOWARDS THE SOCIOGENIC PRINCIPLE"

MAN, ITS OTHERS AND ENVIRONMENTAL CHANGE

The event that was Hurricane Katrina lends itself to the posing of some fundamental questions, not only with respect to the infrastructure of US society, but as well regarding the organization and priorities of contemporary global society. Indeed, given the tremendous impact of Hurricane Katrina, it can be useful to employ the moment to reflect upon the historical origins and the implications of the storm. As such a heuristic device, issues related both specifically to New Orleans and the Gulf region and, more widely, to current and urgent concerns of climate and social change, can be raised.

The title of this essay alludes to Ted Steinberg's analysis of the climatic effects of the urban development in South Florida. To explain the transformation of Miami Beach from a low ridge of dunes and dense swamp of red mangroves into a tropical tourist paradise, Steinberg employed the term *manscape* to emphasize the political forces, (that is, of economically powerful men, such as magnates Carl Fisher and Henry Flagler), that helped to create a high-risk environment in South Florida, where 36% of all hurricanes make landfall. For instance, in the early twentieth century, not only did Fisher bulkhead and pave over the swamp at Miami Beach, but he had artificial islands created in the middle of Biscayne Bay. Such developments led to a considerable increase in high-density urbanization and in tourism, and while they generated enormous profits, especially for real estate developers, this growth also became, according to Steinberg, central to creating the "unnatural history of natural disaster", which consequently in the event of extreme weather can create a "deathscape" (2009: 401-405).

The *manscapes* created by this kind of urban development can also be characterized as a logical and systemic consequence of our present global civilization's particular relation(s) to nature. Indeed, such stems not only from the understanding of the natural world, but equally from the specific conception of ourselves as human. Although forces and processes of nature exist beyond human control, there is nonetheless no single interpretation of nature that can be removed from a cultural representation of it, an understanding which then motivates an ensemble of behaviors that produce and reproduce human societies. Otherwise stated, the social and the symbolic remain inextricably linked. The interpretation of nature that in a large measure determines that the contemporary relation with the planetary environment is generated from the governing *topos* of *Man*, encapsulated in Jefferson's contention that as masters of our own persons, each generation can justifiably manage the proceeds from the earth as they please. This understanding of what it means to *Be Human* was based in part on Enlightenment notions of reason, which then recently liberated from the dominance of the organized Church and the centralized State (if nonetheless gradually and partially), became fully autonomous, self-authorizing, self-governing and, if unacknowledged, transcendental. However widespread, and seemingly impermeable to philosophical attack and to change, it is nevertheless a *conception;* and, as the epigraphs from Foucault and Wynter suggest, one that in its first iteration emerged at a particular historical moment and within the frame of a particular culture, that is, toward the end of the Middle Ages in the secularizing field of thought of Judaeo-Christianity.

Wynter noted that the first variant of *Man* appeared in the wake of the intellectual movement of lay humanism, which eventually led to the displacement of the hegemony of Scholasticism. The *studia humanitatis*, shifted the gaze, even if not completely, from the supernatural/theological to the natural realm. In so doing, the 'sacred letters' and scripture that had previously defined the scholastic *episteme* (to borrow Foucault's formulation) would be reoccupied by a new order of knowledge whose objects of inquiry (language, grammar, rhetoric) reflected a prioritization of the study of things human over the formerly hegemonic study of things divine.

Nature in this context would take on a particular meaning. As occurred in other fields of study, such as politics where the Platonic and Aristotelian *politeia* would be reconfigured in the discourses of republicanism (cf. Pocock 1975),[2] a significant strain of Renaissance thinking returned to and built upon Greco-Roman modes of knowing. With regard to the question of the natural world, a reinterpretation and reorganization of knowledge led to the establishment of proto-academic fields of botany and zoology in which plants and animals would be described and taxonomically classified (Debus 1978: 52-53). In the field of scientific medicine, a similar shift occurred. Whereby from the twelfth century, "physicians sought to assure themselves and their students or readers that at least some part of medicine, usually medical theory, met the Aristotelian criteria for true knowledge," after 1450, "a series of intellectual upheavals" called such an approach into question. Renaissance humanism displaced the preoccupation with reconciling Aristotle and Galen, bringing to light not only "hitherto unknown or less studied medical books," but as well "a range of non-Aristotelian philosophies from Plato to skepticism" (Siraisi 2012: 496-497).

New fields of geography and cartography also emerged. Born in part as a result of the fifteenth-century Portuguese voyages in the eastern Atlantic and those of Columbus beginning in 1492, these encounters brought Europeans into sustained contact with societies on the continent of Africa and in the Americas. As they interacted with the populations in these "new worlds," Europeans, having themselves undergone a transformation of their self-conception, came to identify these peoples, not only in religious terms (i.e. as heathens, pagans and idolators), but also as *Indios* and *Negros*, that is, in terms not to be found within the pre-Encounter Christian narrative. These ascriptive models of identity, the epigraph

---

2 Pocock's seminal study *The Machiavellian Moment: Florentine Political Thought and the Atlantic Republican Tradition* (1975) traces the rebirth of the discourses on citizenship as they reemerged in the ideas of civic humanism in the fifteenth century, and then later in the eighteenth century. As responses to the universality asserted by Judaeo-Christianity, these political vocabularies had to confront what he defined as the secular particularity of the 'Machiavellian moment.'

from Wynter intimates, transformed these populations from understanding their social worlds within their own autocentric cosmogonies, to being *Human Others* in the cosmogony of nature of *Homo politicus* (political *Man*). Such classifications served as the basis upon which the enslavement of those of African hereditary descent together with the dispossession of Indigenous peoples of the Americas would come to be perceived as legitimate and just.

Expropriation of the lands domesticated and inhabited by the Indigenous peoples consequently transformed the landscape of the Americas. Before the coming of Europeans, a specific ecology, or set of them, populated the hemisphere. Recent scholarship has returned to the interpretation of the first settlers and explorers who initially encountered the Indigenous peoples and noted their use of fire, which had profoundly shaped the landscape. Although in the nineteenth-century understanding of Indigenous societies, the use of fire was often denied, now scholars have come to agree that the Indigenous peoples utilized fire for many purposes, such as for hunting, which entailed encouraging undergrowth to increase the presence of herbivores and their predators or surrounding animals with fire to trap them. For pastoralists, burning was useful for moving animals around as well as "to drive off noxious insects." It would also be centrally used to control and harvest crops, as fire "reset the ecological clock" by encouraging plants that need sunlight to grow and "to increase the production of berries, seeds, nuts, and other gathered foods." Fire could also be used as an offensive and defensive weapon, driving away strangers and enemies. It could be utilized to clear routes for travel and as a mode of communication, "propelling messages from one group to the next, and could be 'read' as far as one hundred miles from their source in as short a time as one-half hour." Moreover, among the many uses of fire, not all of them were strictly utilitarian, as it could be used in rituals or, according to one explorer, for the most trivial of reasons. Such is because within the "myriad indigenous understandings of the natural world," fire was constituted "as a powerful force or being" which remained indistinguishable from their specific self-conceptions and relations with natural and supernatural forces (Krech 1999: 101-122; Mann 2006: 250; Pyne 2001: 46-64).

From a global historical perspective, the use of fire by Indigenous peoples of the Americas was not unique. Fire, Stephen J. Pyne has argued, has been fundamental to the existence of both nature and human cultures: "the living world runs on combustion and has co-evolved with the open flame" (2012: 9). And, whilst fire can exist without humans, "it has been a species possession – a defining trait" (ibid.), which no other species has been able to manipulate. Consequently, fire has remained central to the shaping of landscapes, that is, to the adaptation of ecosystems based upon the "prescriptions and codes" (ibid.) of a multiplicity of ways of being and behaving in the world. Moreover, according to the scholars who argue that "the Earth has left its natural geological epoch," the Holocene, it was "the mastery of fire by our ancestors... that puts us firmly on the long path toward the Anthropocene" (Steffen/Crutzen/McNeil 2007: 614). But, was it such a natural and seemingly inevitable process?

In the context of Louisiana and the wider Mississippi River valley, it has also been established that the Indigenous landscape was marked by the impressive (social and technical) engineering feats of earthen mounds. These elevated surfaces were "a form of monumental architecture, constructed eminences on which activities were conducted or buildings were placed." Extending from southern Canada and the Great Plains to the Gulf of Mexico and the Atlantic coast, estimates of their antiquity vary from 100 BC to Charles C. Mann's assessment that "the earliest known examples appeared in northeastern Louisiana 5400 years ago, well before the advent of agriculture." In addition to being the residences of chiefs and other elites, mounds could serve as burial sites, as communal spaces for the performance of rituals and ceremonies as well as centralized facilities for extensive feasting and food storage (Lindauer/Blitz 1997: 170, 192; Mann 2006: 254-255).

The building of mounds and the use of fire represent for Mann "two paradigmatic examples" of the Indigenous peoples "on a very large scale, transforming huge swathes of the landscape for their own ends" (2006: 248). Such should perhaps lay to rest the once frequent romantic notion that before the arrival of Western Europeans in the Americas the Indigenous peoples existed in an Edenic setting. Arguing against this "pristine myth", William Denevan has noted that the Indigenous people made imprints on the vegetation, wildlife, agriculture, and the built environment, whereby not only were cultivated fields common, but in various locations, so were houses, towns, and roads, all of which consequently "had local impacts on soil, microclimate, hydrology, and wildlife" (2003: 5). Archaeologists employing the panarchy theory of interacting physical and social systems, have reached a similar conclusion:

Paleoecological and archaeological studies reinforce the conclusion that throughout the late Pleistocene and Holocene, environmental change has been the rule rather than the exception. Climate changes on all scales in space and time, and changes in the distribution and composition of both flora and fauna occur continually in response to changes in climate. (Delcourt/Delcourt 2004: 164)

This understanding of Indigenous modes of environmental change in the Americas necessarily challenges as well the representation of the "ecological

Indian," a variation of the equally static Noble Savage stereotyped image; both expressions, of what Johannes Fabian has characterized as the denial of coevalness in which the anthropologist (as observer) and the ethnographic object (as the observed native) do not share the same time (Krech 1999: 14-19; cf. Fabian 1983).[3] The notion that the Indigenous peoples were natural ecologists and conservationists was most iconically conveyed in the popular imaginary by Louisiana-born actor Iron Eyes Cody's portrayal of the Crying Indian for the 1970s "Keep America Beautiful" anti-pollution campaign.[4]

Moreover, transformations of ecology have not only been restricted to human modes of existence. In his now classic and highly-influential 1967 essay, "The Historical Roots of Our Ecological Crisis," Lynn White Jr. noted: "All forms of life modify their contexts: The most spectacular and benign instance is doubtless the coral polyp. By serving its own ends, it has created a vast undersea world favorable to thousands of other kinds of animals and plants" (1203). Thus, the phenomenon of climate change itself is neither recent nor exclusively a Western attribute nor restricted to an industrial form of social organization.

Although environmental change can be seen as a phenomenon of all living beings and cultures, all imprints are not created equal, nor do they all generate the same kind of ecological change. Indeed, whilst societies that pre-existed the industrial world "influenced their environment in many ways, from local to continental scales," the impacts that these ways of being in the world have "remained largely local and transitory," and according to some environmental scientists and historians "within the bounds of the natural variability of the environment." Such was due to modes of being, believing and behaving that did not produce the "social and economic organization, or technologies needed to equal or dominate the great forces of Nature in magnitude or rate" (Stephen/ Crutzen/Mc Neill 2007: 615).

The emergence therefore of secular economic *Man*, that is, of *Homo œconomicus*, the Being whom Adam Smith defined as primarily motivated by a "propensity to truck, barter, and exchange"[5] constituted a singular departure with

---

3   Fabian coined the term allochronism to describe this conceptual approach to understanding non-Western societies.
4   Cody's Cherokee/Cree heritage has been disputed, although his commitment to causes of the Indigenous peoples has not. See Angela Aleiss, "Native Son," *The Times Picayune*, May 26, 1996, D1.
5   Smith noted: "This division of labour, from which so many advantages are derived, is not originally the effect of any human wisdom, which foresees and intends that general opulence to which it gives occasion. It is the necessary, though very slow and gradual

respect to the ecological transformation of the planet. Although associated with Smith, he did not actually employ this term, and moreover, Mary S. Morgan has argued, Smith's understanding of this figure, unlike that of Thomas Malthus (and many later proponents), comprised additional and complex motivations beyond self-interest, although such was nevertheless a precondition of modern social organization. Critiques of this social theory began from its early articulations, with it being characterized as a "fictional construction to motivate a virtuous story about commercial society" (2006:3-4). However, regardless whether its explanatory power with respect to "human nature" and motivations can deliver on its claims, over time with the force of many theorists and practitioners, an economic self-interested human nature has become the dominant principle to account for human behavior, one according to which, the realization of full humanness is evidenced by the attainment of ever-increasing, higher and higher standards of living. In other words, it is the postulation of an 'economic' definition of socio-human orders, an interpretation which was first systematically articulated within the Scottish Enlightenment stadial theory, which hypothesized the evolution of societies from nomadic hunter-gathering to pastoral herding, to agricultural farming to a commercial/exchange basis for social organization (cf. Meek 1976).[6] Moreover, Marxist formulations of history (as being based on shifts from feudalist, to capitalist, to socialist *modes of production*) together with the argument for the nationalization of the means of production, do not deviate from an understanding of the human past primarily through modes of subsistence. Yet, it is the definition of the human in predominantly economic terms that legitimate mass consumption and the accumulation of surplus and abundance as virtuous behaviors on the one hand, but which on the other hand, bear a direct relation to the question of climate change.

The identification of the Anthropocene era, as a rupture with previous human societies correlates with this argument. According to Will Steffen, Paul Crutzen, and John R. McNeill, this shift to a high energy-based industrial world occurred in three stages. Coming on the heels of the Enlightenment, the first stage from the beginning of the nineteenth to the middle of the twentieth centuries can be identified by "the enormous use of fossil fuels, first coal and then oil and gas well" which "as a rule" used "four or five times as much energy as did agrarian

---

    consequence of a certain propensity in human nature which has in view no such extensive utility; the propensity to truck, barter, and exchange one thing for another." ([1776] 1976: 25)

6   Meek's account remains an indispensable work for understanding the complex role and changes of this idea.

[societies], which in turn used three or four times as much as did hunter gatherers." The second stage, coming after the Second World War and continuing to the present moment (2015 according to these authors), can be identified by economic and population growth that proceeded "faster than at any previous time in human history." Central to this process has been the dramatic increase in the use of petroleum, especially for motor vehicles. The third stage posits that "humankind will remain a major geological factor for many millennia, maybe millions of years to come," an assertion that concurs with the conclusion of the Intergovernmental Panel on Climate Change (IPCC), that "most aspects of climate change will persist for many centuries even if emissions of CO2 are stopped" (2013: 27, Steffen/Crutzen/McNeill 2007: 616-618).

Yet, if the first stage of the Anthropocene began in the early nineteenth century, how does one characterize the preceding time period from the fifteenth century to the end of the eighteenth century, when Western Europeans had begun to establish a global, if nonetheless contested, hegemony? A central aspect implicit in the Anthropocene framework, although it is not stated as forcefully and frequently as it could be, relates to another pre-industrial, pre-fossil fuel *use of energy*, that is, enslaved labor, one whose employment remained essential to the conditions of possibility that made such a system realizable (cf. Steffen/Crutzen/McNeill 2007: 615).[7] Moreover, whilst both the analyses of the Anthropocene advocates and the IPCC remain insightful with respect to understanding the depth of the contemporary imprint on the Earth System, further contextualization could be employed to explicate phrases such as "anthropogenic emissions" and "human influence" as well as statements such as "the human-induced contribution to warming" and the "central role of humankind" (ibid: IPCC 2013: 17,19).

The provocative term Anthropocene derived from the Greek, *anthropos* meaning "human, mankind" and *cene*, meaning "new" draws attention to the distinctive intervention on the environment of our present world-system and mode of existence. Yet, it also seems to minimize an understanding in which such an imprint can be seen to have only been possible by the emergence of a distinctly new conception of Being Human. In other words, the contemporary state of the climate can be ascribed not necessarily to actions of 'humankind,' but rather by a specific conception of humankind, an understanding of recent historical origin, and one into which members of all societies are now increasingly being induced

---

7   Steffen, Crutzen, and McNeill note that although fossil fuels would be used during the Chinese Song Dynasty (960-1279) and in seventeenth-century London, these were exceptions.

at a global level to internalize and to enact. Furthermore, this conception has been based on a series of Human Others, who would be initially drawn into its framework either through settler and non-settler colonialisms or racially-based enslavement.

The implications remain that the forecast provided by the Anthropocene proponents of "a bottleneck of continued population growth, excessive resource and environmental deterioration" resulting from behaviors during the era of "Great Acceleration" does not sufficiently distinguish in which sectors of the world excessive resource use can be found (Steffen/Crutzen/McNeill 2007: 620). Nor is it fully articulated that this population growth, most extreme in Africa, is not necessarily a concern over a lack of space, but rather a scarcity of basic necessities, a phenomenon produced by the daily operations of the Western-dominated world system. In other words, much of the world's population is paying a price equal to that of the environment. It is therefore in this context that analysis of the history of the settlement of Louisiana is undertaken in order to illustrate the intersection of ecological and cultural issues before the onset of the Anthropocene era.

COLONIALISM, SLAVERY, AND LEVEE CONSTRUCTION

Hurricane Katrina has been described as the most costly tropical cyclone and, according to some, "natural" disaster in the history of the United States (cf. Blake/Landsea/Gibney 2011: 5, 9; Woolsey 2008: n.p.).[8] The levees, which did not hold in the wake of the storm, were a product of a historic understanding and approach to the environment that dates to the colonial origins of the founding of Louisiana as well as to the formation of the social and economic system that would come to define the Americas. As Jeffrey Owens has argued in his seminal study on the early history of levees on the Mississippi, the Indigenous peoples understood the natural patterns of the river, to which they often accommodated themselves by raising mounds, sometimes "with a temple and chief's house upon

---

8 According to the Insurance Information Institute, "Hurricane Katrina remains the largest single loss event in the history of the global insurance industry, causing an estimated $41.1 billion in insured damages ($45.1 billion in 2009 damages) and 1.7 million claims across six states" (cf. Hartwig, Robert P. and Claire Wilkinson, "Hurricane Katrina: The Five Year Anniversary").

them, which were used as a refuge during flooding" (1999: 20). Another response involved periodic migrations from the floodplains to higher grounds.[9]

Thus, whilst natural conditions heavily influence, and can often circumscribe, the way in which a society comes to be formed, as Owens further noted, there remained no one single approach to the environment in this location: "Native Americans in the floodplain of the Mississippi did not endeavor to prepare large fields for cash crop agriculture, nor did they try to prevent overflows with levees." Indeed, as Daniel Usner has argued, "what became New Orleans had been mainly used by Indians for transport between waterways and seasonal gathering of food sources." Thus, the conditions that "made this site ideal for portage and fishing reduced its potential for permanent occupation" (ibid: 21; Usner 2006: 164). And, for European settlers permanent occupation indeed became the overarching goal, one which according to Jefferson, as noted in the epigraph, meant the 'living generation' could manage the land as they pleased, unless such management, as was the case with the Indigenous peoples, directly contradicted the notion of order of European colonization and expropriation.

The arrival therefore of Europeans, firstly the French, constituted a profound and distinct intervention in the ecological context of the area. With a vision to establish a city in a swampy terrain susceptible to flooding, a particular attitude toward land and a specific set of social arrangements for those who would inhabit such a space would be required. As Eleonora Rohland notes, despite being informed by the Indigenous peoples of the Mississippi's flood-regime, "the sources yield no evidence regarding the transmission of 'hurricane knowledge' from one group to the other" (Rohland 2014: 5). In Craig Colten's formulation, New Orleans was "an unnatural metropolis" (cf. 2005), one that had to be wrested

---

9   Owens relies here on a description of Native American homes given by a member of Hernando De Soto's expedition, who suggested that the Indigenous peoples built homes on high ground when possible, but raised artificial mounds in areas that tended to overflow (1999: 107). As previously noted, mounds could serve several different purposes. Most discussions of the mounds do not mention them being used as refuge against flooding, and given that some were presumably built where flooding was not a concern, such would make sense. In the wake of the Great Mississippi Flood of 1927, the archaeologist Alfred Kidder was cited in an article in *Science* also stating that the Indigenous peoples built mounds as refuges from floods. See "Indian Mounds as Flood Refuges," *Science* 65.1688 (6 May 1927): xiv. An assessment regarding Cahokia, a large settlement with most impressive mounds, also obliquely relates to such a possibility: "There is little indication that the Cahokia floods killed anyone, or even led to widespread hunger." (Mann 2006: 265)

from nature. So, from the beginning of the European colonization of what would become Louisiana, the social issues related to land use had to be negotiated.

Construction of the first levees, "ridges of soil heaped up along the natural high ground to hold back high waters," began in the early 1720s, not long after the French began in 1718 to settle the colony. It was a project executed under the direction of the Company of the Indies (*Compagnie des Indes*), the trading company charged with colonial settlement and development of French Louisiana. Popularly known as the Mississippi Company, it was established in 1719 by the Scottish financier John Law, and was an expansion of the Company of the West (*Compagnie d'Occident*) which had been created two years before from a merger of the organization with the other overseas trading companies: Company of the East Indies, Company of China, and Company of Africa (Murphy 1997: 188-212).

The Company of the West had taken over the direction of the political affairs of colony, together with a commercial monopoly, from the colony's first proprietor, Antoine Crozat. It was created in order to address the financial situation produced by Louis XIV's economic policies, which had led to a substantial accumulation of debt. Modeled on the British South Sea Company, it had "the dual objectives of (1) debt management and (2) development of colonial trade" and for these reasons, "was granted a trading privilege in exchange for the company's conversion of depreciated government debt, at a lower interest rate, into company stock." In its agreement with the Crown, "the company was given exclusive trading rights to French Louisiana for twenty-five years, while the Crown benefited by the company's conversion on the part of the floating debt into shares at a lower interest rate." Law's ambitious investment scheme furthermore involved the absorption of the country's mint as well as the tax farmers (*fermiers généraux*), the system by means of which taxes were collected for the government. Moreover, after several unsuccessful attempts with other central governments, Law convinced the French Crown in 1716 to allow to establish a privately-owned bank, the General Bank, which was nationalized in 1718 as the Royal Bank (*Banque Royale*), increasing its power according to his "grand design." Law considered the Mississippi Company and the bank "not as distinct separate entities but as one unique enterprise," whose merger would solve France's monetary and financial crises (cf. ibid: 112, 167-169, 185).

By 1720, Law's Mississippi System, "a new El Dorado" based on an "orgy of speculation," had collapsed, although not before making some extremely rich; indeed, from this event, the term millionaire would be introduced into the modern lexicon (Thomas 1997: 242-243; Murphy 1997: 3). As a result of Law's failure, the Company of the Indies surrendered its authority and was eventually forced in 1731 to retrocede the colony to the Crown. The intervening years ushered in an era of new governance, which began in April 1723 with the arrival of royal commissioners and new councilors in the *Conseil Supérieur* and *Conseil de Régie* (Giraud 1991: 3). During this time, the Superior Court/Council, which would eventually function as the actual governing body of the colony of Louisiana, conducted primarily judicial functions, whilst the Administrative Council performed legislative duties. As the colonial settlers sought to create a livable habitat out of flood-prone swampy area, the Superior Court/Council needed to determine the kind of labor system that would facilitate this endeavor (ibid: 11-14; Micelle 1968: 85-107).

Although from the beginning of French settlement few colonists were able to procure, through individual means, slaves from Caribbean colonies, it was not until 1719 that enslaved Africans would be imported in relatively more substantial numbers. Approximately 500 were brought to and spread out over the vast colony that then stretched from the Gulf of Mexico to present-day Illinois (Thomas 1997: 242-243). For those subjected to such a tragic voyage, not only would survival of the journey itself become a challenge, but as well the general precarious conditions of existence in the colony that they faced upon arrival. Expectedly, the death toll was extremely high, as evidenced by only a marginal increase in the presence of Africans from 1719 to 1721, when according to the 1721 census 2000 had come during this period. Moreover, it was not only with those experiencing the horrors of the Middle Passage, who encountered a high death toll, but such was also true for the over one thousand European contract laborers (including a distinctive German population) and those convicted of crimes, who came in 1717 under the auspices of John Law's Company of the West (Usner 1979: 25, 28).

Given the harsh environment, immediately upon arrival in a strange new land, the enslaved were compelled to grow crops not only for their own subsistence, but also for that of the slaveholding colonists. Indeed, they would take on much of the agricultural labor as well as perform significant skilled labor to build the society, such that, within the first decade of their arrival, slaves owned by the Company of the Indies and by individual colonists "were apprenticed to brickmakers, joiners, blacksmiths, locksmiths, sculptors, wheelwrights, saddlers, masons, and carpenters" (ibid: 34). Moreover, according to Gwendolyn Hall, "[t]he survival of French Louisiana was due not only to African labor but also to African technology," specifically knowledge of rice and indigo production that slaves brought with them (Hall 1992:121-124).

Another area where slaves of African descent served a crucial role occurred with the building of levees. The initial attempts to use levees in the early 1720s to address the problems in New Orleans of flooding, dampness, and moist ground that caused illnesses, required a substantial amount of intense labor, which the colonists did not want to assume. Consequently, the building process did not advance until the arrival of 200 slaves in October 1723 and January 1724 on the *Expédition* and the *Courrieur de Bourbon* respectively (Giraud 1991: 206-207). Before being auctioned off, the labor of newly arriving survivors of the Middle Passage was under the control of the Company, who would forcibly employ them on their plantations as well as to work on the levees. In fact, in 1728, a *corvée* was instituted, which stipulated that every colonist who had been granted slaves was required to allow their labor to be employed for public works for thirty workdays (cf. ibid: 208; Usner 2006: 32).

The twin birth in New Orleans of levee construction and the expansion of slavery in the colony (and thus in the wider colonial French Louisiana) illustrates the inseparability of questions of ecological change from those of social formation, evidenced at a moment when a new society was quite literally being created; one, of course, that transformed the landscape, as many colonial settlements were actually built on Indigenous ones. Expansion from New Orleans, where the first levee was constructed, into the hinterlands required an extraordinary exertion of labor. As a result, in 1728 and 1743 landowners were required to build levees that linked the growing agricultural localities with the more urbanized area of New Orleans. Yet, this goal of building an unbroken series of levees could not be realized because the construction of levees "became a sizable investment for landowners and was only feasible for wealthy planters using slave labor" (Colten 2005: 20).[10]

Consequently, as Craig Colten has chronicled, by the end of the first phase of French possession of Louisiana in 1763, privately built structures of varying capabilities were constructed approximately fifty miles along the riverfront above New Orleans, although "floods continued to breach these ever-lengthening earthen embankments." It was therefore becoming increasingly clear that levees could not eradicate the dangerous potential of flooding, and some argued, actually exacerbated the problem, especially since they redirected high water into unprotected territory. These concerns continued through the years of occupation by the Spanish, who had also adopted the contiguous levee policy, and the US

---

10 A parallel exists with the *corvée* and the requirement of planters to build levees with the creation of dike societies on the coast of the North Sea: "Every owner of the land was obliged to take care of the dike, be it individually, for a certain section of the dike *(Pfanddeichung),* or be it collectively with other members of the community *(Kommuniondeichung).* Anyone who violated this obligation could be forced to leave his land. A proverb in Low-German says: 'De nich will dieken, mutt wieken.' (He who does not want to build dikes, must go)." (Kempe 2007: 331-332)

incorporation of the territory in 1803. During the regime of the former, in 1785 a massive flood engulfed New Orleans and the lower valley, and under the latter's administration, successive floods in 1809, 1811, 1813, 1815, 1816, and 1817 also challenged the viability of the levee system. Moreover, by this time, the height of the levees in New Orleans had been raised from four to six feet, structures that were maintained with chain-gang labor. Subsequent high water on the Mississippi in 1823 and 1828 continued to prompt the questioning of the viability of the levee system, but the option of outlets proposed by some was supported neither by the government nor by planters in the hinterland: "Outlets would mean huge expenses for the state, and it would expose plantations along the bayous used as floodways to damaging inundations." (ibid: 20-26)

According to John M. Barry, the debate as to whether to employ levees or outlets to protect against flooding has always reflected two oppositional understandings of the non-human environment: "Levees represented man's power over nature; outlets represented man's accommodation to nature."(Barry 1997: 39) And, here a precision can be proposed that suggests *"Man,"* not as isomorphic with the human, but rather as a specific conception of Being Human. Indeed, levees were not just structures designed to hold back and redirect overflowing waters. At their origins they were fundamental to the viability of New Orleans and the wider Louisiana colony in this specific social formation. In the eighteenth century, inhabited regions for colonists were determined by where levees had been constructed and sustained. As Owens noted, "[l]evees secured Louisiana's principal population centers and guarded the colony's most progressive sectors of development." One of these sectors was agriculture, as the levees were central to protecting crops and farms. Moreover, in the case of New Orleans in the 1720s, the levee "performed special and diversified tasks," including providing docking facilities where cargo could be loaded and unloaded, serving "as a commercial fixture where trading and warehousing occurred," functioning as fortification in the event of attack, and becoming the site of the first French market in the colony. In other words, without a levee no life was possible in New Orleans (Owens 1999: 40, 76).

And, so to build such a social order in such environmental conditions, Black slave labor was deemed necessary. The slaves of Joseph Villars Du Breuil were "known to have helped clear the site of New Orleans and also worked on the city's first levee" (ibid. 36). Across the Americas, slave labor was often utilized for public purposes, and in New Orleans this pattern was followed. To secure such labor, another Black Code (*Code Noir*) was issued in 1724, following upon the original act of 1685 drafted by Jean-Baptiste Colbert, which had been designed to address slavery in France's Caribbean colonies. The 1724 act concerned French

Louisiana and contained many of the same provisions: requirement of slaveholders to provide for slaves materially and religiously, status of children born under slavery followed that of the mother, and severe penalties for striking a White slaveholder. The act also forbade White subjects of both sexes from marrying with the slaves. Although functioning in a context defined by some historians as being fluid where contempt for the poor also existed (Hall 1992: 128), and being careful not to overemphasize the effects of laws in determining the social reality (Johnson 2000: 122), the 1724 act nonetheless made clear that slaves lacked any political subjectivity. It was stipulated in Clause XXIV:

Slaves shall be incapable of all public functions, and of being constituted agents for any other person than their own masters, with powers to manage or conduct any kind of trade; nor can they serve as arbitrators or experts; nor shall they be called to give their testimony either in civil or in criminal cases, except when it shall be a matter of necessity, and only in default of white people; but in no case shall they be permitted to serve as witnesses either for or against their masters. (qtd. in French 1851: 92)

LEVEES, SLAVERY, AND THE 'EMPIRE OF LIBERTY'

In the wake of the Louisiana Purchase in 1803, the co-existence of the issues of land use and slavery remained central for the U.S. government as it took control of the territory. Philosophically, unlike empires in the past that over time degenerated and collapsed, the Louisiana Purchase for President Thomas Jefferson "promised to preserve the fundamentally agricultural, and hence republican, character of American societies for centuries to come." Being highly impressed by and also diverging from Malthus's theory of population, Jefferson's westward expansion would serve as "the only effective antidote to population growth, development through time, and the corruption that accompanied." Therefore, by "enlarging the empire of liberty," new sources of renovation could be provided, which would maintain the virtue of the nation (McCoy 1980: 190-203). Jefferson's "empire for liberty," which almost doubled the size of the nation, proclaimed to spread happiness through self-government and economic prosperity, except for Blacks (for whom he favored colonisation) and Indigenous peoples, and even to a secondary degree, Spanish and French citizens. It was, according to James Murrin, a gallant attempt to combine "expansion, hegemony, and small government" (Murrin 2000: 2-4).[11]

Moreover, the Louisiana Purchase reignited the inflammatory question of slavery that the ratification of the U.S. Constitution had merely deferred with its compromises. In the 1804 Senate debate, James Jackson representing Georgia insisted that, "Slavery must be established in that country or it must be abandoned." Otherwise, as the New Jersey senator Jonathan Dayton claimed, the territory would revert to a state of wilderness (Rothman 2005: 27-28). In other words, a link between a particular understanding of the environment and slavery was being forged now from the beginning of the U.S. occupation of Louisiana.

After Louisiana entered the Union formally as a state in 1812, slavery remained quite essential for its development. Just the year before, the largest slave rebellion in the United States occurred in St. John the Baptist and St. Charles Parishes, located just above New Orleans. This event occurred in the midst of the sugar boom, which had begun being cultivated under Spanish rule during the 1780s, and which created large plantations that displaced smaller ones producing indigo and rice (ibid: 106). On the eve of the Civil War, sugar had become the principal crop of southern Louisiana, where some of the richest and largest plantations in the South could be found; this, although sugar estates constituted only just over a third of all plantations, and of these, where less than half of the lands were used to cultivate it (McDonald 2003: 486). The increase in sugar production also led to the growth of New Orleans as the site of the largest slave market in North America, which was located adjacent to the levee (Johnson 2000: 2). The slave market, according to Robert Evans Jr. "performed for the antebellum South some of the functions now performed by the New York Stock Exchange, i.e., it served in the eyes of the public as a sensitive reflector of current and future business prospects. As a consequence, the price of slaves, especially in other parts of the South, was often mentioned by local newspapers and by local citizens in letters and diaries, which are sources of conceptions of the general movement of slave prices." (1962: 197-198)

---

11 As Murrin noted, Jefferson first used the phrase in December 1780 in his instructions to George Rogers Clark (older brother of William Clark of the Lewis and Clark expedition) and then subsequently in a letter to James Madison in April 1809, where he asserted confidently that like Louisiana, the Floridas, Cuba and Canada would be annexed, establishing "such an empire for liberty as she has never surveyed since the creation." Jefferson further declared that "no constitution was ever before so well calculated as ours for extensive empire and self-government" (Murrin 2000 3-4).

U. B. Phillips's provocative contention that slavery was "less a business than a life" since "it made fewer fortunes than men," implicitly acknowledged the ontological centrality of slavery in shaping the identity of Whites, and given its role in the Northern economy, not only in the South (Phillips 1966: 401). In this regard, as Walter Johnson has shown, the business of the slave market played a key role: "All of the values associated with the antebellum South – the poses and posturing, the whiteness and independence, the calculation and mastery, the hospitality and gentility, the patriarchy and paternalism [...], the honor, brutality, and fancy – were daily packaged and sold in the slave market." In addition to the very powerful economic motivations therefore, slaveholders "bought slaves to make themselves frugal, independent, socially acceptable, *or even fully white*; they acted in accordance with the necessities of their business or the exigencies of their households; they covered the contingency of their own identities in the capacious promises of paternalism, [...] they obscured the dependency of their fantasies with the brutality of their mastery." Slavery therefore enabled the realization of Whites, here slaveholding men (even if not fully industrial bourgeois *Homo œconomicus*) but nonetheless, as fully human, as *Man*: "Using the ideological imperatives of slaveholding culture—whiteness, independence, rationality, necessity, patriarchy, honor, paternalism, and fancy, they produced, in the classic formation, freedom out of slavery." (Johnson 200: 122)

Moreover, in the context of antebellum Louisiana, the issue of sustaining the viability of a slave society had significant environmental implications. At its peak of prominence in the 1840s, New Orleans, due to its location near the mouth of the Mississippi River, where "it collected the output of midwestern farms and southern cotton plantations," competed with Baltimore as the second largest city in the nation (Vigdor 2008: 138). During this time, the levees continued to be utilized as the primary mechanism to manage inundations. Their use had increased after the flood of 1828, when the government initiated a campaign to build additional ones: "Parishes raised taxes to pay for the construction of levees and passed laws requiring proprietors along the river to maintain them properly." (Pabis 1998: 426) Yet, as the result of a devastating flood in 1844, a change occurred with the passage of the Swamp Land Acts of 1849 and 1850, in which the Federal Government granted state governments swamp and overflow lands, which had previously been viewed as impediments to land cultivation and to development in general, when not, in fact, seen, in Harriet Beecher Stowe's terms, as "dangerous and evil places" (Colten 2005: 33).[12] Technically, the public lands

---

12 This aesthetic is powerfully rendered in Stowe's novel *Dred,* whose very title invokes the swamp as an abode of otherness. The swamp therefore represents for Stowe also a

were donated so that the state governments could sell them to investors, for which the proceeds would be used for flood control.

Despite the corruption that led to most of the funds falling into the hands of land speculators, the process produced a debate between civil and military engineers concerning the nature of a comprehensive flood control policy. This discussion resulted from the decision in 1851 by Secretary of War Charles Conrad to grant the state of Louisiana's request for a federal survey of the Mississippi River. The civilian survey was conducted by Charles Ellet Jr., who came with impressive credentials, such as having built the first suspension bridge (over the Schuylkill River in Philadelphia) as well as extensive engineering experience in Europe. In his 1853 report, *The Mississippi and Ohio Rivers*, Ellet argued that the Mississippi flooded for four reasons: "the expansion of cultivation, the extension of the levee system, the creation of cutoffs, and the natural elongations of the Mississippi into the Gulf of Mexico." To address the issue, he also proposed four approaches: "build stronger levees, improve natural outlets, create artificial outlets, and install a system of reservoirs" (Pabis 1998: 430-434).

Ellet's report received mixed reactions. While lauded as masterful by some, Captain Andrew Humphreys of the Corps of Topographical Engineers, who led the Mississippi Delta Survey, concluded that the evidence substantiated neither Ellet's claims of the role of cultivation, nor of reservoirs, nor of expanding natural outlets. Ellet himself had claimed that further data would be needed to verify his theories. Moreover, in all these cases, Humphreys asserted, even if they were implemented, the costs were prohibitive. Thus after conducting a thorough survey of every aspect of the river related to flood control, through a process of elimination that offered a strong evidence-based critique of Ellet's survey, Humphreys determined that levees remained the most effective way to control flooding. And, one could surmise probably from his standpoint the most cost-effective as well, though Humphreys did acknowledge that they were expensive to build and to maintain (ibid: 435-449).

In the wake of the rise of proto-scientific management, where hydraulic engineering played a role in the development of internal improvements, the "levees only" approach was solidified. By the onset of the U.S. Civil War, the

---

corruption of morals, and thus became an impediment to social progress. In describing the characteristics of Dred, the son of the rebel Denmark Vesey, she notes: "The wild, dreary belt of swamp-land which girds in those states scathed by the fires of despotism in an apt emblem, in its rampant and we might say delirious exuberance of vegetation, of that darkly struggling, wildly vegetating swamp of human souls, cut off, like it, from the usages and improvements of cultivated life." (Stowe [1856] 1968: 273-227)

country had constructed a levee system "built largely by slaves and convicts and paid for by taxes on shippers, mandated contributions from upstream planters, and the state" (Colten 2005: 33). This theory held until the Great Mississippi Flood of 1927 vitiated it. After this disaster, a series of reservoirs, floodways, cut-offs, and spillways – some of the things proposed by Ellet in the 1850s – were adopted. The Great Flood of 1927 also powerfully revealed the intimate relation in the post-slavery context of racial hierarchy and the construction of levees that had previously defined the use of enslaved labor during the antebellum era. In response to the flood, 154 relief camps were created through the combined efforts of the Red Cross, the Department of Commerce, and the National Guard to provide housing and provisions to flood refugees. And, since the South was rigidly segregated on the basis of the "separate but equal" doctrine, one which was codified in Louisiana in the 1896 Supreme Court case *Plessy v. Ferguson*, then so were the camps (Spencer 1994: 172).

Since "separate but equal" often meant "separate and starkly unequal," treatment in the camps differed along racial lines. Whereas in camps for Whites, "National Guard Officers helped in camp administration and performed, at most, an advisorial role to the refugees," on the other hand, the National Guard was armed in the Black camps, which "served as holding pens designed to ensure the retention and preservation of the Southern labor force." As a result, Black refugees were often not allowed to leave the camps and repeatedly "were being conscripted out to local industries against their will" (ibid: 172-173). Such forced labor had indeed defined the post-slavery era, and especially along the Mississippi with respect to the construction of levees. Thus, in Greenville, which suffered severe damage in the storm, "[p]olice and guardsmen impressed every black male they saw and sent them to the protection levee." Such a pattern of Black sacrifice for the good of the levee had occurred previously in Greenville. According to John Barry, in 1912, it was reported in the *New York Times* that when an engineer ran out of sandbags, he ordered several hundred Black prisoners "to lie down on top of the levee and as close together as possible." This action lasted for an hour and half, and "prevented the overflow that might have developed into an ugly crevasse" (Barry 1997: 131, 207).

Although the *Times* reporter described this idea as brilliant, LeRoy Percy, an influential former U.S. Senator and planter/patriarch in Greenville, disapproved of such actions as "men were economic units competing with other men, not with sandbags." Despite such disagreement, however, Percy, who had fought against the Ku Klux Klan and those attempting to deprive Blacks of voting rights, manipulated his son, William Alexander (whom he had the mayor of Greenville appoint as head of the flood relief committee) into adopting the policy of keeping

Blacks in Greenville during the flood to work on the levees and to unload (without pay) Red Cross rations for Whites. According to Barry, the Great Flood threatened the society that Percy's family for generations had worked to create, and their struggle, which "began as one of man against nature [...] became one of man against man." Meanwhile, down the river in New Orleans, the elites decided to blow up a levee at Caernarvon that would destroy St. Bernard and Plaquemines Parishes and immediately transform 10,000 residents into flood refugees. Business leaders felt that "[p]erhaps the city would have been safe without dynamiting the levee. But its reputation, would not have been." And, so they initiated a public relations campaign about safety (ibid: 17, 131, 234-254). These actions illustrate that the role of levees functioned beyond the environmental, as they also structured the social order.

THE SUSTAINABILITY OF *HOMO ŒCONOMICUS*

Given Louisiana's history of attempting to control flooding, the response to Hurricane Katrina, as the most devastating and costly storm in U.S. history, has profound implications. Scholars collaborating on an examination of the reconstruction of New Orleans after Katrina from a comparative and historical perspective have concluded that the approach over the *longue durée* has not substantially improved security from the flooding: "For three centuries, New Orleans has sought to lessen the impacts of its recurrent floods and hurricanes by providing marginal increases in safety." The irony remained, however, that by "doing so, they laid the groundwork for the next catastrophic failure." As an example, the improvement of the levees and floodways that successfully divert high waters seem "to make the city safer from river floods but not from hurricanes." Yet, historically safety has been compromised at the expense of development. Moreover, for these same three centuries, the reconstruction strategy has been to "rebuild the familiar" even if "in safer, better, and more equitable ways." However, reconstruction has often exacerbated some of the issues that led to the problem itself such as after Katrina more land is required to replace housing and infrastructure, which should conform to higher standards. The residents themselves "almost universally reject" any proposals that suggest, for example, a moratorium on building. And, to make the city safer, it appears heretical to propose any changes in land use or the restoration of wetlands (Kates/Laska/Leatherman 2006: 14653-14660).

What is even more heretical is the argument put forth by Jacob Vigdor. Whilst some environmental scientists might question whether rebuilding New Orleans after Hurricane Katrina would be a sensible thing to do, according to Vigdor, "given the city's precarious geological position and the contribution of past land reclamation to the city's current vulnerability," the more basic question remains "fundamentally an economic one." Employing a comparative analysis, he has pointed out that Chicago after the 1871 fire, San Francisco after the 1960 earthquake, and Hamburg after the 1943 bombing during World War II, were all able to rebound following their respective disasters. However, New Orleans's recovery will be difficult because the city has been challenged by certain economic factors with which the city was plagued before the devastation caused by Hurricane Katrina (Vigdor 2008: 135-138).

For instance, not only was there a declining population, "white flight," occurring from the city center, but as well from the wider metropolitan area, which suggests a general deficit in jobs resulting from a shortage of economic opportunity. Moreover, the existing opportunities tended to be "concentrated in industries with little potential for long-term advancement or productivity growth." The New Orleans labor market has traditionally been overrepresented in the transportation, entertainment, and public sectors, having essentially derived its economic strength from its port location and from tourism. Whilst the pre-Katrina lack of economic opportunity might have offset the price of renting or owning a house, which was lower than the cost of construction, a suppressed housing market would be difficult to maintain with the kind of new building that would be needed to conform to codes that could withstand the potential damage from future storms (ibid: 140-143).

Vigdor concluded his examination with a controversial assertion: "the plain economic reality is that [New Orleans's] rationale for existence has been dealt an irreversible blow." Noting that in comparison to other cities with colonial heritages, New Orleans remains distinct in its self-presentation. For instance, as New York became a center of manufacturing and subsequently of the postindustrial economy, it "lost almost every vestige of its Dutch colonial origins." Also, perhaps overstating the example, he claimed that contemporary San Francisco "shows few traces" other than its name, of Spanish colonialism. Yet, "[b]ecause New Orleans did not industrialize, it has no reason to plow under its historic core." Indeed, its residents "can claim ties to a colonizing nation that ceded jurisdiction more than 200 years ago," which means that its "ability to retain this heritage through the centuries is, ironically, a reflection of its economic failure." Vigdor does not remain convinced that simply because the city is a "precious cultural artifact" that "it must be restored to its slowly declining former self." Thus, whilst political pressure to rebuild the city remains strong, he insisted, "the economic pressure is nonexistent" (ibid:151,153).

Therefore, the question of reconstruction remains inextricably linked to attempts to reimagine the social order. Whilst Vigor's provocative conclusion might be neither feasible nor convincing, especially to residents of New Orleans, nonetheless, the current policy of "rebuilding the familiar," evidenced by the speed and the manner of funding in which the Superdome was built, will most likely reproduce the same social and ecological issues. The Superdome was rebuilt because it was based on the premise that what is good economically for the middle and upper classes (as the 'job providers') is also good for the general society, as the behaviors of these groups embody *Homo œconomicus*, *Man*, the referent subject of the order, the basis for securing the social stability. And, yet if such were the case, then all of the policies designed to secure the interests on the non-middle classes as part of the 'general interests' of the society, should have indeed lifted the poor out of their precarious situation by now. Instead, many post-Katrina policies have had deleterious effects on the Black and poor residents in New Orleans and the Gulf area, a central one being their permanent displacement.

Moreover, prioritizing the reconstruction of the Superdome formed part of the enacting of the overarching objective of fostering 'economic growth,' the supraordinate *telos* (goal) and seemingly unquestionable assumption of our present modern world-system. The challenge remains difficult because the discourse of economics, as Robert H. Nelson has demonstrated, functions in the similar theological manner as a religion, and thus for us as *Homo œconomicus*, it remains "the ultimate source of meaning," one with its own secular salvation schema (soteriology), that of, economic redemption by not succumbing to the forces of natural scarcity (Nelson 1991: xxv). It is also in this context that the hegemonic relationship to nature can be understood. To return to Jefferson, it belongs to the living generation. *Belongs*. Consequently, the prescriptive role of the dominant global financial institutions (Wall Street, International Monetary Fund, World Bank, European Central Bank, Federal Reserve) must be above all to secure this metaphysics, and to do so in such an absolutist manner, as Nelson argued, due to its monotheistic Judaeo-Christian intellectual origins. As an example, structural adjustment policies that emphasize privatization, deregulation and austerity of central government spending must necessarily subordinate the social and 'human' interests (health, education, housing, civil service sectors) in order to achieve the goal of an efficient economy. Rather than viewing this in moral terms as simply the greed of the one percent, it can be seen in logical culture-centric terms. A nation's gross national product (GNP) and its economic growth do not necessarily need to correlate with the real-life conditions of the non-middle classes. Indeed, the strain on our planetary habitat and the structural inequality remain systemic to the instituting of economic growth. Thus, in order to come to terms with the vast and global disparities of wealth and the devastation of the earth, it becomes increasingly difficult to see how these can be approached without a fundamental reconfiguration of our present self-understanding as *Homo œconomicus*, Man.

In his now classic 1970 "Address to the Board of Governors," then World Bank President Robert McNamara made a series of stunning statements that might qualify as apocalyptic (a very American intellectual tradition) being situated in what Nelson has more recently described as the "new holy wars" between economic religion and environmental religion (with its worship of a pristine nature and its Calvinistic preaching against greed, human corruption, and excessive pride) (cf. Nelson 2010). Nonetheless, given that much of the speech fitted within the normative discourse of economics, especially his discussion on population control, it makes McNamara's assessment all the more stunning.

Quoting the Nobel Prize recipient and distinguished Canadian statesman Lester B. Pearson, McNamara asserted that "'a planet cannot, any more than a country, survive, half-slave, half-free, half-engulfed in misery, half-careening along towards the supposed joys of almost unlimited consumption.' In that direction lies disaster, yet that is our direction today unless we are prepared to change course – and to do so in time." Despite his commitment to neo-classical economics, McNamara did not see the solution primarily in economic terms: "There are really no material obstacles to a sane, manageable, and progressive response to the world's development needs. The obstacles lie in the minds of men. We have simply not thought long enough and hard enough about the fundamental problems of the planet. Too many millennia of tribal suspicion and hostility are still at work in our subconscious minds." Here one might want to challenge the terms laid out as many have indeed thought long and hard, but perhaps it may be a question of the terms of the diagnosis and the prescription to solve the issue. Nonetheless, he does not remain fully epistemologically resigned to the current explanation of the social reality (McNamarra 1977: 21, 23).

McNamara concluded his speech with a call for the formation of a new community, noting that our global civilization is "in fact an inescapable community, united by the forces of communication and interdependence in our new technological order." Therefore, the situation can neither be solved merely within the social science paradigm of economics, nor by utilizing more technology. Rather, it remains a question of redefining the altruism underlying our present global system of social relations: "Thus the challenge of the scientific revolution is not a tremendous technological conundrum like putting a man on the moon. It is much more a straightforward moral obligation, like getting him out of a ghetto, out of a favella [sic], out of illiteracy and hunger and despair. We can meet this challenge if we have the wisdom and moral energy to do so. But it we lack these qualities, then I fear, we lack the means of survival on this planet." (ibid: 23)

BIBLIOGRAPHY

Barry, John M. (1997): *Rising Tide: The Great Mississippi Flood of 1927 and How It Changed America*, New York: Simon and Schuster.

Blake, Eric S./Landsea, Christopher W./Gibney, Ethan J. (2011): "The Deadliest, Costliest, and Most Intense United States Tropical Cyclones from 1851 to 2010." NOAA Technical Memorandum NWS NHC-6 (National Oceanic and Atmospheric Administration, National Weather Service, National Hurricane Center), February 26, 2015 (http://www.nhc.noaa.gov/pdf/nws-nhc-6.pdf).

Colten, Craig E. (2005): *An Unnatural Metropolis: Wresting New Orleans from Nature*, Baton Rouge: Louisiana State University Press.

Debus, Allen G. (1978): *Man and Nature in the Renaissance,* Cambridge: Cambridge University Press.

Delcourt, Paul A./Delcourt, Hazel R. (2004): *Prehistoric Native Americans and Ecological Change: Human Ecosystems in Eastern North America since the Pleistocene*, Cambridge: Cambridge University Press.

Denevan, William M. (2003): "The Pristine Myth: The Landscape of the Americas in 1492." In: Louis S. Warren (ed.), *American Environmental History,* Malden: Blackwell Publishing, pp. 5-26.

Evans, Robert Jr. (1962): "The Economics of American Negro Slavery, 1830-1860." In: *Aspects of Labor Economics: A Conference of the Universities-National Bureau Committee for Economic Research*, Princeton: Princeton University Press.

Fabian, Johannes (1983): *Time and the Other: How Anthropology Makes Its Object*, New York: Columbia University Press.

French, Benjamin Franklin (1851): *Historical Collections of Louisiana, Embracing Translations of Many Rare and Valuable Documents Relating to the Natural, Civil and Political History of That State*, New York: D. Appleton and Company.

Foucault, Michel (1973): *The Order of Things: An Archaeology of the Human Sciences*, New York: Vintage.

Giraud, Marcel (1991): *A History of French Louisiana, Volume 5: The Company of the Indies*, 1723-1731, Brian Pierce (trans.), Baton Rouge: Louisiana State University Press.

Hall, Gwendolyn Midlo (1992): *Africans in Colonial Louisiana: The Development of Afro-Creole Culture in the Eighteenth Century*, Baton Rouge: Louisiana State University Press.

Hartwig, Robert P./Wilkinson, Claire (2010): "Hurricane Katrina: The Five Year Anniversary." New York: Insurance Information Institute, February 26, 2015 (http://www.iii.org/sites/default/files/1007Katrina5Anniversary.pdf).

"Indian Mounds as Flood Refuges," (1927). In: *Science* 6/65. p. xiv.

Intergovernmental Panel on Climate Change (IPPC) (2013): "Summary for Policy Makers." In: Thomas F. Stocker, et al. (eds.), *Climate Change 2013: The Physical Basis: Contribution of Working Group I to the Fifth Assessment Report of the Intergovernmental Panel on Climate Change*, Cambridge: Cambridge University Press, pp. 3-29.

Jefferson, Thomas ([1789] 1984): "Thomas Jefferson to James Madison, 6 September 1789." In: Merrill D. Peterson (ed.), *Jefferson: Writings*, New York: Literary Classics of the U.S.

Johnson, Walter (2000): *Soul by Soul: Life Inside the Antebellum Slave Market*, Cambridge: Harvard University Press.

Kates, R. W., et. al. (2006): "Reconstruction of New Orleans after Hurricane Katrina: A Research Perspective." In: *Proceedings of the National Academy of Science* 103/40, pp. 14653-14660.

Kempe, Michael (2007): "'Mind the Next Flood!': Memories of Natural Disasters in Northern Germany from the Sixteenth Century to the Present," In: *The Medieval History Journal* 10/1-2, pp. 327-354.

Krech, Shepard III (1999): *The Ecological Indian: Myth and History*, New York: W. W. Norton.

Lindauer, Owen/Blitz, John H. (1997): "Higher Ground: The Archaeology of North American Platform Mounds." In: *Journal of Archaeological Research* 5/2, pp. 160-207.

Mann, Charles C. (2006): *1491: New Revelations of the Americas Before Columbus*, New York: Alfred A. Knopp.

McCoy, Drew R. (1980): *The Elusive Republic: Political Economy in Jeffersonian America*, Chapel Hill: University of North Carolina Press.

McDonald, Roderick A. (2003): "Independent Economic Production by Slaves on Antebellum Louisiana Sugar Plantations." In: Gad J. Heuman/James Walvin (eds.), *The Slavery Reader*, London: Routledge.

McNamara, Robert S. (1970): "Address to the Board of Governors," President's Address, World Bank Annual Meeting, February 26, 2015 (http://www-wds.worldbank.org/external/default/WDSContentServer/WDSP/IB/2011/11/

24/000333037_20111124024100/Rendered/PDF/557810WP0Box360y0Robert0S.0McNamara.pdf).
Meek, Ronald L. (1976): *Social and Ignoble Savage*, Cambridge: Cambridge University Press.
Micelle, Jerry A. (1968): "From Law Court to Local Government: Metamorphosis of the Superior Court of French Louisiana," In: *Louisiana History* 9/2, pp. 85-107.
Morgan, Mary S. (2006): "Economic Man as Model Man: Ideal Types, Idealization and Caricatures." In: *Journal of the History of Economic Thought* 28/1, pp. 1-27.
Murphy, Antoine E. (1997): *John Law: Economic Theorist and Policy-Maker*, Oxford: Clarendon Press.
Murrin, John M. (2000): "The Jeffersonian Triumph and American Exceptionalism." In: *Journal of the Early Republic* 20/1, pp. 1-25.
Nelson, Robert H. (1991): *Reaching for Heaven on Earth: The Theological Meaning of Economics*, Savage: Rowan and Littlefield Publishers.
Nelson, Robert H. (2010): *The New Holy Wars: Economic Religion vs. Environmental Religion in Contemporary America*, University Park: Pennsylvania State University Press.
Owens, Jeffrey Alan (1999): *Holding Back the Waters: Land Development and the Origins of Levees on the Mississippi, 1720-1845*, Unpublished Louisiana State University Dissertation.
Pabis, George S. (1998): "Delaying the Deluge: The Engineering Debate over Flood Control on the Lower Mississippi River, 1846-1861." In: *Journal of Southern History* 64/3, pp. 421-454.
Phillips, Ulrich Bonnell (1966): *American Negro Slavery: A Survey of the Supply, Employment, and Control of Negro Labor as Determined by the Plantation Regime*, Baton Rouge: Louisiana State University Press.
Pocock, John Greville Agard (1975): *The Machiavellian Moment: Florentine Political Thought and the Atlantic Republican Tradition*, Princeton: Princeton University Press.
Pyne, Stephen J. (2001): *Fire: A Brief History*, London: The British Museum Press.
Pyne, Stephen J. (2012): *Fire: Nature and Culture*, London: Reaktion Books.
Rohland, Eleonora (2015): "Hurricanes in New Orleans: Disaster Migration and Adaptation, 1718-1794." In: Bernd Sommer (ed.), *Climate Change in North America*, Leiden: Brill.
Rothman, Seth (2005): *Slave Country: American Expansion and the Origins of the Deep South*, Cambridge: Harvard University Press.

Siraisi, Nancy G. (2012): "Medicine, 1450-1620, and the History of Science." In: *Isis* 103/3, pp. 491-514.

Smith, Adam ([1776] 1976): *An Inquiry into the Nature and Causes of the Wealth of Nations*, R. H. Campbell/A. S. Skinner (eds.), London: Oxford University Press.

Spencer, Robyn (1994): "Contested Terrain: The Mississippi Flood of 1927 and the Struggle to Control Black Labor." In: *Journal of Negro History* 79/2, pp. 170-181.

Steffen, Will/Crutzen, Paul J./McNeill, John R. (2007): "The Anthropocene: Are Humans Now Overwhelming the Great Forces of Nature?" In: *Ambio* 36/8, pp. 614-621.

Steinberg, Ted (2009): "Do-It-Yourself Deathscape: The Unnatural History of Natural Disaster in South Florida." In: Paul S. Sutter/Christopher J. Manganiello (eds.), *Environmental History and the American South: A Reader*, Athens: University of Georgia Press, pp. 400-432.

Stowe, Harriet Beecher ([1856] 1968): *Dred: A Tale of the Great Dismal Swamp*, Boston: Phillips, Sampson and Company.

Thomas, Hugh (1997): *The Slave Trade: The Story of the Atlantic Slave Trade, 1440-1870*, New York: Simon and Schuster.

Usner, Daniel H. Jr. (1979): "From African Captivity to American Slavery: The Introduction of Black Laborers to Colonial Louisiana," In: *Louisiana History* 20/1, pp. 25-48.

Usner, Daniel H. Jr. (2006): "American Indians in Colonial New Orleans." In: Waselkov, Gregory A./Wood, Peter H./Hatley, M. Thomas (eds.), *Powhatan's Mantle: Indians in the Colonial Southeast*, Lincoln: University of Nebraska Press.

Vigdor, Jacob (2008): "The Economic Aftermath of Hurricane Katrina." In: *Journal of Economic Perspectives* 22/4, pp. 135-154.

White, Lynn Jr. (1967): "The Historical Roots of Our Ecological Crisis," In: *Science* 155/3767, pp. 1203-1207.

Woolsey, Matt (2008): "America's Most Expensive Natural Disasters." In: *Forbes*, September 13, 2008 (http://www.forbes.com/2007/10/29/property-disaster-hurricane-forbeslife-cx_mw_1029disaster.html).

Wynter, Sylvia ([2001] 2009): "Towards the Sociogenic Principle: Fanon, Identity, the Puzzle of Conscious Experience, and What It is Like to Be 'Black.'" In: Mercedes F Durán-Cogan/Antonio Gómez-Moriana (eds.), *National Identities and Sociopolitcal Changes in Latin America*, New York: Routledge, pp. 30-67.

Lewis Watts: *Uncle Lionel*, Bass Drummer of the Treme Brass Band who died in 2012, New Orleans 2002

The photo depicts Uncle Lionel of the Treme Brass Band. Uncle Lionel was a fixture in New Orleans and a force of nature. He played the bass drum and he could always be found at events and hanging out on Frenchman street. When he died in 2012, his family had him standing in full band uniform at his wake. Eric Porter and I decided to use this image as a cover for *New Orleans Suite* (2013).

Authors

Brown, Nikki, is an Associate Professor of History at the University of New Orleans. She is also a professional photographer and documentarian. She works on African American history and visual culture of the twentieth century, particularly the African diaspora, art, global feminism, and gender studies. Her photographs have been on exhibition in the United States and Austria.

Bucher, Michael, is writing his dissertation on the work of John Rechy at the University of Cologne, where he has also been teaching courses on American literature and queer theory. He has co-edited the essay collection *Between Science and Fiction: The Hollow Earth as Concept and Conceit* (2012), and currently lives in Berlin.

Carmichael, Katie, is an Assistant Professor in the Department of English at Virginia Polytechnic Institute and State University in Blacksburg, Virginia. She is a sociolinguist who studies how language practices vary across social and cultural contexts, and how that variation is reflective of broader social processes as well as individual acts of identity. Her current research agenda focuses on post-Katrina Greater New Orleans, and other communities in South Louisiana.

Dickel, Simon, is a Juniorprofessor at Ruhr-Universität Bochum. He is the author of the book *Black/Gay: The Harlem Renaissance, the Protest Era, and Constructions of Black Gay Identity in the 1980s and 90s* (2011). He is currently working on phenomenology and embodiments of difference and co-editing a book on Queer Cinema.

Eudell, Demetrius L., is Professor of History at Wesleyan University, where he specializes in U.S. history and the history of Blacks in the Americas to the end of the nineteenth century. In addition to a number of essays and articles on Black intellectual and cultural history, he also is the author of *The Political Languages of Emancipation in the British Caribbean and the U.S. South* (2002) and co-editor with Carolyn Allen of *Sylvia Wynter: A Transculturalist Rethinking Modernity* (2001), a special issue of *The Journal of West Indian Literature*. His current research project examines the role of ideas of history, nature, and human differences in the eighteenth-century Enlightenment with special reference to the German *Aufklärung*.

George, Courtney, is an Assistant Professor in the Department of English at Columbus State University in Columbus, Georgia. She also serves as director of the Carson McCullers Center for Writers and Musicians. She obtained her Ph.D. from Louisiana State University, and has published widely on representations of the South in literature and popular culture in journals such as the *Southern Literary Journal*, *Television and New Media*, and *Studies in American Culture*. She is at work on a book tentatively titled *Hurricane Katrina in the Popular Imagination*.

Kindinger, Evangelia, is an Assistant Professor for American Studies at Ruhr-Universität Bochum in Germany where she teaches American Cultural Studies and American Literature. She has published various articles on diaspora theory, transnationalism and gender, including her monograph *Homebound: Diaspora Space and Selves in Greek American Return Narratives* (2015). Currently, she is working on class, popular culture and the American South.

Letort, Delphine, is an Associate Professor in the English Department at the University of Maine (France) where she teaches American civilization and film studies. She studies notions of race and class through the construction of stereotypes in Hollywood productions. She published *Du Film Noir au Néo-Noir: Mythes et Stéréotypes de l'Amérique 1941-2008* (2010) and edited *Panorama Mondial du Film Noir* (2014). She also co-edited various journal issues devoted to the study of documentary filmmaking (*InMedia, Lisa*). She serves on the advisory editorial board of Black Camera (Bloomington, Indiana) and her latest book devoted to the study of Spike Lee's documentaries will be published in 2015.

Piskurek, Cyprian, is lecturer for British Cultural Studies at the University of Dortmund. His research and teaching interests include football fan culture, detective fiction, popular music and Irish Studies.

Siepmann, Philipp, finished his dissertation "Inter- und Transkulturelles Lernen im Englisch-Unterricht der Sekundarstufe II: Das Modell der Transnational

Cultural Studies" ("Inter- and transcultural learning in the advanced EFL classroom: A didactic model of transnational cultural studies") in 2014. His research interests comprise EFL methodology, intercultural and transcultural learning, cultural and literary studies in foreign language education and global education.

Strube, Miriam, is Professor of American Studies at the University of Paderborn. She has published on Gender Studies, Visual Culture, modernist poetry and American philosophy. For these projects, she was a research fellow at Harvard University, visiting professor at Oglethorpe University, Atlanta, and visiting scholar at Princeton University and Columbia University.

Watts, Lewis, is a photographer, archivist/curator and professor emeritus of Art at the University of California Santa Cruz. His research and artwork center primarily on the cultural landscape, focusing on communities of African descent in the San Francisco Bay Area, New Orleans, Harlem, Jamaica, Cuba and France. He is co-author of the books, *Harlem of the West: The San Francisco Fillmore Jazz Era* (2006) and *New Orleans Suite: Music and Culture in Transition* (2013).

Printed by Printforce, United Kingdom